T0123238

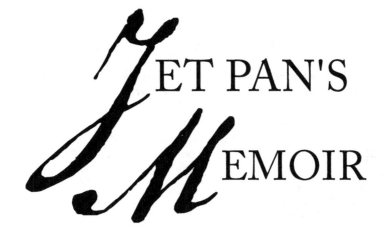

JET PAN'S MEMOIR

DORIS BOURGEOIS-DARLING

authorHOUSE®

AuthorHouse™
1663 Liberty Drive
Bloomington, IN 47403
www.authorhouse.com
Phone: 1 (800) 839-8640

Published by AuthorHouse 07/10/2019

ISBN: 978-1-5462-6150-6 (sc)
ISBN: 978-1-5462-6148-3 (hc)
ISBN: 978-1-5462-6149-0 (e)

Library of Congress Control Number: 2018911373

Print information available on the last page.

ACKNOWLEDGEMENTS

Sincere thanksgiving to my husband David for his patience and constant encouragement in my endeavor to produce this manuscript, especially for the many evening meals prepared for us while I stayed at my desk for the past three years. Through prayers and God's grace, I finally accomplished what I always desired to do: write my life's story.

I dedicate this manuscript to my six children: Marcel Joseph, Janice Marie, John Francis, Jamie Patrick, Mark Jason and Lori-Ann. You are the reason for its creation.

I appreciate all the good wishes from my family and friends and I am indebted to all my sources of reference.

To my awesome cat Toby, who faithfully supervised the ongoing task of this project while sitting quietly on my desk, and obviously enjoying the tapping on the keyboard, and who will probably wish it would continue...

No, Toby. This is THE END.

REFERENCES

Google Wikipedia - General Information

The Mayo Clinic - Multiple Myeloma

James Johnston, Historian - Town of Franklin

Dr. Arthur Sgalia MD - Milford Medical Center and Dana-Farber

The New Brunswick Provincial Guide

The Boston Athletic Association - Boston Marathon Tragedy

The Milford Daily News - Local Events

The Country Gazette - Local Events

The Cape Cod Times - Cape Cod Events

The Boston Globe Newspaper

CONTENTS

CHAPTER I

The Orphans

Thirteen months ago, when Mrs. Léger gave birth to her tenth child, a girl, she almost lost her life. Today her tiny little Dori, cuddled on her grandfather's lap, is weeping. She does not understand why her mother does not come when she calls her and why there are so many people around and hugging her tenderly when she is only longing for her mommy.

She does not know that this morning her mother, in the prime of her life, peacefully left this world. Alas, Dori will never remember her mother's smile, her embracing arms, her warm kisses, the color of her eyes or of her hair. She will never share, like most little girls do, intimate secrets with her mother. After awakening from her first nightmare, Dori will face her misfortune with a cast of players who will do their best to make the game of life as pleasant as possible for her, although the main character has been dismissed.

Similar thoughts were filtering through Delina's mind, little Dori's loving grandmother. She paused for a moment, leaning against the tall white kitchen stove, staring at the burning small birch logs, now in full process of accomplishing the dual role of heating the old farm house and cooking the family meal. The eyes of the septuagenarian filled with tears as her wrinkled hands covered her face. She repeated to herself the last words spoken to her on the previous day: "Mom, are you preparing food for my journey?" As ironic as it seemed at the time, for Laudia had been bedridden for a few days, now it was clear: Laudia had a premonition of her own death. "What a pity!" she exclaimed, startling her husband Marcel who was rocking little Dori. He was a kind and religious man and well respected in the community. He reached for his faithful wife's

Doris Bourgeois-Darling

hand and, bringing it to his trembling lips, whispered: "Courage, Délina. Everything will be alright; we will take good care of the children." "Oh! the children. They have to be fetched from cousin Lionel's house; they do not know yet." On that comment, she signaled to her mate to bring the baby back to her crib.

Meanwhile, in the spicy, cold and wintry day, an echo could be heard from afar: "Easy, Big Tom. Easy, now." Although it was mid-April, the heavy-set horse was struggling to pull the red sleigh through the blizzard which hurled the snow fifteen feet into the air. The year was 1941; it marked another rigorous winter in Canadian history. Willie held the reins firmly in one hand while adjusting his warm handmade woolen hat over his ears with the other. Seated next to him was Amédée, a small nervous man, the new widower.

Although he had suffered a back injury in his childhood which had left him hunchback, Amédée always managed to provide for his family either by working on the family farm or as a door-to-door peddler. He was now lost in his thoughts, staring in the endless cloud of swirling snow that blanketed the fields ahead. With a heavy heart and teary eyes, he gave in to sorrow. "Why me, Lord? You took away six of my ten children in infancy; then my little three-year-old Oscar, who was my pride and joy. Now, my sweet Laudia. You know how much I loved my dear wife. Forgive me, Lord, for being so selfish. May your will be done." Wiping his tears with his thick gray mittens, and turning towards a third passenger sitting in the back of the spacious sleigh, he broke the morbid silence: "Are you alright, Father?" Father Gallant, clutching his precious black case in his gloved hands, nodded affirmatively. "I wonder if Amédée will keep the children", was on the pastor's mind. "He certainly has had his share of sorrow and pain in life. Dear God, please give him the grace and strength to keep his faith in You."

It was only two miles from Saint-Marcel to the rectory in Grande-Digue but on that day, to Willie, it seemed like an endless road. It was only the day before that, as a good neighbor, he had brought Doctor Dumont to the Léger's house. But today it was all over. Young Laudia's only surviving

2

lung could not win the fight against that pneumonia. "She was much too young to die at thirty-six. And leaving a husband and three young children. What a shame; she loved life so dearly!" So were the thoughts on Willie's mind. "Whoa, Big Tom. Here we are." After helping the priest off the sleigh, Amédée mumbled: "Thank you, Father, for coming", to which the priest replied: "We will make the funeral arrangements tomorrow. Keep your courage, Amédée."

Willie and the forty-eight-year-old widower disappeared into the blizzard, now at its worse. At the Léger's house, a few neighbors and relatives had gathered as it is common in a small community to come together as one family. At the sight of her Papa, Dori hurried towards him, but precautious Grandma picked her up gently in her loving arms and said: "It is not healthy for you to go near Papa when he looks like a snowman right now."

CHAPTER 2

The Early Years

1941 - 1950 Hermance, age eight; Ronald, aged six; and Dorice, thirteen months; all three orphans stayed at the homestead with Papa, Grandma Délina and Grandpa Marcel. He was the patriarch of the Léger family and also of the small quaint seaside village named after him. Saint-Marcel was a small community consisting of about twenty families, most of which were related, a small village in the parish of Grande-Digue in Southeastern New Brunswick, Canada, where you earn your bread by farming and fishing. I was a very small, frail child who adored her Grandpa and who was the apple of his eye. Grandpa was respected by the whole community as he was on the school board, was the tax collector, owned a large farm and helped everyone in need. Through the years many young men found work at Grandpa's farm.

My siblings and I were to call our father "Papa" per Grandma's order. Papa was semi-handicapped due to a hunchback condition, the cause of which is unknown to me to this day. He helped on the farm and, in the summertime, would become a seafood peddler to towns away from the seashore. Memramcook was one of those towns. It was where my favorite aunt Marguerite lived near the railroad tracks. My brother, sister and I took turns going on the thirty-mile trek with Papa to visit. I have always loved trains.

Grandmother Délina was a devoted mother to us three orphans: a diligent woman who had raised her own family of eleven. She knew hard work and she knew the joy of a house well kept. She made butter with the big old churn after separating the milk and the cream with the separator that was kept in the shed adjacent to the kitchen. Grandma made boudin (blood sausage) from fresh blood from the slaughtered hog. I can smell it and taste it now. Arthur was the hog slaughterer in our neighborhood. Grandma made my dresses cut and hand-sewn from pretty flour sacks. I loved them. She also made her own lye soap for laundry, to use on the scrub board. Although Grandma was always busy with household chores, she always found time to knit socks and mittens for us as well. And she was always ready to teach us good Christian living. Ever since I can remember, Grandma had vertigo and she staggered a lot. Whenever we, children would go to the seashore, which was within walking distance from our house, we would bring salt water from the sea for her to bathe her aching feet and legs.

Everyone called me la p'tite Dorice: Little Doris. I was always well treated as I was pitied for being an orphan. Sometimes Grandma threatened to send me to the gypsies if I misbehaved but Grandpa was always on my side. I was very tiny for my age and as a young child could fit between the legs of the kitchen stove. I would take winter naps there with my faithful companion Tom, my tiger cat, or my old teddy bear Brownie. I did not have many toys. What toys we did have were handmade. I remember my Grandpa had carved me a cone-shaped doll, which I liked. I would have to wait till I was about eight years old for a real doll, a doll given to me by my cousin Rita. Oh! How I loved that big doll… so special to me. There were not many children to play with in our neighborhood besides my cousin Bernard and his sister Rachel, as we were close in age.

As in any normal childhood, there were mishaps. As a very young child, around two years old, I sustained a deep laceration on the right side of my throat from falling on a broken bottle near the bulkhead of our cellar. My brother claimed responsibility for that one. He was seven at the time. I still have a scar on my right chin. (As I grew taller the scar changed position.) To the best of my knowledge, there was no medical intervention; the cut healed naturally.

I never learned to swim due to an incident involving my brother and cousins pushing me out of a canoe when I was five years old. Even though it was in shallow water, it left me scarred for life. I am still afraid of water and to this day, this Pisces does not swim.

Our property had many attached buildings. Aside from the twelve-room family home, there was a woodshed which housed the out-house which was attached to the main house. An outside stairway led to the grainery above the shed. It was like an attic. That place was always interesting to me. There were four divided bins serving as grain storage for the cows' winter ration. There was also a makeshift altar which my brother used to pretend to celebrate mass for us. He loved to imitate people and did a good impersonation of our bishop Monsignor Norbert Robichaud. Ronald and cousins Lionel and Roger used this hideaway for smoking, practicing their singing and playing the guitar. I once kept a dead kitten there in a shoe box, embalmed with baby powder. I thought I could keep it forever until Papa found out and that ended that mourning period.

Among the other buildings on the property stood our very unusual barn which had a huge hay area with a pitchfork set up at the ceiling of the barn that could move bales of hay from one end of the barn to the second story mow. This was made possible with the help of a horse; and this was fascinating to me.

There was a small car garage which housed Papa's Model A Ford. My Papa had several cars through the years. I remember the Model A and the 1939 Plymouth.

Between two barns was the manure pit, a beneficial asset to the vegetable garden but a hazard to little children. My little brother Oscar died after complications from falling in that pit. There were stables and barns, a large hen house and a pigsty to house our horses, cows, chickens and pigs. There was also a rooster that enjoyed chasing me right to the kitchen door.

I loved that old homestead with its twelve-room farmhouse, its grain fields, its gardens and orchards.

In the summer of 1946 there was a great forest fire which started in the raspberry patch in our woods, apparently set by teenagers smoking. Raging flames came as close as one hundred yards from our barn. It was traumatic for a six-year-old. A lot of prayers were said and many gallons of water were used. To this day I do not recall seeing any firemen. There was tremendous damage to the forest, some cottages were destroyed but no family homes were burned and there were no fatalities. That summer also marked the year that my uncle Edouard, the prodigal son, returned home after going missing for over twenty years. Grandpa probed into his marriage status as he brought home a wife.

Grandpa was very protective of me and would not permit me to start school at age six like other children, in part due to my small stature and in part due to the distance to the school, just short of two miles. I would have walked to school by myself at times, as most of the other children were older than I was.

However, on May 1st, 1947, I started school as an observer (Papa was also on the school board) in the one-room schoolhouse managed by my father's cousin Évangéline Léger. About twenty-four pupils from grades one to four were taught in that school. The little schoolhouse had a pot belly stove in the middle of the classroom and that stove heated the school and was also used by the teacher for reheating lunches for the pupils before the noon hour. It was a different way of life in those days.

In September of 1947, at age seven and a half, I started first grade and met Paul Bourgeois, my rival for the next eight years. I was a fairly good student and Paul and I alternated for first place position with high averages. Oh! How I miss those report cards! Paul was a very intelligent boy from a large family and had a sibling in every grade. He became an educator and the author of nine historical manuscripts and of his autobiography. His literary collection is presently displayed at the little school, "la p'tite école", which is now a museum. In his middle years he also became a great runner and qualified to run the Boston Marathon in 1987.

Being one of the youngest girls in our neighborhood, I do not recall sharing the two-mile trek to school with many children in the winter. It was easier to walk in the fields than the roadway. Sleighs being our only mode of transportation in winter, there was no plowing of the roads. Our school year would extend from early September to June thirtieth, every year. July First was called Dominion Day, like our Fourth of July in this country. It is now called Canada Day.

Christmas at our house was quiet. A tree was cut from our woodland and decorated by us children with simple handmade ornaments. The presents were scarce: clothes, mittens, hair accessories. We had a special meal with Grandma's pies for dessert. Christmas Day was one of the rare occasions when we enjoyed certain foods that we now take for granted and have daily such as nuts, grapes and oranges. One Christmas night, upon returning from midnight mass with Papa, my brother and my sister, I was handed an orange by Grandpa and he told me that Baby Jesus had sent it to me. I must have been a good girl! My favorite cousin Emery felt pity for his little cousin and would send a gift at Christmas time when I was a bit older, like eight or nine. I received a large coloring book and crayons, a Parcheesi game and a sweater, a dark green cardigan. I was very grateful for all that attention.

My aunt Marguerite, Emery's mother, was my favorite aunt. She would come and visit on Sundays and bring a large bag of puffed wheat, which I still love to this day. She was Papa's sister and lived in the town where Papa was peddling seafood. Her daughter, cousin Rita, was the donor of my very first doll.

It was always an exciting time when Papa would get ready for his peddling trip. He would go to Cocagne, the next village, where he picked up the shellfish, mostly lobster, directly from the fishermen's boats. He cooked these poor creatures by immersing them in boiling water but prior to their sudden death, they were free to crawl on the floor, which scared me. They were then packed on ice in large metal coolers. Other shellfish such as clams, quahogs, mussels and oysters (my favorite!) were also available sometimes. Memramcook was the town about thirty miles away where my aunt Marguerite lived near the railroad tracks and where my father's customers were. My sister, my brother and I took turns accompanying our father on his peddling trips. We loved to pick cherries from my aunt's garden and get treats from the little corner store. But I particularly loved the trains speeding by my aunt's house, especially their loud whistle. Those are fond memories from my childhood.

On one cold February afternoon, upon my return from school, my dear eighty-year-old Grandpa was lying on the kitchen floor, paralyzed from a stroke. Grandma was waiting for Papa to return from getting firewood from our woodland area. Grandpa lay resting his head on a pillow. He was conscious but had difficulty speaking. On Holy Saturday, March 27th, 1948, my special Grandpa went to his reward. I was devastated. On his deathbed he had told me I should become a nun. That phrase was imprinted on my mind. I pondered those words in my heart and reviewed them in my mind frequently over the following ten years.

I missed my Grandpa. He had been a central influence on my young life. He had told me so many stories. Like the time, while away on business during a wintry night, he had to share a room with another gentleman. Being exhausted, he was soon sound asleep. In the middle of the night, he was awakened by the sound of prayers being recited in the room. To his surprise, a young woman was seated at a small table and was reading out loud from a book by the dim light of a lamp. When he realized the content of the prayers, he jumped out of bed and, wearing his white long johns, scared the woman, who ran towards the stairs and fell, fracturing her leg. Grandpa realized he was in a room with a dead man, and the lady thought she had seen a ghost.

My Grandpa told me, as I was too young to remember, about the summer evening when Henriette and Marie-Louise came to visit with their trainer. The two bear entertainers were part of a traveling show going from town to town. While their master slept in the house, the two stars stayed outside our kitchen door. I wonder if they were restrained. Those were the 1930s and 1940s.

I remember the day my grandfather was attacked by a porcupine while was working in the upper field near the wooded area. How painful were those quills embedded in his leg as Grandma was trying to pull them out, as I was watching. Poor Grandpa.

Another time, I recall Grandma medicating Grandpa's back with some ointment to relieve the pain from shingles. Those are some of my memories of my dear grandparents and their devotion to each other.

Grandma held up well with Papa and kept the household together in spite of her chronic vertigo. The Sunday night card games of Little 45s continued with the neighbors and relatives arriving with their lanterns for the weekly get-together. Although it was exciting to have a lot of company, I did not appreciate the noisy and rowdy demeanor of all those men interfering with my sleep in the bedroom, next to the card room.

Papa had married my mother when he was thirty-two and she was nineteen. He was now the head of our household at age forty nine, a widower with three young children to raise. He was Grandma's first-born with ten siblings. He had a fourth-grade formal education, was self-educated and an avid reader. Papa was always interested in learning especially on world events and politics. He was a good Christian; he made his first communion at age twelve, which was common in that era. He had a devotion to the Holy Souls in purgatory. He was a churchgoer. Papa also loved a good time with family and friends: he loved music and singing. And he loved the seafood that he peddled. Papa smoked the pipe, liked beer, and raisin pie. At age seventeen, he got his driver's license and, according to town records, there were only four automobiles in the parish at the time. The owners were: the pastor Monsignor Belliveau, Marcel and Dominique Léger (they were brothers), and the local physician, Dr. Olson. One of the first autos in the Léger family was a 1912 Ford Model T.

There was no electricity at our farmhouse until my favorite cousin Emery, who worked for the Canadian National Railroad, wired electric power in our kitchen, but in the kitchen only. I was eight years old then and it was a great help for me doing my school homework.

In second grade, at age nine, I got eyeglasses for reading. I remember every year at Mother's Day I had to recite a poem about an orphan. I soon got tired of it.

There was one time, I was falsely accused by one of the children of stealing tomatoes from a garden on my way home from school. There was no need for such a thing as we had a vegetable garden at home. I was punished by the teacher. I still claim my innocence today. My grandmother had instilled in me a sense of honesty and a sense of responsibility. She had taught me at a very young age that taking anything without permission was stealing - even food at home (a little exaggeration!). She often said: "Ask and you shall receive". Grandma always quoted Bible verses to explain rules to us, children.

I remember one fourth of March, on my ninth or tenth birthday, our neighbor Mrs. Bourque, who had a house full of boys, gave me a freshly baked raisin bread. Sometimes a peddler would give me a fruit, which I loved. Those were the days of simple things bringing simple pleasures with neighborly love. Simple things, simple pleasures were the fabric of my young life in Saint-Marcel.

Although I was a tiny child, I was growing strong in other ways. In our evening prayers, my Grandma assigned me the litany to the Blessed Virgin Mary followed by the prayer to St. Joseph. I learned these at age ten. I was very devoted to our Blessed Mother Mary as a child, as a preteen, as an adolescent and beyond. I always carried my rosary beads in my pocket. In spring and summer, in this large room above our kitchen which was called "the old grenier", I would erect small altars with statues and holy images and would adorn these with wild flowers. One of the two staircases in our house led to this special room while the other led to the four bedrooms. This open room served as a workroom where vegetables and fruit were laid on newspaper around the kitchen stovepipe to dry and preserve for the winter. I helped Grandma with the drying of shelled peas and beans, and cranberries. This room served as my chapel and as my playroom. In this special room I could be a nun, a nurse, a teacher, a princess or whatever I wanted to be. THIS WAS MY OWN LITTLE WORLD!!!

Life was always interesting. The farm well must have been near an oil well (ha!) because the water smelled and tasted like kerosene. No joke. How awful!!! We were getting our drinking and cooking water from our cousins' house across the road. They were very accommodating, even Lionel, who was a grumpy old man, was always nice to me. He would say: "You can borrow water only if you bring it back." That made a ten-year-old girl think. Ozélie Léger, Lionel's wife and mother of fifteen, was the village postmistress. I helped to deliver the mail bag to their house from Ovila Després' mail truck for a nickel or a dime, depending how heavy the bag was. Cousin Ozélie was a saint (in my opinion). She was my sponsor at my confirmation, which I made at eight years of age, the same year I received the Eucharist for the first time. The reason for being confirmed so young (compared to today's standards) was that the Bishop visited the parishes only every four years and if you had received the Eucharistic sacrament, you were allowed to be confirmed.

After a few years praying for an apparition from our Lady, my disappointment turned me towards the Lord Himself. Reading The Passion from my father's book The Imitation of Christ was a delight at age ten or eleven. I prayed to St. Maria Goretti, a martyr at age twelve, as I desired to imitate her virtue of purity. I was not attracted to St. Thérèse de Lisieux as most young girls were. That changed later on. I felt I needed my rosary beads as a weapon in my pocket. I was verbally sexually assaulted as a preteen by a relative and others. I was so ashamed! I confided to my confessor only. Being very trusting and naïve, later when older, I was in several dangerous situations where I could have lost my virginity, which was preserved until my marriage in 1962. The rosary in my pocket protected me. I swear to that. Thank God for the precious gift of His mother to us. I was pious even as a young child and I had a devotion to my guardian angel whom I named John Patrick, but I always called him JP. I talk to him daily.

At age ten, in fourth grade, I was doing well in school and was still competing with Paul Bourgeois for top of the class. I was studious. I loved to read and to make scrapbooks with interesting newspaper and catalog clippings. I loved world events and became very interested in the British Royal Family as the Queen was our sovereign but delegating her orders through government officials such as the governor-general and the lieutenant-governor in each province. I also loved to write short stories. I wrote a booklet about an elderly couple named Bourlinguette and Bourlinguot. I believe it was what old age signified to me at that young age. I always wanted to be an author (of something). In later years and through middle school and high school, I was assigned to write for different occasions such as birthdays and farewells to teachers. I wrote essays on music and nursing. I enjoyed writing. I liked to write letters and corresponded with children my age from a newspaper column listing birthdays. I had a few penpals.

In elementary school, in late spring or in June, we would have field trips and picnics on the school grounds. It was so much fun. I was blessed with many friends. I recall going to Magnetic Hill near Moncton, our nearest city in New Brunswick. A small stream of water seemed to be running uphill. Such an optical illusion. In middle school, I was still competing with Paul. One of my teachers, Lucie Gallant, once gave me a home hair permanent at her home after school. The odor of the strong solution was very unpleasant. Her grandma entered the room and said: "You have to suffer to be pretty."

Winters in New Brunswick were harsh sometimes, although I did enjoy playing in the snow. We had a skating rink on the frozen pond in our yard where I learned to skate with my brother's skates and seven pairs of socks. The frozen pond was the village attraction for the youngsters especially during winter break.

But summers were my favorite times. I learned to ride my brother's bicycle in the backyard. One summer, a distant cousin my age was visiting her grandparents across the road. Cousin Diane taught me to speak English. We had so much fun playing on our farmer's porch called a "veranda." We loved to play dress-up and once I sneaked my first communion dress to play with. The party was over when Grandma caught me. In an upstairs closet were my mother's clothes which I was allowed to play dress up with. Some were still new. Papa told me my mom was never in a hurry to wear her new clothes. I do the same today.

The best part of the summer was when my cousins from Massachusetts came to visit along with their mother, aunt Sara, my father's sister. My cousin Leo was a natural musician. He played background steel guitar with famous musicians such as Willie Nelson and Buck Owens, among others. Helen, six months my junior, played the 12-string guitar and she and her sister Jeannette sang. Richard, the little brother, was the comedian. And still is. I was so looking forward to their annual visit. It was so much fun to have them around for about a month each summer.

One summer I met my mother's brother Thomas and his wife Fernande visiting from Chicoutimi, Québec. That was for me a new addition to my relatives on my mother's side of the family. My grandparents Hébert had died from influenza, which plagued many families during the Great Depression. I had many cousins from my aunt Judith's and uncle Arthur's large families. I did not know my mother's relatives well.

My brother, who was five years my senior, was nice to me most of the time, except for the canoe incident. When I had pneumonia at age five, Ronald prayed very hard for my recovery and made a deal with God; so I was told. My brother had all the toys our family could afford. He loved to skate and he played hockey and baseball. He loved to sing and learned to play the guitar with our cousins. He had a lot of friends, learned to drive young and had an old car, which had always worried our Papa. As a teenager he would recite the rosary so fast after supper so he could go out with his friends. Ronald finished eighth grade and then helped on the farm. At age seventeen he went into the army, forging our father's signature on the application form.

I never liked my name but I still prefer it to my sister's name: Hermance. She was pretty, popular, promiscuous and caused our poor father much worry. I shared a bedroom upstairs with my sister but often when she was out at night, I slept downstairs on a little sofa in the corner of our large kitchen. I was not a brave girl in the dark. I can still hear the ringing of that old country clock on the shelf above the sofa. It rang every half hour; we were used to it. On our bed upstairs we had a buffalo skin to keep us warm and cozy on those cold Canadian wintry nights. Hermance was not always around but when she was, she was nice to me. I remember her curling my hair and explaining some of the mysteries of life, including the birds and the bees saga. She might have felt that she needed to replace our mother in some ways. She told me one night she saw our mother standing at the foot of our bed in a white gown. Pregnant at seventeen and a half, Hermance went to a Sisters' home for unwed mothers in Saint John, New Brunswick, and gave birth to a very handsome boy. We met Daniel at age two. I fell in love with this special nephew and taught him the basic prayers and how to read.

In 1952 Papa started getting sick with stomach cancer. This explains his self-medicating with baking soda solutions for stomach upset and heartburn. He was so sick at times, even unable to attend my sister's wedding. He needed my help tending the little village post office. He had what he called a "milk leg", which is an inflammation of the femoral vein. By the time Papa got medical attention, it was too late. The surgery was of no use. Six months after the surgery, on the eve of his death, he called me to his bedside to tell that he would teach me to drive so we could go for rides. On Saturday May 16th, 1953, I was sent to the dirt cellar for vegetables to make him a soup. When I returned upstairs, Papa was on the floor near the kitchen sink. He had a bump on his forehead but there was no bleeding. After having alerted Grandma and uncle Hypolite, I ran as fast as my legs could carry me to my uncle Léo's house, about two-tenths of a mile up the road. I was so scared, my poor dad had suffered so much in silence already. I'm sure I prayed; I loved him so much. Father Brideau arrived too late. I knew that the sacrament of the sick could be administered only on the condition that the person was still alive. I prayed that God would save my father's soul.

Grandma was eighty-five and her brother Hypolite was eighty-two at the time. Uncle Léo took care of all the funeral arrangements. I was told that the plain wooden coffin had cost forty dollars. What a difference from today's cost!

At the time of our father's death, my sister was married with two children. My brother was stationed in Valcartier, Québec, with the Canadian Army and he did not make it home in time for the funeral. I was distraught by his absence.

After my father's death I ran the village post office for two months until it was moved down the road to the Bourque's family home. Yes, I was thirteen. It was a very small community; therefore it was doable.

Grandma moved to her daughter's house, aunt Lina, who had a family of sixteen children. Uncle Hypolite went to uncle Léo's house and I moved with my sister near the church and schools in Grande-Digue, our parish.

Senator Aurèle Léger, my father's cousin, took over the old homestead as it was repossessed by the government for unpaid taxes. The taxes were my brother's responsibility as he had inherited the property. A cleaning crew was hired to prepare the property for sale. Well, to my great surprise and disappointment, all my personal belongings were destroyed including my trunk full of treasures so important to a young girl! I was very saddened and upset by the discovery, especially the loss of all my elementary school report cards that I was so proud of. One day after school, I walked to the old house and found a pair of red shoes on the floor of a small closet near the kitchen. That finding scared me. I left running and ran all the way to my sister's house, almost two miles away. To this day, I'm still puzzled about those shoes as no one I knew owned them. The mystery still remains.

CHAPTER 3

The Teenage Years

At age thirteen, I was in seventh grade and still doing well and competing with Paul. In September of 1954 I entered the eighth grade in the secondary school located near our church. We often had unexpected visits from our pastor Father Brideau, who was a very stern priest and made us nervous sometimes. A new school, up to high school, was being built and was to be named after our pastor.

1954 The day prior to my fourteenth birthday, I became an aunt to my sister's third child and third son, Maurice. I also became his godmother with my cousin Peter as his godfather. At age two, little Maurice was scalded over about ninety percent of his body with third degree burns. He had been accidentally pushed by the family dog against a bucket of hot water which was to be used to prepare the livestock's feed. The poor little toddler was hospitalized for several weeks and was left severely scarred but he was able to lead a normal life. He has been happily married for over four decades, has fathered three sons and he recently told me that he does not remember the accident, the hospitalization, or the suffering.

My teenage years were spent living at my sister Hermance's house, going to school and helping out with the household chores and with the care of her children. We lived within walking distance of the church, Notre Dame de la Visitation, which stands high above the sea, its steeple guiding the fishermen and its bell calling the people to pray. The church was built in 1830 and had many additions and renovations through the years. I loved its beautiful stained-glass windows and its very ornate tall altar. That altar was replaced in later years by one from a church in Lynn, Massachusetts, which was being demolished and its altar was transported to Grande-Digue by a former Visitation Church parishioner. Very impressive! That parish church witnessed the reception of all my childhood sacraments. The cemetery where my parents, grandparents and many other relatives are buried next to the church is composed of two parts, the old and the new, and it extends from the road to the sea. Across from the church was the local post office in the Gallant's house.

As a young teen-ager, while living at my sister's house, I used to visit the Haché family often. They were distant relatives. There I met Eric, a guitar player with whom I became infatuated. He proposed to me. I was fourteen at the time. What a boost to my ego! I soon found out that he was a Big Flirt and my first crush was crushed. I got over it quickly. My other teenage loves were Elvis Presley, rock 'n' roll, and country music. I was keeping up with the latest in the country music world by reading magazines featuring the artists. I enjoyed Sunday evening strolls to Shediac Bridge with my friends Corinne and Lorraine and sometimes Corinne's brother Elie. Another fun time for us teens was the Lobster Festival in the town of Shediac which was named the Lobster Capital of the World. That was the yearly July Big Event in our area.

In January 1955, the top seven of the eighth grade class were promoted to ninth grade in the newly opened high school. I believe it was to better allocate the students to the newly available rooms. Students from other school districts from the parish joined us in the new school and now Paul had a new competitor in Hélène Boucher. I was by then in a love-hate relationship with math. Algebra I could understand but it was different for geometry, which was a totally foreign language to me. Now Paul and Hélène were at the head of the class.

For the first time in our schools, some of our new teachers were religious sisters: Sister Marie-Géraldine and Sister Marie-Raymond. They were great, well-liked and respected. Sister Marie-Géraldine became my mentor. I loved her. They were members of the order of Our Lady of the Sacred Heart, with the mother-house in Moncton, our nearby city.

In September of 1955 I entered the tenth grade and my struggle with geometry continued through high school. I became so preoccupied and stressed out about geometry that I was sleeping with my textbook under my pillow in the hope of figuring it out upon awakening. It was a nightmare!

In eleventh grade we had a male teacher for the first time in our school: Mr. Melville Landry. I was getting help with math but I became frustrated with my progress and wanted out of school. Due to this inability to cope with geometry, I decided to quit school. During the Christmas break 1956, I told my friend Corinne's parents about my decision and they suggested that I contact my father's cousin Senator Léger for help to continue my education somewhere and somehow.

A young woman from our town was studying Home Economics in Saint-Jérome, Québec. Yolande Léger (no relation) was in her third year of a four-year program. She was contacted and as we learned more about L'Institut Familial, I became very interested. Arrangements were therefore made for me to attend that school with the religious sisters of Our Lady of the Good Counsel. It is amazing to me how quickly I was accepted to the program, without an interview. All the process was made long distance. No doubt the Senator had some influence in the matter. This little orphan was happy to ride the train to Montreal with Yolande in January 1957. At the time, I wanted to pursue a career in home economics. I mostly wanted to learn how to cook, motivated by my secret love for my soldier friend Ed, who had said that he wanted a wife who could cook. That was to be me...

Oh! How lucky I was to have such gracious and generous relatives to help me in my time of need. My sister and brother-in-law, while raising their family, were unable to help me financially and neither could my brother. My only income was a small government pension.

Saint-Jérome was a lovely town thirty-three miles north of Montreal. While I was studying there, I lost my thirty-two-year-old cousin to meningitis. It was very hard for me to be so far from home at that sad time. My friend Ed and I had been corresponding for three years. He was a good writer and was always respectful. It was the postal service which was responsible for the end of our relationship due to lost letters.

I had a great time at school. I made new friends, did well, and received a first-year diploma with some awards in six months. After my return home, I spent the summer at the Senator's home helping with chores. Mrs. Léger was a warm, motherly woman who taught me to be a young lady. I admired her. As for the senator, he was intimidating, being a perfectionist, and he made me feel uncomfortable. During that summer, I expressed the desire to finish high school. Mr. and Mrs. Léger were very pleased with my decision. In September 1957, I entered a local boarding school for girls in Bouctouche, New Brunswick, about twenty miles from home. This school was also under the direction of the religious order of the Sisters of Our Lady of the Sacred Heart.

Life was good for me as a student at the sixty-plus-year-old Couvent Immaculée-Conception, which lodged about one hundred students ranging from eighth to twelfth grade. We had wonderful sisters who sincerely cared about us. They were great role models to what young ladies should aspire to become: Good Christian Women. Under the direction of Sister Marie-Lydia, Sister Aurèle-Marie, our great eleventh and twelfth grade teacher, of Sister Marie-Joanne and others, we were in very good hands. We were thirty students in our class including one young man, Jacques Michaud, who lived in the neighborhood. He was a walker. We had many talented girls in our class: Anita Pellerin, Gloria Keenan, Nélida Maillet, to name a few. We had choir, plays, concerts, sing-alongs, movies, and passes to downtown on Saturdays. I had a friend who came from Hartford, Connecticut, which I thought was strange coming from so far away, but her mother had studied at Convent Immaculate-Conception (CIC) when she was my friend Helen's age and she wanted her daughter to attend also. Estelle Manuel was another friend of mine who would come with me to visit my cousin and family down in the village.

During the month of May we assembled around the outside grotto in front of a statue of our Blessed Mother Mary where we prayed a beautiful prayer that I still recite today during the whole month of May (in French of course). Although I had a good year at the school, I was ill for some time. I was very fatigued and had to rest during recess while my classmates could enjoy their time off. I had to return to class at the sound of the bell. That went on for about a month but I was not diagnosed or had to be hospitalized or dismissed from school, fortunately. I worked very hard and with the help of Sister Aurèle-Marie, you guessed it, yes! I passed geometry on the provincial exam, which we had to take before we could graduate.

In the months prior to graduation, I was approached and asked to order our class rings. I obliged and our rings were purchased from a jeweler in Shediac. I still have mine today and I wore it until a few years ago. It is a thin gold-plated ring with a blue design of a graduation cap and a diploma. My granddaughter Brianna likes it and it can be hers someday if she wants it.

Graduation day finally arrived on June 25th, 1958. The day started with mass attendance in the lovely chapel, a special breakfast and then, free time. Most of the local girls went home to their family. I got a ride to Shediac with one of my classmates, Thérèse, and her family who lived near the center of that town. From their house I walked approximately two miles to my aunt Lina's house, wearing high heel shoes and my graduation dress, in a pretty turquoise color, which Mrs. Léger had helped me pick. I was going to visit my grandmother. Unfortunately, she did not recognize me. That was painful; but at age ninety-one, Grandma had lost some of her faculties, understandably.

I returned to the convent with Thérèse and her family for the graduation ceremony which took place at the town's high school as it was more spacious and could accommodate the large number of guests. The ceremony was very impressive as we were privileged to receive our diplomas from the hand of our beloved archbishop Monsignor Norbert Robichaud of Moncton. The Senator and Mrs. Léger could not attend as the senator was at work in Ottawa at the time. My sister and my brother-in-law attended, which made me very happy. My brother was away working in Quebec. My family was proud of my accomplishment as I was the first in my immediate family to graduate from high school. Both my brother and sister had finished eighth grade. I received awards of distinction for French and good language, two subjects related to my studies in Saint-Jérome. Our class of thirty students completed eleventh and twelfth grades together in one scholastic year. I ranked ninth in my class.

While I was at the convent in Bouctouche, my aspiration was to continue on to nursing school. The discernment of a religious vocation had been dormant in my heart for some time however, and during a retreat at the end of the school year and under the direction of the spiritual director, I decided not to wait until I had finished nursing school to enter religious life.

After graduation, I returned to my sister Hermance's house. My relationship with Ed, which had ended while I was in Saint-Jérome, was hard to forget, especially when watching a movie with Troy Donahue, his look-alike. My brother was dating Ed's sister Muriel, which made it difficult for me at the time. On August 1st, 1958, my sister was at the small hospital in Shediac to give birth to my fourth nephew and while there, she witnessed Ed's wedding to a local girl at the church across from the hospital. I got over it. Actually, one month later I entered the novitiate.

CHAPTER 4

The Novitiate

On September 8th, 1958, I entered the Novitiate of the religious order of Our Lady of the Sacred Heart in Saint-Joseph, a village on the outskirts of the town of Memramcook, my childhood dream place. My cousins, the Légers were very supportive.

My brother-in-law drove me to the convent, which was about thirty miles away. My sister could not attend as she had a new baby and four children at home. I had felt that I should postpone my entrance that year and stay with my sister to help her but Mrs. Léger pointed out to me that she knew someone who did that and never attained her goal of becoming a nun. I decided it was time for me to enter religious life. So, with my small trousseau, I entered a new way of life.

The life of a religious is one of prayer, silence and work, whatever you are assigned or trained to do, and recreation. Even though it was a great change for me, I believe I adjusted well. I had difficulty with being silent at times: I was heard singing in the basement bathroom. There was a Mr. Bourgeois, a janitor, who reminded me of my uncle Léo. He was so jumpy. It was hilarious!

Our habit consisted of a long black dress with a black veil over a white coif. It was fairly comfortable. We had guardians for the first year to help us along; mine was a lovely second-year novice named Sister Anita. There was another sister in our order with my name, therefore mine was changed to Sister Dorice-Marie Léger. For my feast day I picked March 19th as I always had a devotion to St. Joseph, probably because of the novena prayer recited by Grandma after the rosary during my childhood.

Our daily routine started with rising at 5:30 am and on to chapel for morning prayers followed by the mass. After mass was breakfast and then chores; my favorite was being the chaplain's dining room attendant but we were given alternating chores. I worked in the kitchen, cleaned stairs and had laundry and pressing room duty. We picked vegetables from our own garden and strawberries from a nearby farm. It was very hot in our heavy habit in the scorching sun on some days.

There were classes throughout the day. I was assigned to teach catechism to a group of girls ages sixteen to twenty-four who were in a home economics course given in the same building. That morning class was intimidating to me, a small nineteen-year-old nun teaching to girls some of whom were older than myself. There were thirty students. I was also teaching French grammar to my fellow novices and postulants. At noontime there were prayers in the chapel, the Angelus. All prayers were recited in French, instead of in Latin. After lunch, the afternoon program was quite similar to the morning's. I was also in the choir and we had frequent practices.

After dinner we had recreation which included conversation, card and board games, music appreciation, and small skits performed by our very talented classmates. I recall the play Joan of Arc, beautifully acted by Sister Gloria.

On December 6th, 1958, my beloved grandmother died at age ninety-one. I was allowed to go to the funeral in Shediac, accompanied by my favorite sister, Sister Marie-Berthe, the laundry supervisor. We stayed at one of our community convents in Shediac. It felt so good to visit with my family and friends at the funeral home.

While I was in the Novitiate I suffered a pain in my pelvic area which required hospitalization in a Moncton hospital where I underwent some medical tests. I was sent to the hospital with Sister Antoinette, a novice who was leaving the convent. Her family gave me a ride to the hospital. It seems odd to me now. Once in a while, one of our classmates would leave; although nothing was said, we noticed, felt badly and missed her.

Another postulant, Sister Mélinda, was also hospitalized at the same time as I was. My pastor Father Albert Brideau was a patient as well. I visited him once. My classmate and I received several cards and letters from the sisters at the Novitiate.

In 1961, a young Catholic senator from the State of Massachusetts was running for President of the United States. Everyone was happy about it even behind convent walls in Saint-Joseph, New Brunswick, Canada. Little did I know that someday he would be my President.

While I was a novice I was in an advent play. I loved performing and was picked for another play to be done in the spring, but I left beforehand.

Our mistress of novices, Sister Marie-Antonine, was like a real mother to me: kind, understanding and loving to all. She was celebrated as she retired from her post and Sister Léo-Marie became our new leader.

Each year on August 15th, the feast of the Assumption of our Mother Mary, members of the religious order take their vows. After one year of postulancy we received the white veil and became a first-year novice. In 1960 I had become a second-year novice. I was then required to prepare and study to take my temporal vows in August 1961. I was not comfortable with taking the vows and got cold feet. Therefore, after a discussion with my mistress of novices, Sister Léo-Marie, it was decided that the religious life was not my vocation. I had spent two years and five months in the novitiate and I had loved it. I had been happy there. It is much easier to be a religious than to be a mother, in my opinion.

On a cold but sunny afternoon, on February 4th, 1961, I left the novitiate. My cousin Emery and his wife Gloria, who lent me a winter coat, took me home. It had been a very snowy month of January and mountains of snow surrounded us. They brought me to my sister's house, which was full of children. While I was away, my sister had given birth to two daughters, naming one after me. I was introduced to my two-month-old niece with my namesake.

Here I was starting my new life in a secular world, at one month short of my twenty-first birthday. I got a job at the Poirier Corner Store, a small convenience store owned by a distant relative and conveniently close to my sister's home. After a month or so, I became a nanny for the Kennedy family in Sunny Brae, a suburb of Moncton. I was caring for Lynne and Brian, ages six and four. Their mother worked at the employment office in Moncton; that is how I got that job. She was very nice to me and taught me how to make meatloaf! Brian was a handful; he tied me with a jump rope once when I was talking on the telephone.

In that summer of 1961, I came to the United States to visit my brother and his wife Cécile, a lovely girl formerly from New Brunswick. My niece Diane was just born. They lived in Waltham, Massachusetts, where I decided to stay and make a living. I worked at different jobs for the next three months such as the Ranch House, a fast food restaurant, Candyland, and a small factory making screws and nails. It was too difficult working two jobs, therefore I was happy to leave the old dusty factory and go to work for the Gallant family taking care of their two children. I slept at my cousin Alain's upstairs apartment, which was very convenient. I recall being so hungry and with so little money to spare I had crackers and grape jelly for my evening meal sometimes. That was my realization that money does not grow on trees, not even in America. I frequently visited my aunt and uncle Frank and Sara LeBlanc who lived near the Italian Church, which I loved. During that summer, I met a young gentleman, Euclide Brun, from New Brunswick. He was a kind and gentle soul and a respectful man. Once, at my brother's apartment, we were caught reciting the rosary together. My brother loved to tease us for being too serious. We were just friends.

I returned to New Brunswick to conclude my passport process in October with a former novitiate classmate of mine, Pauline Goguen and her husband Hervé Babineau, in his old jalopy. We made it there safely. I stayed at my sister's again and worked at obtaining my legal papers in order to become a legalized alien in this country.

CHAPTER 5

The Accident

On November 12th, 1961, a beautiful Sunday afternoon of a holiday weekend, on a dirt road in Rexton, New Brunswick, two young couples were laughing and having a good time returning home from a pleasant ride in the countryside. After stopping for a delicatessen delight, the foursome was on its way home, in the Volkswagen Beetle operated by our friend Patty, who did not have a driver's license but her friend Casey let her drive whenever she wanted to.

Suddenly something went wrong, but only God knows what, for it happened so fast. Crash! Bang! "Oh! Please, God, save us", whispered a voice. After a few seconds the vehicle came to a stop and rested on its roof. Patty was in the middle of the road but conscious. Casey came out staggering from the trees along the road, bleeding profusely from a laceration on his forehead. Euclide's leg was stuck under the car. I got out of the car and had minor cuts and bruises on my legs and hands. Help arrived and we soon were on our way to a nearby dispensary.

Euclide's legs were sore but there were no broken bones. Patty suffered a fractured thumb. Casey's forehead needed sutures. As for me, it seemed at the time that I was the least injured of us four. After our medical examinations we were released and were picked up by our relatives, respectively. The following day, we found a physician in his office in Shediac. After the doctor had extracted pieces of glass from my finger and legs, I complained about my neck being sore. I was told that I could expect that for a while.

On November 26th, 1961, I entered the USA with my visa. I was now legal! Earlier, while I was working without my legal papers (green card) I had always felt guilty and felt that I was cheating the government and that I did not belong here. I even discussed the issue in confession. On one occasion I went to confession to an old Italian priest who rushed me off and, not having understood him well between the French and Italian accents, I returned immediately to the booth to get more satisfaction and receive my penance.

The day after I returned to the USA, I got employment at the Clevite Corporation, a well-known electronics plant in Waltham, in the city where I would live with my aunt Sara and my uncle Frank. I had already met Phil at my brother's apartment. He also was employed by the same company. Meanwhile, the pain in my neck persisted, sometimes excruciating pain. Car rides were the worst punishment for my pain.

Phil and I started dating in December 1961, our first date being at the Clevite Christmas party. He was very compassionate, and shed a few tears with me at times. He insisted that I had radiography done as it never happened in New Brunswick at the time of the accident. So I did have my neck x-rayed, in July, eight months after the injury.

The x-rays revealed that I had sustained a fracture of two bones in my neck, C1 and C3. A cervical spine injury may be not only painful but also crippling or at least can become arthritic at a later time. Now the hairline fracture was healing but I needed treatment to alleviate the pain and suffering. Dr. Semenza, my aunt's physician, ordered tractions. These were purchased for $12.50 at the pharmacy and were installed above my bedroom door by my brother and my uncle. The tractions reminded me of the guillotine. My aunt kept saying: "Poor Doris, I know what you are going through. I had a broken bone in my back once which required an operation." That was exactly what I needed to hear...

Needless to say, I was very distraught about the whole thing and was a little resentful about the situation with the accident. The vehicle's owner was Casey's sister and Patty was driving without a license but with Casey's permission. On the night of the accident we had all agreed that we would not say anything about the accident to anyone. Apparently, months later, I was the one who sustained the most serious injury after all. Thankfully, my employer came through with the health benefits and I could finally breathe easier, for I had been worried sick about the financial burden.

I was hospitalized for ten days in tractions since the home treatment had not improved the healing. My orthopedist was Dr. Mulroy, and he informed me that I would have to wear a cervical collar for about six months.

Phil and I had been engaged since February and our wedding was planned for September 8th. Therefore, five weeks prior to our wedding, I was in tractions in a Waltham hospital with dreadful weights pulling at my neck, whether I was in a sitting or lying position. I was scolded several times for being out of my tractions too frequently.

At the hospital I spent my time in conversation with my roommate, a lovely Irish lady suffering from a back injury. I also had time to read and to write letters, and I kept busy planning our wedding. The visits, the cards and gifts cheered me up. Phil visited me faithfully each evening and he was frequently reminded of the visiting hours by the nurses as he abused the rule. Together we were planning our future.

Phil was of small stature, dark complexioned and witty. He had always been called "Little Phil" and I "Little Doris", therefore we made a compatible couple, apparently. He treated me right most of the time but he was a smoker and a drinker, which I detested; but, starving for affection, I tolerated it. He had recently returned from a tour of duty in Germany with the American Army.

After leaving the hospital I took a sick leave from Clevite to allow for my neck to heal. I had formed friendships with several coworkers from New Brunswick, among them were Maria LeBlanc and Nora Boudreau, who became my bridesmaids, and Diane Arsenault, a distant cousin, who would be my maid of honor. We kept the relationship for some time; then they returned to Canada and we lost contact with each other. Except for Diane, we still keep in touch.

Phil was told to stay out of the sun by our photographer: he was so heavily tanned. A week after Phil's return from army camp, our Big Day arrived!

CHAPTER 6

The Wedding

On a beautiful warm and sunny early autumn Saturday morning, on September 8th, 1962, Philbert J. Bourgeois and Doris M. Léger were married at St. Joseph's Church, a French church, in Waltham MA. The ceremony was officiated by Father Charles Aubut. It was an impressive ceremony and we were a happy couple surrounded by our family and friends. My uncle Frank gave me away; Phil's friend Ernie Russo was his best man; while my cousin and friend Diane was my maid of honor. Phil's brother Arthur and my brother Ronald were the groomsmen and Nora Boudreau and Maria LeBlanc were my bridesmaids.

Phil's mom Laura and his younger brother Elie had arrived from Canada the previous afternoon and had been picked up at the airport in Boston by a very nervous groom-to-be. Elie was to be the best man but his tour of duty in the Congo with the Canadian Army delayed his arrival. Phil is from a military family, his dad in his military career served in both World War I and World War II.

The wedding reception was at the French American Victory Club, in Waltham. The gorgeous 75-degree temperature brought many friends and relatives to celebrate with us. The music and dancing were still in full swing when we left the club to change into our going-away clothes. My outfit was a turquoise dress probably purchased at Grover Cronin Department Store, on sale no doubt. I was very thrifty even then. I wore white medium heels with accessories to match, including gloves.

Phil had an apartment on Cushing Street where we were going to live upon our return from our honeymoon. There we picked up our luggage and we were on our way to Canada in his two-tone '58 Chevy. Our first night was spent in Westminster MA, a small country town about one hour west of Waltham. The next day being Sunday, we attended a local church where the priest was facing the congregation while celebrating mass. This was our first time witnessing the new ritual change from the Second Vatican Council which was about to start; we were astonished.

We proceeded towards Canada via Vermont, Quebec, and Montreal, where we visited with Phil's brother Bob and his wife May. They had organized a little celebration, which was very nice. We also visited L'Institut Familial in Saint-Jérome where I had studied in 1957. And we visited L'Oratoire Saint-Joseph and another religious pilgrimage site called Notre-Dame-du-Cap at Cap-de-la-Madeleine.

The next day we continued on our journey along the Gaspé Coast, to the little motel where we stayed. I was startled at the sight of a fur coat left behind in the closet. In New Brunswick, we visited Phil's family and mine as well as relatives in Prince Edward Island. My sister and my brother-in-law came with us to the Island as they were celebrating their tenth wedding anniversary. One of my novitiate classmates, Anita Pellerin, was hospitalized for the amputation of a cancerous leg. We paid her a visit as well.

After our two relaxing weeks, we returned to 107 Cushing Street, Waltham, our new home. We continued to work at our respective jobs at Clevite Corporation. I wore my collar for two months more and I had nineteen outpatient physical treatments for my neck injury. It healed well, finally. Deo Gratias!

CHAPTER 7

Early Family Life

By the middle of November I was pregnant. More pregnancies were to follow in the next thirteen years.

I had a good pregnancy although it was a very hot summer. I was given a baby shower at my sister-in-law Rita's house. I received almost all I needed. I gained twenty-two pounds during my pregnancy and wore a shift dress to the hospital. I had a family doctor, not a gynecologist, Dr. J. Merola, who took good care of me. I was at the hospital for fifty-one hours prior to delivery, about twelve hours of labor, then I gave birth to my son Marcel Joseph on Friday August 23rd at 3:12 am. He weighed six pounds six ounces and was nineteen inches long. I was elated! He was a healthy baby, with long dark hair.

I had a lot to learn as I had no experience in the care of a newborn. My aunt Sara, who had had eight children, and aunt Marguerite, who had moved from New Brunswick to care for an elderly lady in Newton MA, as well as Phil's aunt Annie were all very helpful. Phil, being from a large family, was more comfortable with a small baby than I was. Marcel was a charming baby, content and easy to care for. Surprise! when Marcel was two and a half months old I found myself pregnant again. Since I felt very tired, I was advised by the pediatrician to stop breastfeeding.

I enjoyed motherhood with my calm good-natured and healthy baby. Marcel was three months old when our President was assassinated on November 22nd, 1963. I learned the news while on a walk with the baby in his carriage on that dark afternoon. What a sad tragedy!

Marcel's first haircut was at about one year and it was given to him by his godfather, uncle Arthur, a barber. We moved to 100½ Prospect Street in the center of Waltham, in a nice four-room first-floor apartment, across from an elementary school. The apartment owners were Phil's cousins and they were very good landlords.

At age twenty-four, I had two babies in eleven and a half months. On August 8th, 1964, Janice Marie was born at 11:59 pm weighing six pounds nine ounces and nineteen inches long, with dark curly hair and a dark complexion. Uncle Jim said she was the prettiest baby he had ever seen. She certainly was daddy's little princess. Janice was baptized on Marcel's first birthday. Her uncle Ronald and aunt Cécile were the godparents. It was such a joyous occasion.

Marcel did not walk until he was thirteen months old. Then he had to give up the crib to his sister and be promoted to the Big Boy's Bed. Having an allergy to the milk formula, Janice was very unhappy, suffering from colic, until it was remedied. She also had motion sickness which made car rides difficult. Marcel welcomed his little sister by powdering her face once, otherwise he was good with her.

At four months, Janice was hospitalized with pneumonia. I forgot to leave her pacifier with the nurse before leaving so she got used to falling asleep without it in the oxygen tank. Poor baby! When it came time to wean her from the baby bottle during the night, which was difficult, a few sleepless nights did it. At seven months she outgrew the motion sickness.

I loved to fix Janice's beautiful dark curly hair and to sew clothes for her. She liked to tease her brother and pull on his pants and make him fall sometimes. Marcel loved to play with his twenty-seven matchbox cars, all lined up on the coffee table. I still remember him coming out of his concentration on his caravan every time a commercial would come on television. He especially liked the one about the Chunky candy bar: "Open Wide For Chunky".

During a fight with his neighbor playmate, Marcel bit Paul, and what a reaction from the mother and the Italian grandmother! I was mortified! I apologized, of course, and life went on. Marcel and Janice got along fairly well most of the time. We enjoyed them a lot. Phil was working at the General Motors Corporation in Framingham MA. I was a stay-at-home mom and life was pretty good then. We visited relatives on weekends so the children would get to know their cousins. We also visited great-uncle Jim and aunt Annie, who was a great cook and had a beautiful flower garden.

We went to visit our family in New Brunswick every summer. In 1965, I went with the two children and I was to stay for about one month but Janice got sick. After a few visits to the doctor's and a few sleepless nights, it had become a nightmare. My in-laws were very hospitable and understanding but it was very difficult so Phil came back for us sooner than planned.

During that visit, I visited the religious sisters in Moncton. A few of the sisters had been in the convent with me. That was special. In that same time I met and became good friends with my cousin Reggie's wife Marie-Anne. We had a lot in common, especially children the same ages. That friendship lasted until her death in 2013.

On November 26th, 1966, John Francis was born at six pounds ten ounces and nineteen and a half inches long, with blue eyes and a fair complexion. He was a healthy child and developed rapidly in mind and in body. At age four months he was crawling from one end of our four-room apartment to the other. He was tiny and agile. Phil had picked the name John and I picked his middle name.

I now was the busy mother of three children in a little over three years. We lived on Prospect Street in Waltham until John was sixteen months old. Then we moved to our 86 Pine Street Franklin MA ranch home in March of 1968. My first year in Franklin was not too great as I could not walk with the children with the baby stroller, as there were no sidewalks and also no street lights which I was accustomed to in Waltham. Evenings were scary for me as Phil was working and the neighborhood was pitch dark.

John quickly learned to master stairs and climb the fence separating our yard from our neighbors', the Lapios. John and I had a lot of time together when Marcel and Janice were in school. We played board games and read books. He was a fast learner and retained the ending of his favorite book: ...they did somersaults all over the yard. That book was read to him every night. He did not speak much until his second birthday. At age three, he walked with me to the John F. Kennedy School, a distance of one and one third mile each way, to bring his brother's much needed mittens for recess. He seemed to enjoy the walk.

In 1969, I got myself a typewriter and started writing songs and short stories. Getting a lot of rejection slips did not deter me from keeping on trying. The Man With Charisma was written after Robert F. Kennedy's assassination. I obtained a copyright and three promotional 45 vinyl records for the song. I also took a writing test and got a B grade and received the visit of the representative of the Writers' School but I could not pursue that dream at that time as my family was my priority.

John became an avid Sesame Street and Electric Company viewer. When he was glued to the television screen, that was my writing time. My typing was poor, slow and difficult as I never had typing lessons in school.

At age three and a half, John could add and subtract equations up to twenty. It was amazing! John and Christine Berardi, our little neighbor who was about one and a half year older, were best of friends until they were twelve years old. Her mother was one of my best friends until her death in 2012. She often said that we would have a great big French / Italian wedding someday for John and Christine.

My active little John was always outdoors in fair weather, chasing or kicking a ball of some sort. One early evening, he was retrieving a ball from under his dad's car, in our driveway. Phil started the vehicle to be on his way to get milk at the corner store, unaware of John's whereabouts, until he heard a thump and a cry. Needless to say, Phil was visibly shaken as he carried his frightened and crying little boy into the house after this scary near-tragic incident. Miraculously, three-year-old John sustained only a small abrasion on one finger. He soon recovered; all he needed was his mother's comfort and his siblings' sympathy.

In the 70s there was no kindergarten in our town. We were told however that being a French-speaking family, we were eligible to send our young children to a preschool program at no charge. Therefore, four-year-old John went to Project Swing on Saturdays, while his playmates were home from school. On one occasion, the school bus driver's husband took the students home and he did not know where the children lived. When John was asked, he said he lived in Franklin. Finally the driver's wife identified John and provided his address. You bet John was taught his home address promptly following that incident.

Marcel and Janice started school in 1969 and 1970, respectively. They were doing well and liking school. Marcel joined the cub scouts and Janice was a brownie. Then came the little league baseball and the Franklin Rangerettes, a drum and marching band which was competing with other similar drum and marching bands. Janice was the flag carrier. We were busy every weekend during the summer with baseball or Rangerettes.

Our backyard was the neighborhood playground. Phil was very strict and wanted his children on their own property. Some of the neighbors' children were not very comfortable with my husband but they played with my children and behaved in our yard.

On July 15th, 1969, I got my driver's license, at age twenty-nine. I had taken driving classes at the Franklin High School adult program with Mr. McCall. I had failed the first attempt but felt liberated once I got my driver's license. Phil was busy working and I was busy as a stay-at-home mom. I joined the Women's Club at our St. Brendan Church in North Bellingham. On weekends before I had my driver's license, I had gone to mass at the Fatima Shrine in Holliston MA with my good friend Therese. I met a lot of new friends through the children's school activities and my friendly neighbors.

Marcel, Janice and John were all fairly healthy except for John's frequent ear infections.

I started teaching catechism (CCD) for our St. Brendan Parish. I taught Marcel's first grade class. One time, then three-year-old John answered a question that had the other children baffled. Unfortunately, I do not recall the question at this time. My neighbor Mrs. Wilcox, who was helping me with the large class, was very impressed with John.

On January 23rd, 1972, we welcomed Jamie Patrick at seven pounds and seven ounces and twenty inches long. He was born with long dark hair and what was called "the devil's horn" on his head. The pediatrician informed me that it would disappear in six months or so. It was all gone within three weeks. Even though John had been the baby of the family for five years and two months, he accepted his little brother with open arms. Once, he picked up his newborn brother from his crib, carried him to the living room and sat on the sofa, holding and consoling him. Upon my return from the basement laundry room, I was shocked to find John, a small five-year-old holding Jamie Patrick. When I explained to him my concern about safety, he said to me: "But, Mommy, the baby was crying." Even at that young age, he showed his kind and caring nature. I can say the same about all my children. Jamie was our pride and joy. Janice was like a little mother to him.

CHAPTER 8

The Practical Nurse License

I had first applied for the nursing program in 1970. After reviewing my math with library books and honing my language skills with the word power section of the Reader's Digest, and after taking a mandatory psychological test, I had been accepted into the program. I had earned money to pay for my school books and uniforms by coloring coats of arms for a neighbor. I was then ready to start school in the fall of 1971. I needed to be a US citizen to take my state board exam, however. Therefore, on October 18th, 1971, Phil and I became American citizens. Aunt Annie and uncle Jim were our sponsors. Now I had to wait to enter the class of September of 1972. I was so anxious to go to school. I called Mrs. Knight, the nursing school coordinator from the maternity ward after Jamie was born. She told me I could go in the program until I was sixty-five years old. I did not like that comment. At the start of classes in September 1972, Jamie was eight months old. My next-door neighbor Geri was to take care of Jamie, as John was starting first grade. That only lasted one month for they moved to Mississippi to be with family there. Their son David, John's close friend, was leaving also. How sad for John. My best friend and neighbor Therese, and Jamie's godmother, took great care of my baby.

So in September of 1972, I entered the nursing program at Henry O. Peabody School for Girls in Norwood MA, approximately eighteen miles from my home. The town of Franklin paid my tuition of $700.00 and reimbursed my mileage costs as the school was an accredited vocational school and my town was included in its district. Lucky me!

Although school was difficult for me after being out of high school for fourteen years and not having had anatomy or biology in school, I loved it and certainly made a lot of new friends, some of whom I remain in touch with today. Our family life changed some: Phil changed his work schedule and worked the second shift at General Motors. When I was leaving for school at 7:00 am, Phil was coming home from work, the older three children were getting ready for school. After they had taken the school bus, Phil would take Jamie next door to Therese and then go home and sleep until 2:00 pm. When the school bus brought the children home, he would pick up Jamie. I was coming home around 4:00 pm. At that time there were chores, supper, the children's activities and homework (including mine). For eleven and a half months I had three hours of sleep each night except on Fridays, my night free from studies. It was very hard for the whole family, but I knew that it would pay off someday. And it did.

I had a good attendance at school: I missed only one day of class when Phil had to use my vehicle to bring John to Framingham for adenoids surgery. On that day there was also an ice storm but apparently the whole class was present except me. On that day, my classmates voted for the Eager Beaver Award, which was a piece of wood prepped by a beaver and found near Lake Winnipesaukee in New Hampshire, by Ms. Keady, one of our instructors. At our February capping ceremony, I was the recipient of that award, which had been stained and polished by my friend Victoria's father. I was happy with that special sign which led me to believe that my classmates and teachers appreciated my efforts and might even have felt sympathetic towards my struggles in class and my busy home life.

Soon after capping, I was with fifth child and, afraid of not being allowed to finish the school year, I tried to conceal my baby bump by wearing a tight girdle. Mrs. Knight got wise to my situation and kindly reassured me that I could continue the classes if I did not miss too many days. I was so relieved and continued my regular schedule and did not miss another day of class.

Baby Jamie was thriving. He was smothered with affection from his godmother and from his family. He was the youngest of his siblings to learn to walk, at eight and a half months, and could speak sentences at seventeen months. Being clumsy, he suffered many cuts and bruises with enough sutures on his face along the way. While growing up he had more injuries than his adventurous brother John, who at age three required seven sutures on his hand after sliding down a tree, but had avoided a major catastrophe by his fast moving out of the way of his father's car while darting out of our driveway after a rolling ball. Those were the never-a-dull-moment days in our household.

My fifth pregnancy was going well and I was thankful to some of my classmates for their generosity in lending me larger uniforms. I loved the hospital rotation and caring for the patients. When I was asked if I had any previous medical experience, my answer was: "I have none". Ms. Keady corrected me saying: "You have plenty of experience by being a mother". On July 20th, I was given a surprise baby shower at the school then on August 18th we had our graduation banquet at the LaFayette Club in Foxborough MA. My friend Sarah and I took a train ride to Boston to purchase a dress-style white uniform, the kind of uniform which along with the nurse's cap are presently obsolete.

Graduation Day was September 20th. The ceremony was at the school and was attended by the superintendent of the Norwood School District among others. For me the most important people in attendance were my family: my husband Phil, Marcel 9, Janice 8, and John 6; after all they helped me to get through that extremely busy year by doing their part in whatever they were asked to do. It had been a difficult year for the whole family. Bedtime had been set at half past seven during school nights so I could do my homework and laundry. The three older children were my occupied-bed models during my practice at home in order to demonstrate to the class on the following day. I received a standing ovation when I stood to receive my diploma as an expecting mother of four. I was elated! I had made it. I was a nurse! My family and friends were proud of my achievement.

On October 20th, 1973, Mark Jason was born, weighing only five pounds eight ounces and nineteen inches long, but he was a healthy baby. All was going well and I kept busy with my family and still kept up my studying for the State Board's exam which was to be on November 20th. On that day, I got a ride with Dale Anderson from Franklin, our nursing class' youngest student. It was a difficult day for me as I had been up during the night with my one-month-old baby's feedings. The temperature in the exam room was about 90 degrees Fahrenheit, but I passed the difficult exam. It was such a joy to receive my hard-earned nursing license. Yay! I was now ready to use my nursing knowledge to help heal people. I applied at the Milford Regional Hospital for part-time employment as a Licensed Practical Nurse. I was very persistent in pursuing that sought-after position. Finally I was called for an interview with Mrs. Recchia and I was hired to work in the Intensive Care Unit. Pretty scary! Mark J. was then three months old. Jamie turned two on January 23rd and I started my orientation on January 28th, 1974, working daytime shift. Phil was home that week and toilet-trained Jamie. What a guy!

Henry O. Peabody School
Nursing Class of 1973

CHAPTER 9

Milford Whitinsville Regional Hospital

I loved working in ICU but I was uncomfortable at first as I was a new LPN fresh out of nursing school. The unit was small, ten beds in all. The staff was very helpful. In spite of my feeling inadequate, it felt good being able to help in the care of sick patients. I was working the evening shift, three times a week. This included weekends, which Janice disliked a lot as she was home with her four brothers and her dad and had to help with the care of the little ones and also help with the chores. Her favorite pastime was playing with paper dolls and of course teasing her older brothers and getting them in trouble. Janice was always very helpful in every way, she was my big helper. She used to beg me not to go to work sometimes as she missed my company. We were close. My income was necessary at the time as the family had grown to five children and I now had a profession. A profession that I loved.

I worked for a year and a half in the Intensive Care Unit, then it became a policy that only registered nurses would work in ICU. I was transferred to the Maternity Floor. I was assigned to care for the post partum patients and sometimes I worked in the nursery with Mrs. Lynch and Mrs. Mazzini. I really enjoyed working with those exemplary nurses who taught me so much. Mrs. Haynes and Mrs. Maffia were also great.

This was 1975, prior to the 1990s when a major renovation made the Milford Regional Hospital a modern state-of-the-art maternity department, the envy of surrounding area hospitals. Milford Hospital was founded in 1903 and had become a full service non-profit 121-bed acute care facility serving twenty plus towns. Through the years it had grown and became a teaching hospital in the 1990s, affiliated with the University Massachusetts Medical Center in Worcester MA. In 2007, a

$25-million Cancer Center was established near the Hospital, a satellite of the Dana-Farber Institute and Brigham and Women's Boston-based hospitals. In 2009, a Breast Health Center also became part of the hospital, now known as Milford Regional Medical Center which has been in the top one hundred hospitals in the country along with other hospitals with the same criteria. Administration and staff pride themselves of their 145 beds and nearly two hundred physicians on staff and another hundred courtesy and consulting physicians. Presently, a two-year project is in progress for expanding the medical facility. This is the hospital where I gave birth to my three youngest children.

When working on the maternity floor I was expecting my sixth child. I was given a baby shower at the hospital, courtesy of my coworkers. It was lovely. On August 19th, 1976, my second little girl was born, weighing in at seven pounds and seven and one quarter ounces (one quarter ounce on you, Jamie!). Lori-Ann was a nineteen-inch pretty bundle of joy.

Janice was besides herself at the thought of finally having a little sister to spoil. She even disguised herself to look like a fourteen-year-old (she had just turned twelve) and broke the hospital visiting rules in order to bring her gift, a pretty aqua-colored outfit, to her baby, to the maternity ward.

Mark, age two, was a patient on the pediatric floor, after being diagnosed with a blood disorder called Idiopathic Thrombocytopenic Purpura, which means a decreased number of platelets in the bloodstream. It manifests itself with bruises over the body. Mark, at his young age, impressed the nurses with his knowledge: he could read his full name on his medical chart. He was also very tolerant of the daily blood draws, which amazed the staff as well. He was hospitalized for nine days and treated with prednisone then he continued to be monitored closely by his pediatrician Dr. John Cocchiarella MD. The normal platelet count is between 150 and 400. Mark's was 25. Although there is no known cause for ITP, there is a cure. Sometimes the removal of the spleen is performed but not in Mark's case. About forty years later, a nurse who had cared for Mark remembered him, as well as his diagnosis. I was amazed!

Mark's discharge from the hospital happened the day following the mother and baby's return home. It must have been traumatic for this toddler to realize that he was not the baby in this family any longer. During the following days he repeated the words "I love you, Mommy" as many as twenty-five times a day. Yes, I counted. He never hurt his baby sister, but the rivalry between the two siblings intensified through their childhood. They became friends in their teens and grew even closer in their adulthood.

Lori-Ann was a very calm baby, so much so that Janice thought she was deaf. Janice helped to care for the baby and spoiled her when their father was hospitalized for open-heart surgery for the repair of an aortic aneurysm at St. Elizabeth Hospital in Brighton MA, where he stayed for nineteen days. Lori-Ann was then three months old and her big sister Janice was a huge help to me.

== CHAPTER 10 ==

Phil's Medical Emergency

On November 10th, 1976, on a snowy evening, Phil returned from his work at the General Motors Plant complaining of left arm and left jaw pain. I took him to the Milford Hospital where he was diagnosed by cardiologist Dr. S. Razvi with aortic dissection and aneurysm. He was immediately transported to Boston for emergency surgery. He was seven weeks shy of turning forty-one years old. This was a difficult time for our family. The surgery was performed during the night and I was told on the telephone there was only a two percent chance of survival. Pretty scary. I thought for sure I was going to become a widow on that long night. I called my neighbor and best friend Therese to come and stay with me; we got busy cleaning the house. Therese was a very neat lady.

I drove to Boston the next day to visit Phil, and subsequently I drove again with Therese, who was my navigator. On Thanksgiving Day I took all the children to visit their dad. They brought best wishes cards and letters. There were food baskets and other donations from friends and neighbors and from staff of Milford Hospital departments who knew us.

I was working part-time on the maternity floor at the time, on the evening shift. Friends and relatives helped with child care. When Phil returned home he had to be on a restricted activity program. He did well but he had to take a disability pension from General Motors after one year on sick leave. The Knights of Columbus were also a great help to our family, especially at Christmas time. It was very hard for Phil to be unable to work at such a young age with a family of eight to support. He had always been a workaholic and a good provider.

I increased my working hours at the hospital and also was transferred from the maternity to a medical surgical floor, 4 West. That was a fun floor with family-like staff, where I made some lifelong friends, such as Louise Nelson Fitzgerald, with whom I share a birthdate. We had a lot in common even though I was eighteen years her senior. While working on 4 West I took a Framingham State College course at the hospital. Although it was difficult, I got an A- on Sociology of the Family, a course that I enjoyed very much.

It was a busy time in the Bourgeois household as our family grew older (and wiser). The five-year difference between the three older siblings and the three younger made it easier in some ways but harder in others.

Well, as they participated in different activities and sports, life went on as in any average normal family. The children were doing fairly well in school, especially John who was excelling in math and was an avid reader. He got the Most Read Books Award once; his reward... a book. He still likes to read today. Marcel and John were in the Boy Scouts Organization and their dad was involved helping with the Webelos; he and the boys won the cake decorating contest and the model race car contest. All good for the boys.

In 1977, Grandpa Bourgeois passed away in New Brunswick, Canada. By Lori-Ann's third birthday, the children had lost both grandparents. Grandma left us on the second anniversary of Elvis Presley's death, on August 16ᵗʰ, 1979. Her funeral was on Lori-Ann's third birthday. All six children were placed in a different friend's home while Phil and I drove to New Brunswick to be with the family at that sad time. I loved my mother-in-law and we sorely missed her. She loved all her grandchildren dearly, but Marcel was special to her as his birthday was the day previous to hers.

Those were years filled with loss for Phil.

CHAPTER II

Facts about the Bourgeois Family

Marcel was very pious in church, especially after he made his First Communion at age seven. Janice was the only sibling who made her First Communion on a rainy day and her dad had to work on that day. She was never attracted to religion, perhaps because at age three, her dad punished her for not behaving in church, one Sunday.

When John turned four years old, he started making his bed; therefore when his younger siblings turned four they were expected to do the same.

All started to learn their prayers at age three. We always prayed together at bedtime and during lent we recited the rosary as a family.

John became an altar boy, serving mass, when he was in sixth grade. Jamie and Mark followed suit. Our son Jamie was the only mass server with facial hair, a ponytail and a dog chain around his wrist. What a way to make a statement as a teenager!

Jamie also got in trouble in school for imitating the chicken sound and for wearing ripped jeans. I even hid the torn jeans in question in the trunk of my car, which he found.

Mark was spending much time at his friend Tracy Gavel's house, where he was learning French, learning good music appreciation, getting free piano lessons and going to concerts. That friendship lasted from second to seventh grade.

Lori-Ann was the youngest of the family to skip school, in second grade. She also guided her blindfolded brother Mark to crash into a cement incinerator located in the middle of our backyard while playing Hide and

Seek. Fortunately for Mark, it was not catastrophic; but he wore a lump on his forehead on his First Communion day.

Mark also suffered the effects of a bad haircut, courtesy of brother Jamie, as the hair gluing was unsuccessful.

In 1978, while vacationing in New Brunswick and staying at a trailer park in Shediac, my home town, then six-year-old Jamie was very active. In order to keep track of him, I started running after him all over the park. So after our return home, I kept on running in early morning and John started to run with me: he wanted to increase his speed for his soccer game. John, at twelve, did not keep it up for long, but I did and became hooked on running. September 1978 was the beginning of my running career, which spanned over thirty years. It was very hard at first and much discipline was needed, but I loved running, and wanted to pursue that hobby. I was thirty-eight years old and had never run before except when, as a child, I would run from my village of Saint-Marcel to my school in Grande-Digue. There were no school buses in those days.

Marcel, John, Jamie and Mark all played baseball. Janice was a girl scout and in a drill corps, the Rangerettes. John, Jamie, and Mark played soccer. Lori-Ann also played soccer, was a girl scout and played softball.

Lori-Ann was also a gymnast for many years. She and I were fortunate to enjoy a trip to Europe in 1988 with her gymnastics team. That was a memorable time; we visited Luxembourg, Austria, Germany, Switzerland and Lichtenstein. Her team practiced with other teams and we attended many fun events in beautiful countries on a nine-day tour. I was very grateful to my family for allowing me to go with my daughter by providing the funds as I was not working at the time due to an injury at work. Lori-Ann earned her own way through fundraisers.

Jamie loved to draw and at kindergarten pre-registration, he was asked to draw a picture of himself. He drew a lion and insisted that was him. At ages three and four, every morning Jamie would say: Who will I be today? He would pretend to be a policeman, a fireman, a cowboy, a clown, or other child hero. He would use whatever clothes and props he could find: his imagination was wild. He loved to sing, dance and act. He was in many school plays and at age eleven he played Kurt in The Sound Of Music with the St. Mary's playgroup in Franklin. The play was a huge success. We were so proud of our little thespian.

Lori-Ann was in the children's choir of the same play, The Sound of Music, with the nuns at the Abbey. Having to stay up so late at practice, she was allowed to rest in the nurse's office at school on the next day. She was six and a half.

Jamie was in the play The Music Man and along with Mark had minor roles in Annie. They both were in a small play called Save my Garden in which Mark played a villain.

Jamie directed his own plays with his friends and neighbors. In the summer, our backyard became an outdoor theater and our picnic table was transformed into a stage.

John and Mark were jugglers, in their own way. John juggled three balls and Mark juggled three bowling pins. Very interesting!

February 12th, 1978

Here is how tall we were:

Lori-Ann	32 inches	18 months
Mark Jason	39 ½ inches	4 years 4 months
Jamie Patrick	44 inches	6 years 1 month
John Francis	53 inches	11 years 3 months
Janice Marie	62 ¼ inches	13 years 6 months
Marcel Joseph	5 feet 6 inches	14 years 6 months
Doris Marie	5 feet	37 years 11 months
Philbert Joseph	5 feet 6 inches	42 years 2 months

CHAPTER 12

The Blizzard of '78

The great blizzard hit New England hard, especially Massachusetts. It formed on Sunday February 5th, 1978 and it started snowing on Monday February 6th in mid-morning and the snow continued until Tuesday February 7th in the evening. Our meteorologists, Harvey Leonard of Channel 7 and Dick Albert of Channel 5, both warned us: "It is going to be a BIG one".

School and work facilities were dismissed early on Monday. I left the hospital after my day shift was over at 3:00 pm. After leaving my vehicle in the hospital parking lot, my friend and coworker Louise Nelson drove us safely home to Franklin. My family was safe at home.

Marcel was then fourteen and a half years old, Janice was thirteen and a half, John was eleven, Jamie was six, Mark was four and Lori-Ann was one and a half year old. We had plenty of food and heat. Fortunately we did not lose our electrical power.

Tuesday was my day off from work. Phil was home, on disability since 1977, and he was very helpful in the care of the children, enabling me to work during the day. As I recall, we spent time playing board games, making puzzles, listening to news reports, and watching the enormous snowstorm with wind gusts of hurricane force reaching 75 mph in Boston and 93 mph in Chatham MA.

Highways, such as Route 128 and Interstate 495, became parking lots with 3,000 cars and 500 trucks stranded. The white-out conditions lasted about thirty-two hours. Roads were impassable and snowplows had difficulty clearing them therefore emergency vehicles only were allowed.

Snowmobiles, 4-wheel drive Jeeps, and sleds were used to bring medical staff to work. Our governor Michael Dukakis urged everyone to stay home as it was too dangerous to be outside, and for people not be interfering with the snow removal equipment.

The Civil Defense and the National Guard were of great help at this time of need.

Some facts of this Great Blizzard:

Visibility was reduced to near zero.

Beach erosion and coastal flooding occurred.

Portions of Rhode Island and Massachusetts were declared disaster areas by President Jimmy Carter and federal help was sent to clean up.

Sea levels were more than 16 feet above normal at some places.

Death tolls:	Massachusetts: 73	Injuries and illnesses: 432
	Rhode Island: 28	Injuries and illnesses: 232

Damages:	Massachusetts: $500 million
	Rhode Island: $11 million
	New Hampshire: $14 million

Beginning February 6th and 7th, 1978, the whole State came to a standstill for a week. When the sun finally reappeared, the children enjoyed frolicking in their snow-blanketed backyards and the parents got to know their neighbors better.

CHAPTER 13

A Busy Mom's Time Away

I kept very busy with my nursing career and my family. On March 17th, 1980, I was invited by my good friend Antanet Shaw to come visit her in West Palm Beach, Florida. Waving a welcome sign and later we enjoyed a cake at home. That was a great getaway for a busy mom.

The flight from Logan Airport Boston to West Palm Beach, which was my first time flying, was pleasant. Ann was waiting for me at the airport.

The next morning, off we went to Riviera Beach on Singer Island. It was a beautiful day but I got a little too much sun. My dear friend had a colitis flare-up and, although feeling miserable, made sure that I had a good time. This is a lady with a heart of gold! My friend Ann Shaw was a retired school teacher and my friend Therese Berardi's sister, and my friend Beverly-An's loving mom.

I jogged everyday, met with her friends, went to the orange grove, to the dog track (no winnings). We saw The Coal Miner's Daughter movie. We visited the famous hotel The Breakers. And we went shopping for family gifts.

At the Red Lobster Restaurant, I had a Pina Colada… Yes, I did! I have a photo to prove it.

Ann always prepared simple, nutritious and great tasting meals.

Unfortunately, my dream vacation soon came to an end. The flight home was fine even with two stops: one in Atlanta and the other in New York. My entire family welcomed me in Boston, waving a welcome sign and later we enjoyed a cake at home. After that nice reception, the children enjoyed their gifts as well as the fruit I brought back from Florida. That was a great getaway for a busy mom; thanks to my family and a super friend.

CHAPTER 14

A Busy Life

The following weeks were busy ones: Jamie's First Communion, the completion of the psychology course I was taking at the hospital and the oral presentation of the essay Communications in the Family, on which I got a good grade and a standing ovation from my classmates. I believe they sympathized with my effort in spite of my French accent.

Another paper was written about The Problems of Adolescents, which was typed for me by my good friend's daughter Teri, which was much appreciated. Therese was always there for me when I needed her, like on the evening that my car keys disappeared in the road drain in front of the John F. Kennedy School where I was attending a meeting. Phil was called and came to my rescue, and Therese stayed with my children. We later on laughed at that episode as we reminisced on the "Old Days" on Pine Street in Franklin.

After an evaluation from my head nurse, I got a raise in pay, which brought my hourly pay rate to $5.24. (That was 1979.)

Life was always busy in our household with the many children activities, playing board games and reading to the younger ones every night, or being read to by the children.

Mark was an avid Sesame Street fan as his brother John had been before him. He learned to make the letter M at the age of fifteen months and could read the newspaper fluently at age four by sounding the words.

I kept jogging as often as I could, according to the available time and energy. Sometimes one of the children would come with me.

CHAPTER 15

Idiosyncrasies

I have some weird habits, my family would agree...

Apples: I love them; when I am through eating an apple, there is nothing left of it. I eat the core, the seeds and the stem. No waste.

Empty spaces: I dislike bare walls and bare floor spaces, unless there is too much clutter.

I am a Pack Rat, saving everything, especially paper products such as: greeting cards, letters, newspaper clippings (obituaries, weddings and important current events).

I have old magazines of presidential inaugurations, papal elections, wars, royal coronations, natural disasters, and famous personalities.

I have saved through the years thousands of photos and clippings, hundreds of 8-track cartridges, and also a 1975 stereo player. On which, I can still play my favorite country music tapes as well as records.

I also saved my tag number of every road race I ran, as well as clippings of the Boston Marathon News.

Sponges of every kind, I despise.

Window shades, I turn upward versus downward to block the light better.

Comforters or bedspreads must be removed from the bed at night.

Blankets should not touch the face.

I dislike locked doors. I do not lock my car or the house all the time.

Toilet seat covers should be closed when not occupied.

Food should not be wasted. I will eat something I do not like or is unhealthy for me so not to throw it away.

I feel I have to occupy every minute of the day and I feel guilty if planned chores or projects are not completed as intended. Therefore I have stayed up late to finish what was started. TIME is precious. I try not to waste it.

I'm unable to relax until all is done, that means never! for as you know, a woman's work is never done. I was multitasking when the word wasn't cool. I must admit that as I grew older I have become more lenient (or lazy) with myself.

I collect small bells.

I recycle boxes (all sizes), bags and wrapping paper.

I love mail and consider it a sad day when the mail is not delivered. I usually receive on average eight to ten pieces of mail daily; but I have received a record high of thirty-four pieces in one day, and not on the day after a holiday. Most of the mail consists of catalogs and greeting cards from different agencies or religious missions demanding donations. That explains why I have a multitude of greeting cards of all kinds. Recently I have been receiving a large amount of political mail.

Since age thirteen, I have been wearing my wrist watch on my right wrist with the watch facing the anterior aspect of my arm rather than facing upward.

I still use the old-fashioned cleaning method of Elbow Grease.

I have an aversion for shopping carts left close to vehicles in parking lots.

I dislike umbrellas and pocketbooks and use them sparingly. I love to wear raincoats and hooded jackets, with pockets, instead.

My Flaws:

I am very obstinate; I will search for the correct answer to prove that I am right.

I am afraid of rejection and failure; I want to make a good impression and I want to be the best I can be.

Sometimes I use excuses to make me look better.

I have difficulty accepting compliments.

I can accept constructive criticism graciously, but I feel terrible afterwards.

I am naïve and trusting, sometimes to my disadvantage.

Guilts:

I feel that I should have been more affectionate, understanding, patient and a better listener when I was raising my children.

CHAPTER 16

Teenagers

From 1976 to 1980, the three oldest children became teens. They all had been good students until high school. John was very active in sports and as a freshman played three sports. He played baseball and soccer and he wrestled. He was recruited to play soccer on the varsity team. When playing against the varsity team he scored the only two points to win the game. Once, while on the wrestling team, he had to lose weight for the category requirements, therefore he had to run in place on the bus on the way to Hyannis. He qualified but missed defending the State Championship by a few points. Too tired from running, perhaps? Marcel played baseball and tennis in school and received an award for tennis at graduation. Janice competed with the Rangerettes for four years.

Early employments included newspaper delivery: four boys and one delivery girl, Janice. Marcel also worked at inserting newspaper ads in a local newspaper prior to working at Speroni's Restaurant in Medway MA where his brothers Jamie and Mark served time at kitchen duty as well, along with their friends Steve and David, David Jr., Tracy and other teenagers from our church community.

Janice had babysitting assignments in the neighborhood and was a busgirl at the Colonial Restaurant in Bellingham and worked at Regina Pizzeria in Franklin as well, while taking food trades at our local vocational school, the Tri-County Regional. John's first employment was parking cars at a flea market in Franklin, under John Tregoning's leadership, and he did some iron work later on as well as he worked for the Guitar Therapeutic Glove Company, for the same employer.

Marcel, at age nineteen, taught fourth grade CCD class for one year. His all-boy class included his brother Mark, David Rapko and Danny Marsh, among others.

CHAPTER 17

Separation Divorce and Annulment

In 1981, Marcel graduated from Franklin High School in Franklin and the following September he started business studies at Mass Bay Community College in Wellesley MA. At this time Lori-Ann started kindergarten (half days). As I was working during the day, I needed daycare for my five-year-old daughter. Marcel helped on his time off from classes. A neighbor, M. Steinborn, as well as a nearby daycare center were my other options. The reason for this need was that on August 8th, on Janice's seventeenth birthday, Phil had left our home.

The last few years had been difficult; our marriage was suffering. After family and individual counseling and under the guidance of a Catholic priest, it was advised that having fared well on my own with the children for the past six months, it would be better for the children's welfare if Phil and I would stay apart and continue our guidance classes. Father C. also agreed there were reasons for divorce, unfortunately.

That was not an easy decision to make. Lori-Ann asked: Why did you send my daddy away? Her daddy had been her caretaker since she was one year old. He braided her long hair, cooked for her, listened to music with her and took her for car rides. The bond had been interrupted and she missed her daddy. I felt terrible.

After three years of separation, in 1984, the divorce was finalized with some help from Suffolk University Law School for the total cost of FIFTY dollars. On a fine July day, Phil and I drove to the Dedham District Courthouse to obtain our divorce papers; all went well. Afterwards, we had lunch, then Phil drove me home. It might seem strange to some but that was the way best suited for us. No grudge.

I got full custody of the four minor children. It was agreed to consult each other in regards to education, health and welfare for the children's best interest and to discuss our concerns in a harmonious manner. The children and I were to remain in our home until the youngest child would turn eighteen, at which time the property was to be sold.

Flexible visitation rights were agreed upon. It was by mutual agreement that either one of us would encourage respect for both parents from the children. Health insurance was provided by Phil's former employer, the General Motors Corporation.

It was a challenge to raise a family, maintain a household, and engage in a full-time nursing profession. Although it was difficult financially, my income was supplemented by child support provided by Social Security from Phil's disability pension - which was a godsend for us - until the children's eighteenth birthday as long as they were in school (which they were). They all graduated from high school: three from Franklin High School and three from Tri-County Vocational, located in Franklin as well.

Phil moved to Milford and found it very awkward to pick up the younger children in the driveway for visits. I agreed that he could come into the house. On the weekend that I worked, he watched the three younger children, he took them with him to meetings, and entertained them the rest of the day. He was the good guy. He also brought them to their activities, such as scouting or sport events.

Phil and I had a good mutual understanding involving all aspect of the children's welfare, which I was grateful for and the children were as well.

There were many home improvements done in the early 1980's, such as vinyl siding on the house, town sewage hook-up, new windows, new driveway, and the addition of a mud room. Later on, a new roof and new carpeting were installed, and a new stove and a portable dishwasher were purchased.

An annulment from the Catholic Church was granted in 1985 and obtained from the diocese of Worcester with the assistance of my friend Father Robert Wondolowski.

CHAPTER 18

The 1980s

This was a time of adjustment for our family. The children were seeing their father frequently and they were happy with the relationship.

The 1980s were busy as I was a full-time employee and in the prime of my running. I became very busy at work as I got involved with several committees such as the smoking policy committee and the evaluation form committee (forms reviewed and reformed). I also helped with the hospital road race committee.

Besides teaching religious classes at St. Brendan Church, I volunteered with the Boston Archdiocese Bishop's Fund collection (door to door) and continued for several years. I volunteered at doing cholesterol testing, under Dr. A. Sgalia's guidance, for The American Heart Association at the Franklin Annual Home and Trade Shows. Those were all interesting projects.

During these trying times, I did some extra shifts at the hospital and at local nursing homes (day, evening and night). For a period of six months I worked the graveyard shift on Sundays. It was tough driving home on Monday mornings. I fell asleep once, but no problem, thank God!

Janice worked for Medical Resources, an elderly home care agency. She did house cleaning and personal care and ran errands for the elderly. She liked her work and learned to speak very loudly, even when at home. She had to be reminded that we were not deaf.

In the summer of 1983, our best friends and neighbors, the Berardis, along with Janice's friend Christine, moved to San Diego, California, to join their oldest daughter Donna and her family. That was a sad time for our family. But our friendship of fifteen years did not end however, it was reinforced through the years by our communication and it continued after their return to New England a few years later.

Marcel worked at Axton Cross, a chemical plant in Holliston MA, while attending Mass Bay College in the evening. In 1984, he became an ice cream machine operator at the Sealtest Company in Framingham, where he remained until the plant closed its doors in 2011.

Marcel, at age nineteen made me a proud mom when he taught religious education to 4th grade neighborhood boys. In 1984, Marcel was seriously injured in a motor vehicle accident which killed the operator of the vehicle and left another passenger paralyzed.

I loved my work as a licensed practical nurse and I had a special attachment to some patients, especially the elderly; for some it was mutual.

Arthur Bertorelli, was my patient for ten months. At that time there was no limit on the length of stay for patients, as there is today. Mr. Bertorelli knew me well and could tell when something was wrong at home. Upon returning from a long weekend off, at approximately fifteen minutes into my shift, he expired. His wife assured me that he waited for my return to leave this world. I attended his funeral with some of my children.

Another patient offered to hire me for private duty. Many others expressed their appreciation by notes of thanks. As for Anthony's family, flooring store owners, their generosity was well received in the form of a generous discount on floor covering and installation in my home, in gratitude for the care given to their father during his hospitalization. He called me Rose, saying: "You remind me of a Rose I once knew..."

Nursing is a very rewarding profession. It is a calling. I believe that. Well, I never regretted the hard work that got me there.

In 1984, I was diagnosed with PIE syndrome, which means a Pulmonary Infiltrate with Eosinophil increase and translates to Eosinophilic Pneumonia (in modern medical terms) which manifests itself like pneumonia but is treated with steroids instead of antibiotics. It is a chronic condition which may occur at any time without warning but at times is preceded by stress or strenuous activity and starts with a sore throat but seldom with a fever. It progresses to congestion and heavy, sometimes bloody, phlegm (mucus) expectoration. It lasts approximately twelve to fifteen days. It occurs two to three times a year, therefore I have the wonder drug Prednisone on hand at all times. And I have great faith in my pulmonary physician, Dr.DeMarco, who diagnosed my problem over thirty years ago and still treats me today.

In 1985, John got his high school diploma after making up the academic credits. John was a free spirit. Mr. Parsel, a teacher and counselor, took an interest in him and helped him as much as John allowed. Besides spending a lot of time in the "Rubber Room", the suspension room, John was interested in astronomy and in drums. Unable to afford a set of drums, he played bongos with his friends Terry and Frankie. Mr. Parsel took him to play racquetball in Milford once after school and also made arrangements with his friend in Holliston to let John and Terry use his small astronomy lab. A nice gesture.

In early April 1987, I injured my back while lifting a patient at the hospital. Dr. Alan Bell, a neurologist, helped me to recovery with several methods of treatment for my bulging disc, which included physical therapy, acupuncture and exercises at the Milford Racquetball Club; it was a long process as I was out of work for eleven months.

On April 12th, 1987, the Milford Whitinsville Regional Hospital's first 5K Race for Health originated. The race was organized by Bill Flynn, Dr. John Hoell, Elaine Boardman and myself. Unfortunately, because of my injury, I was unable to participate or even help on that day.

Janice, Jamie and his friend Scott ran in the one-miler race. Jamie finished in nine minutes and eleven seconds and finished third overall. Scott ran eleven minutes and twenty-eight seconds, while Janice ran eleven minutes and fifty-six seconds. I was proud of all of them.

When the gun went off for the 5K race at 1:00 pm, Lori-Ann and my niece Nancy started out together but when Lori-Ann spotted out Bob Bettuelli, a hospital employee, she did what she was instructed to do and left her nineteen-year-old cousin and took off in pursuit of Bob and, giving all she had, beat him to the finish. She was the first junior female finisher (18 and under) with a time of 24:02 and pace of 7:45. She finished fifty-fifth overall and seventh female among eighty-eight finishers. She was ten and a half years old. Oh! How proud I was.

Nancy finished in a close time of 25:48. She continued running and became a very good runner indeed to this day. As for my little girl, prior to this race she had entered several road races and done well. At ages six, seven and eight she was winning the girls' division in one-milers in fun runs in Franklin. Jamie and Mark ran those races as well and had good times but always had to settle for second and third place in their division.

In mid-April 1987, Jamie and Mark went to San Diego for one week to visit Jamie's godparents, the Berardis, and to spend Easter with them. They enjoyed the fruit of their hard earned money from their paper route. They had a great time.

As a result of my injury in April, I lost my position on the fourth floor surgical unit and I was sent to school to Dean College in Franklin for a typing course. That did not work out: I still cannot type. I refused to take a secretarial position as ward clerk which, in my opinion, is the most difficult task in the hospital, where everyone wants your attention at once. I knew my nerves would not tolerate that activity and those who know me well would agree. I went to court to be allowed to resume my Licensed Practical Nurse career and I won the case. The judge was sympathetic towards my plight and ruled in my favor. I did not want to go on disability.

I continued with physical therapy, wore orthotics, took swimming lessons at the YMCA in Attleboro MA with my friend Jeannette a nurse from Milford Hospital, in the summer of 1987. Although swimming lessons may have helped my back somewhat, they did not improve my swimming skills.

In August, Jeannette, myself and Lori-Ann spent a wonderful day in Boston after an hour-long ride on the commuter train from Franklin.

We enjoyed a lunch cruise and toured the ship "The Courageous". We visited Faneuil Hall Plaza and did some shopping for Lori-Ann's birthday. My friend was very generous! Upon our return to Franklin's Train Depot, we were invited to Jeannette's home for dinner with her family. What a lovely gesture! In addition to that trip to the Big City, Jeannette gave me a small desk, which I still have, and her daughter Jane lent me a typewriter to practice at home while taking the course at Dean. Such great friendship was much appreciated. Even though we lost contact with each other for a few years, due to moving circumstances, we have recently reunited and continue our friendship.

Lori-Ann had the highest score for physical fitness in the history of the Presidential Program at JFK Elementary School in Franklin at the time, with a score of 94, according to her physical education teacher, Mrs. Boudreau. Lori-Ann participated in a Pentathlon at the Hockomock YMCA in Attleboro MA. The events consisted of the long jump, the 100-yard dash, the softball throw, a swim and a half-mile run. There were seven children in her age group of 9-12 year-olds, three girls and four boys. Lori-Ann was ten days shy of her eleventh birthday. She took first place in three events, second place in two events and third place in swimming. She was the first girl overall with 125 points and brought home a ribbon. Good work-out! There was a McDonald's stop on the way home.

Lori-Ann had started gymnastics and dance at the McKeon Academy in Franklin at age seven and was doing well. There were many practices and competitions. She made many friends there and her eleventh birthday party consisted mostly of her gymnastics team, all lovely girls. Lumberjacks (molasses cookies) were a big hit and at 11:00 pm, we were still baking cookies.

After a complete recovery, in early 1988, I returned to Milford Regional Hospital to resume my Licensed Practical Nurse duties, doing what I love best "helping those in need".

The last years of the 80s were challenging for myself and for my children. Lori-Ann, although being an avid gymnast and a fairly good student in junior high school, became a handful for me, especially after her dad moved to New Brunswick, Canada. It was a difficult time for the four younger children and me as there was less supervision at home because of my full-time employment, which under the circumstances was absolutely necessary. That spring, my 1984 bronze-colored Chevy Cavalier was taken for a joyride by teenagers and was much abused and required a new motor. As the General Motors arbitrator did not rule in my favor, my little station wagon with 60,000 miles went to the vehicle graveyard. How sad! There were trying times Lori-Ann had much difficulty adjusting to her parents' divorce. The years between age eleven and thirteen were challenging years for both of us. What a nightmare! when she along with two of her friends were missing for three days. An extensive search by the authorities, family members and friends ensued, which resulted in their safe return home. Thanks be to God!

With a lot of love, soul searching and counseling therapy, we survived and we became a closer family, but for me guilt feelings remained as I labeled myself as a "Bad Mother". With help, I finally was able to admit to myself that I could not do what I did not know how, which was to be more "affectionate".

Through the years, it has become much easier to express our love to each other in our family. Telephone conversations or parting from each other always end in a hug and a friendly "I love you".

Those years during the 1980s were very busy ones for our family. There were three high school graduations and two eighth grade graduations, Jamie's and Mark's.

Lori-Ann and her friend Melissa Wood's trip to Disney World with Phil, Lori-Ann's trip to New Brunswick, Canada, with her dad and to Europe with the gymnastics team and myself, all happened within one year. Quite the little traveler, our Lori-Ann.

A lot of work was being done to the house. Jamie and Mark scraped and painted the house trim and did a fairly good job for inexperienced young men working for low wages. They were treated to a Chinese Food

Restaurant meal and got $10.00 cash each from a cheap and poor mother. These two brothers got along very well, as did Marcel and John. They had many mutual friends: the Rapko brothers, the Haran brothers, as well as many boys from Pilgrim Village in Bellingham. Some were church members, some scout troop members and some coworkers at Speroni's Restaurant.

Jamie was a sophomore in the Tri-County Vocational School plumbing program and was making statements with his appearance and behavior, at times. Even though Jamie was the class clown, he was well loved by his teachers. One of them let him do the famous chicken sound on the intercom for all to hear. He remained an altar server as well as a boy scout until his graduation from high school. Both he and Mark loved camping and skiing. Although he was more outgoing than his brother, Mark being the more intellectual type but also witty, Jamie was a comic. The two together kept me laughing and sometimes crying. As I was ordering new suits and white dress shirts for them for a wedding, Mark left this note to Jamie: "Jamie, Mom wants you to measure your neck size, so the noose will fit properly. No slip = quick death".

John, now a young adult, worked at different skills such as stitcher for the Guitar Glove Company, also doing iron and masonry work for the same employer. He reported that two elderly gentlemen, who were working with him and argued a lot, once threw a hammer at each other. John lived at home and remained friends with his neighborhood high school buddies (and rubber room pals) Terry and Frankie. Many late nights worried me as the aroma of burned food from John's cooking awakened me. Even though he did not like fish, there was a lot of fish sticks cooked during the night hours...

Marcel and Janice were living on their own and for a short time lived together in Framingham. Marcel was working at the Sealtest Ice Cream Plant and Janice was a homemaker for Medical Resources. In 1989, she started her employment with Stewart, a medical and surgical supply warehouse in Franklin, presently Owens & Minor, where she is still employed today.

CHAPTER 19

Our Pets

Toby Biscuit 2011 - Present

After visiting on the Internet Claws of Mashpee, a cat shelter located in Marstons Mills and owned by J. Daley, and after seeing Smudge's profile, we fell in love with him and an appointment was made for the next day. So on March 8th, Dave and I met Smudge, who was being kept in a cage due to his aggressiveness towards other cats.

By 11:30 am we brought Smudge home. He was a large gray and brown striped cat with a white underbody and paws, and a smudge on the nose, his birthmark. He was so handsome: shy at first, then friendly after spending three hours under a bed. We decided to name him Toby Biscuit.

After three disruptive nights, Toby was left outside the bedroom at night. That rule remains to this day.

Toby became more and more affectionate and after a week and a half at our house, he climbed up to my lap and stayed there for about an hour and a half. I was thrilled. Those are the signs of his innocent disposition when all is well and he makes us forget his aggressive character, which only transpires when hunger strikes.

Shortly after Toby's arrival to our home, we attended the Mashpee High School production of Oliver which we enjoyed for the great performance by the cast and the orchestra. Upon our return home, however, Toby was nowhere to be found, and did not respond to our call. We started to worry... Then, as David opened the hallway linen closet, in the midst of pillows, sheets and blankets, a disoriented Toby came crashing down and went exploring the rooms, most likely to reorient himself to his new surroundings. Soon, being his old self again, he slept peacefully all night.

Toby follows my command of "Walk, Walk, No jump," while going to his food dish, where he waits for the ritual: a few sprinkles of water on the food and a splash on his head.

He loves the outdoors and enjoys his early morning excursions in favorable weather. He patiently waits on the front steps for my return from my daily walk and cautiously crosses our lane after looking out for any danger. I repeatedly instruct him to look both ways before coming to greet me. He actually has gone around our condominium complex delivering the early newspaper with me and has stayed on track for approximately fifteen minutes.

He also has his favorite family members which he recognizes by their voice and he comes out of his hiding to visit. He loves to sit on a footstool, in a safely manner, near the front door and watch the world go by.

I believe that cats can learn new tricks, as dogs do. Toby will lie down when we say "Down" but he does not favor a leash.

Spunki 1992-2010

Spunki came to us from the house of one of Lori-Ann's friends, Mike Doyle. He was so tiny, about five or six weeks old, that he had to be fed with an eye dropper. Tracy obliged. Spunki was black with a white upper chest, white paws and the cutest little face ever seen. He adjusted well to our cat Tiffany and our dog Tuchie and they all became friends.

He lived up to his name of Spunki, given to him by Jamie and Tracy. He was very energetic and a great hunter. He made his daily trek to the wooded area across the road and brought to my door his trophies: birds, mice and a chipmunk. He was an accomplished squirrel chaser. He mastered a very bad habit: jumping from the hoods of our cars parked in the driveway into the screened kitchen window. He ruined a few screens.

In my mind's eye I can still see him hanging for dear life and waiting to be rescued and brought into the house.

In 1996, when he stayed behind at my son's house and while renovation work was being done to the house, Spunki became very nervous, agitated and balding. So he moved in with me at my Franklin Crossing condominium where he became an indoor cat. But we had more screen trouble, as he was trying to escape from a second story unit. He became friends with David and the three of us lived happily for the next five years.

In 2002, Spunki moved to his final residence in Mashpee. Once he got over the seventy-mile trip and the initial change (he spent one week under a bed) he became very affectionate. He loved to sit with us but when we left our seat, it was lost. He seemed to enjoy our beautiful backyard with multiple birds and a plentitude of squirrels.

We enjoyed his company for eight more years. On January 9th, 2010, he succumbed to kidney failure after two days of suffering. He was seven weeks shy of his eighteenth birthday. He was a Leap Year Baby and had only four birthdays in his life. His ashes rest on my desk eight years later. He was a great pet.

Tiffany 1983-1994

Our beloved cat Tiffany, a boy cat, came to us in 1983 with Janice from her workplace, the Glen Ellen Golf Course in Millis MA. After Janice graduated from Tri-County with a certificate in food trade, she worked at several places; one being this golf course where Tiffany, our beloved black and white male cat, was found. Unaware of his gender at the time, Janice named him Tiffany and we kept the name. John did not agree and called him Samson.

Tiffany was the neighborhood warrior and suffered several injuries while busy populating the feline world, until medical attention was provided. Tiffany then became the most affectionate and loving kitty. He could sit on the floor like a human and watch television. This has been observed by a bystander and it is a proven fact. He was loved and enjoyed by our entire family for eleven years. His life was cut short when he was hit by an automobile in May 1994. He is now resting under a white rock in the backyard at the Bourgeois' homestead at 86 Pine Street, Franklin MA.

Here are my thoughts on that wonderful pet, penned by myself many years ago:

Tiffany 1983-1994

Awesome Black Furry

Quiet Soft Large

Snores Purrs Cuddles

Fur Balls Lazy A warrior

Affectionate

Loved to be petted

A great hunter Loved cars

Loved music

Greeter in the driveway

Tiffany AKA Samson

the best cat on earth,

was loved and dearly missed by many.

Tuchie 1992-2003

A handsome Golden Retriever, brought home from a pet store as a puppy by Jamie and then girlfriend Tracy. He was so cute and fluffy. Jamie had always wanted a dog since he was a child but he never got one as he had wished.

Tuchie was named after the restaurant where Jamie and Tracy had lunch after the pet purchase at the Mall in Taunton MA.

He and Tiffany got along well. He was a kind and lovable dog and was taken away from us too soon by cancer at age eleven.

Our first pets

Our first pets include a cat named Country Bumpkin. He was a medium-sized white and gray quiet kitty, who was not with us for long as he was accidentally killed in our driveway by a car driven by a family member.

Cupid, a large brown and gray male cat, was friendly with humans but not with other animals. He was hit by a car in front of our driveway and expired in the car on the way to animal hospital with Marcel and myself.

Nicki was a black Labrador, brought to our house by one of Lori-Ann's friends and was discovered hidden in her bedroom closet. Nicki never learned to behave. An ad in the newspaper for adoption proved futile as well as obedience school attendance. We were told that she was taken from her mother too young and therefore had never learned manners. After about one year of furniture destruction and erratic behavior, I had enough and Nicki was adopted by one of Janice's coworkers at Owens & Minor.

CHAPTER 20

Franklin, Massachusetts

The area was first settled by Europeans in 1660. In 1778, what is now Franklin became independent from the town of Wrentham. It was to be named Exeter upon incorporation but in order to flatter Dr. Benjamin Franklin, the town was renamed after him. The statesman was asked to donate a bell for the town's church steeple but instead the town in 1786 was given books for its library, which had been built in 1778 and which was the first public library in the United States.The original library was replaced by the Ray Public Library, built in 1904 and still in existence today. The Franklin Library's Italian architecture is very special with its majestic murals and it remains a prominent establishment in this beautiful town. The library is being renovated at the present time.

The Little Red Brick School, a one-room schoolhouse, was in operation from 1833 until 2008. In later years it became home to a kindergarten class, which my grandson Tyler attended. There is still a dispute between Franklin and Croyden, New Hampshire, where a similar schoolhouse is located, regarding the founding date of the original one-room schoolhouse.

Franklin has many important landmarks including the Dean Academy, founded in 1865, which later became Dean Junior College, and is presently called Dean College, a four-year school.

The Franklin Historical Society, with former high school history teacher and author James C. Johnston as president, hosts the history museum which is open to the public.

The Horace Mann Monument honors the pioneer of the public school system, who was born in this town in 1796.

St. Mary's Catholic Church's high steeple dominates the corner of Main and Highland streets and is the seat of the largest parish in the archdiocese of Boston with 1,500 members.

There are numerous old magnificent homes in this town which were the homesteads of famous people, such as The Oliver Pond House. There are homes of famous men born in Franklin, to name a few: Oliver Dean, founder of Dean College; James Mason, inventor of the coffee percolator; Dr. Emmons, a street was named after him; Dr. Miller and Albert Richardson, both authors and biographers.

The Massachusetts insect symbol originated in Mrs. Johnson's second grade classroom at the John F. Kennedy Elementary School in Franklin MA. The ladybug became the official State symbol in 1974.

Another fact about Franklin is it's Cinema which was later on named Zeotrope (reason unknown) was closed in 2005 and demolished in 2006 What a shame, as it was an antique gem and the town was left without a movie theater.

A very unusual one way main street was changed to a two way street in 2017, after forty years of existence.

Franklin is a major center for transportation and accommodations. Its commuter rail service serves hundreds on their daily trek to Boston. There is an approximate thirty-mile distance between Franklin and Providence RI, between Franklin and Worcester, and between Franklin and Boston. The rail service makes it very convenient for commuters.

Franklin's population exceeds 33,000 and at one time it was the fastest growing town in Massachusetts. In 2014 it was named one of the safest towns in America for its low crime rate. It also had the title of "Boring Town" but the town is great for young families. Franklin has a great school system, in both academics and sports. A multi-million-dollar high school opened its doors in September 2014.

I am proud of this town and thankful for having had the privilege of raising my children in such a distinguished town.

CHAPTER 21

The European Trip 1988

On April 14th, 1988, a gymnastics team from The McKeon Gymnastics Academy, where Lori-Ann had been a student for the past four years, headed for Central Europe to visit and train with other gymnastics schools and bring home new views on the sport as well as new techniques for the instructors.

I was one of the chaperones, along with several other mothers. We were responsible for ten very energetic young girls. I had been entrusted by one of the gymnasts' parents with the care of their daughter Joanne, Lori-Ann's friend. We left JFK Airport in the early evening and arrived at Luxembourg Airport in the early morning. It was a long flight: about eight hours. At our arrival in Luxembourg, we met with our bus driver Norbert and our guide Renate, a young college student from the city of Cologne.

After getting situated in our hotel room, and after calling home, we practiced a few words in the German language. Our first meal was pork with noodles and gravy, a salad, red tea and a fruit cup with ice cream. After the 7:00 pm meal, we visited a gym where the girls checked out the equipment. Then early bedtime after a long tiring day.

Day 2 On our way to Germany, our bus with forty passengers on board broke down, and was promptly repaired by Norbert.

Interesting facts about Germany:

Police (polizei) cars are green and white; license plates are white with black numbers and highway signs are blue and heart-shaped and we noticed polka dots cars.

Autobahn driving was scary as the 130 km (81 miles per hour) limit was indicated in certain areas only, otherwise there was NO Speed Limit. Unbelievable!

On rural routes, the speed limit is similar to ours: 37 to 43 miles per hour.

If a police spots someone speeding, he will pass the vehicle in question. A sign will appear on the back of the police vehicle saying: "Follow Me". Then the police officer will pull over on the roadside and wait for the speedster, who has to pay up then and there.

Signs of Kodak, IBM and Shell were seen along the way. All reminders of home.

Germans are very reserved and dress well, mostly in dark clothing, preferably in black. They have a resting period in mid-afternoon and eat dinner late in the evening and have a late night life. Sometimes, after a 9:00 pm dinner and after a practice or a show, we would be walking to our hotel at midnight and would see a surprisingly heavy flow of traffic.

Most Germans only SLOW DOWN at a red light and do not stop. I acted as a traffic director at times as I was petrified that someone would get hurt.

There were no smoking or drinking age regulations in Germany in 1988.

German boys are expected to serve their country. If, for good reason they are unable to, they have to do three months of social service.

Typical German meals consisted of red cabbage and sauerkraut.

Day 3 After our frugal breakfast of orange juice, bread and jelly, and nutella tea or coffee, we were on the bus heading to Trier. Nice scenery and interesting place. We visited Porta Nicro, an amphitheater, an Episcopalian cathedral and Catholic churches.

Days 4 and 5 While traveling through Heidelberg, we saw a large university with 2,700 students. We passed gothic and renaissance castles on the way. Along the ride from Heidelberg to Munich, we saw Canadian Army trucks on the highway. Phil was stationed there in the late 1950s with the American Army. While approaching Munich, Bavarian Catholic churches with rounded steeples were noticed. Asparagus fields were seen along the Rhine River. Munich, a fairly large city, has many churches whose bells ring at 11:00 am on Mondays. The city is also known for its museums, the train station, the pedestrian plaza, universities, a library with four million books and its famous beer. Munich was founded in the eighteenth century and has over one million inhabitants. It hosted the 1972 Olympic Games at its 5000-seat stadium. One church's congregation consisted of Catholics and Protestants worshiping together.

April 18th, no broken record at the Boston Marathon. Issam Hussein from Kenya posted a 2:08:43 win and Rosa Mota from Portugal won with a time of 2:24:30, as reported by the New York Herald and related to me by Renate at my request.

Everyday, our gymnasts practiced with the German girls, and we, their parents, watched. It was very enjoyable.Training time was around two and a half hours each day. Some of us mothers went to the Wash Salon, the laundromat, one day, while the girls were conditioning at the gym. That was quite an experience: riding in a very small and old BMW taxi, with a non-speaking and non-smiling German gentleman who charged double fare because his small vehicle was overcrowded. Our driver Norbert proved his excellent driving skills with difficult maneuvering on narrow streets. We always applauded him.

Munich is a wine country and we could see vineyards all along the Rhine River as we made our way south. A point of interest was a castle with a mountain in the background where US President Ronald Reagan and German President Carstens and Chancellor Schmidt met in a conference in the early 1980s.

Days 6 and 7 Austria Bound: Innsbruck was a four-hour ride away. We saw impressive small villages along the way with churches surrounded by small brown roofs, brown and white quaint houses. People were seen on beaches on that warm April day. In Innsbruck the houses were slightly different, with red roofs and stucco or wood construction, mostly beige or brown with large religious murals in front of homes. There were farms, large gardens, horses and sheep. Vehicles were the same as in Germany. What a feast for the eyes, with the Alps on each side. Such a beautiful country.

We met many Americans at different places. It is a small world! Austrian folklore music is amazing with horns, bells, accordion and yodeling. Our hotel, the Krona, was new, spacious and nice. There was much excitement with the girls, a late night, and a 1:30 am bedtime.

Days 8 and 9 En route to Lucerne, Switzerland. Small houses in fields for animal shelter, tools or animal food (like our barns, but smaller). Green grass and flowers in bloom; similar houses as in Austria. French signs along the highway.

We arrived in Liechtenstein in early afternoon to spend a few hours touring on foot. We visited a castle and had lunch. The country is one of the ten smallest countries in Europe, a favorite for winter sports, due to the Alps. It is an exclusive and expensive area. The population was 28,089 inhabitants in 1988. Forty percent of the terrain is rock and sixty percent is forest.

Switzerland is very scenic with twin-tower churches, a castle on a hill, hilly terrain, tough for running. Surrounded by those famous mountains, the Alps. Zurich has the biggest hotel, 1,000 beds. As we toured the city, which was very interesting, our tour guide was a distinguished elderly gentleman who had been a Swiss guard for the Pope and spoke English very well. Automobile license plates were white with black numbers with a white or green cross, some plates were red with a white cross. A Bavarian Show, enjoyed one evening with the girls, had performers from many different nationalities, including Canadians. Switzerland's currency was the Franc in 1988.

Lucerne, founded in 1871 and built with many bridges across the Reuss River, has a spectacular train station, nine Catholic churches and seven churches of other denominations. Impressive.

There are four dialects spoken in Switzerland: Swiss French, Swiss German, Swiss Italian and Swiss Romansh. Some English is taught in schools. En route to the Black Forest, we passed the Rheinfall, the largest waterfalls in Europe. The pine trees in the Black Forest being so close account for the darkness. "Vue des Bois", Forest View, a sign indicating a large statue of a deer on a peeked ledge on a mountain side, was visible from the highway. A Visa is required to enter France from Switzerland.

We visited the Normandy American Cemetery and Memorial, where General Patton is buried with his soldiers (by request). The Unknown Soldiers' Grave reads: "Comrades In Wars" and "Known only to God". The field of white crosses and Stars of David were very impressive. The cemetery is large and similar to Arlington Cemetery in Washington DC.

It was time to bid goodbye to our two wonderful friends, our guide Renate and our skilled driver Norbert. Gratuities were presented and souvenir shirts from the McKeon Academy were offered.

During our long wait at Iceland Airport, we did some last minute shopping. I purchased a sweatshirt that read: "University of Iceland" and I still have it today. There was a definite chill in the Iceland air on that April 23rd morning as we boarded the plane to head for JFK Airport in New York.

We arrived home that evening with a contented heart after this fabulous trip. It was great to be home, nonetheless..

CHAPTER 22

Kennebunk, Maine

My first long distance trip driving by myself was to visit my favorite cousin Helen in Kennebunk ME. I was accompanied by Jamie, Mark and Lori-Ann. In spite of the rainy two-hour ride, with Jamie as my navigator, all went well and we enjoyed a great weekend with Mark's godparents and their family.

Kennebunk has always been dear to me as that quaint little coastal town is so charming. There was so much to do for all of us, such as swimming at the beautiful Town Beach, admiring the scenic route to Kennebunkport, and the The Wedding Cake House along the way. That famous mansion was built by a Sea Captain as a wedding gift to his daughter, and had been closed to the public for years but, fortunately, David and I toured it in 2005 at a very special anniversary. It was very impressive.

Kennebunkport was favored by the children for its Penny Candy Store and The T-Shirts Store. Another memorable event for the children was the Old Orchard Beach with its large amusement park in all its glory. The beach is known for its frigid water. Needless to say, no swimming.

There were many more trips to that special place in Southern Maine through the years. My cousin Helen and I were very close since our childhood when she and her siblings, with their mom my aunt Sara, visited us in New Brunswick, Canada, every summer. Helen's husband Hank was a landscaper and he was entertaining. My children enjoyed his company. Three of their children: Stephen, Donald, and Lisa left home at a young age. But June, the third child, was a dispatcher at the local police department and she impressed my children. She later became a police officer herself and married Jeff, a very tall sheriff. June also became a selectwoman and also an entrepreneur, owning a contracting business. She is a well respected Kennebunk resident. I still visit her today with her two children, Ashley and Ryan.

Being legally blind, Helen walked everywhere and accepted rides from her many friends. She was well loved. We enjoyed walking around town with her at each of our visits. We certainly had good times with Helen, picking blueberries in the summer and visiting farm stands, picking apples, gathering pumpkins and getting chrysanthemums (her favorites) in the fall. We went to the Ashland County Fair and the Arundel Playhouse and Flea Market. We enjoyed the Blue Moon Restaurant and walked to the Square Toes Restaurant for breakfast. Those are great memories.

Helen loved her music. She played the accordion and the 12-string guitar and she sang in the St. Martha's Church Choir. She served as music director at the Cursillo Movement weekends for over twenty years. I had the pleasure of participating in the Winthrop, Maine, weekend in December 2008. I enjoyed those three days tremendously. She also took leadership in a few other Christian evangelization initiatives and had group meetings in her home for such as Renew and Faith Sharing. She served as Eucharistic Minister.

She was devoted to her family and took pride in her grandchildren as well as her great-grandchildren.

Although handicapped from birth, she lived her life fully and served others well. We were related by blood but we were best friends by choice. Helen and I spent many hours chatting on the telephone as we both had the gift of gab. I will always cherish the time spent together either at her small but tidy and lovely apartment or walking on the beach. Those were precious times.

Helen battled cancer courageously for over three years, until her treatment became too difficult. For most of that time, she continued working and minister as well. Although she was color blind her clothes always matched; it was amazing to me.

Although Helen was visually impaired, she worked for eighteen years as a housekeeper at the River Ridge Rehabilitation Center, where she deeply cared for all the residents and would provide music entertainment for them weekly for several years and performing all her normal activities, and was so grateful to all who helped when needed. As her illness progressed, she was confined to Gosnold Memorial Hospice House in Scarborough, Maine, for a couple of weeks. She went to her eternal reward on July 13th, 2010.

Helen was from a large family and her funeral was well attended by family, friends, and parishioners. I was honored to be a part of the ceremony by doing one of the readings and David was a pallbearer. De colores, the theme song of the Cursillo Movement, was sung, as she had played it on her guitar so many times.

Helen was an inspiration to all who knew her. My son Mark was privileged to have such an amazing godmother. Hank, his godfather, went to his reward a short four months later. May they both rest in Eternal Peace.

CHAPTER 23

Family Special Events

Eighth grade graduations involved a modest ceremony with school officials and the reception of a well-earned certificate, a special meal for the graduate and a small gift in remembrance of the special day.

I specifically remember Mark's eighth grade graduation as, after having been at my podiatrist for treatment earlier on that day I was unfortunately wearing very uncomfortable shoe orthotics.

Catholic confirmation involved two years of preparation. Our neighbor and friend Jocelyne Rapko was the Religious Education Director in our parish. Ninth and tenth grades were the targeted years.

The confirmation candidates chose a saint's name as well as a sponsor of their own choice. An auxiliary bishop from the Archdiocese of Boston would administer this very important sacrament, which made the recipient a resilient soldier to defend his or her faith. Unfortunately, many confirmed individuals do not keep their promise.

The children's sponsors were :	Marcel J.	Ronald Léger
	Janice M.	Cécile Léger
	John F.	Frank Bourgeois
	Jamie P.	Ralph Berardi
	Mark J.	Marcel Bourgeois
	Lori-Ann	Nancy Bernier

The saints' names picked were: Joseph, Marie, Francis, Patrick, Zachary and Xavier.

High School graduations were also celebrated:

Marcel J.	June 5th, 1981	Franklin High School
Janice M.	June 3rd, 1982	Tri-County Vocational High School
John F.	June 7th, 1985	Franklin High School
Jamie P.	June 3rd, 1990	Tri-County Vocational High School
Mark J.	June 7th, 1991	Franklin High School
Lori-Ann	June 4th, 1995	Tri-County Vocational High School

Every family member's birthday was celebrated in our traditional manner: pizza, cake and ice cream. Ice cream cake for some as their preference.

Other major events were also observed such as Baptism, First Communion, Confirmation and certain achievements and celebrations.

A farewell get-together with family and friends for Phil's move to Canada took place in 1989. He returned to reside permanently in the United States in 1995.

Lori-Ann's fifteenth birthday was very sombre indeed as it happened on the heels of Hurricane Bob, which had caused much damage on the coastline, especially on Cape Cod. More tragically, on that day, Scott Haran was killed instantly when his vehicle was hit by an eighteen-wheeler on a major highway in Foxborough MA. Scott was Jamie and Mark's close friend who spent a lot of time at our house. I was his sponsor at his confirmation.

This was such a tragedy for the Haran family as Scott's mom had succumbed to cancer two years earlier and the father was left with Rick, his younger son.

I recall my ride to pick up Lori-Ann's birthday cake with Janice's antique Chevy Chevelle, which I was unfamiliar with. I had been in an auto accident with my vehicle the previous week, in Bolton MA, while on my way to visit our good friends the Berardis. To our surprise upon checking the cake, the lady had omitted the writing on it, probably disturbed by the hurricane. A reasonable explanation.

This August 19th, 1991, in spite of the sunny day, the atmosphere at the Bourgeois home was very dismal and sad. Scott's funeral took place on August 23rd. That was a somber day for Jamie and Mark, then nineteen and seventeen, as they served as pallbearers for their nineteen-year-old friend.

Mark's wrapped hand was a reminder of an injury sustained while closing our basement window on that dreadful day.

I still visit Scott's grave. He was like a fifth son to me.

CHAPTER 24

Special People in my Life

Although I have never met my own godparents, Victor LeBlanc and Lillianne Caissie, I had many godmothers and many other important people who played significant roles in my life.

First, of course, was my grandmother Délina who was a mother to me and my two siblings, Ronald and Hermance. She insisted on being called grand-mère. Grandma was very spiritual and quoted Bible verses frequently; and even though I do not recall seeing her reading the Good Book, I know she knew it well. Grandma had perpetual vertigo, apparently due to an inner ear problem; she was staggering a lot. I do not remember her ever hugging me or showing me any physical sign of affection, but I was assured of her love for me because she cared for me since my infancy and taught me a lot about morality, especially honesty. One of her favorite verses was: "Ask, and you shall receive", regarding everything, including food. I used to think that taking food without permission was stealing and spreading two dressings on bread was sinful. (A little scruple there!) Grandma was very strict. She was no doubt very tired after raising her own large family and starting over with three grandchildren. Bouncing the ball on the outside of the house was one of those things that were annoying to her. She nursed me back to health when at age five I had pneumonia. And my brother made a special promise to God for my recovery. I recovered completely without hospitalization. Who knows about Ronald's promise?

My Grandpa also played a major role in my childhood formation, as well of course did my father. Grandpa, whom I idolized, treated me to beer at a very young age. I loved it so much that I was licking the empty bottles I found in the shed. YUK! How gross! If only Grandma had found out. The taste of beer left my lips at about age five and I detest it to this day. Thanks, Grandpa. The only toys I had in my early childhood were handmade by Grandpa, except a little yellow teddy bear. I also had a real tiger cat named Tom. I always loved cats and I still do.

My special aunt Lina, mother of sixteen children, and my aunt Marguerite were very dear to me. Aunt Exelda, my favorite uncle Léo's wife, was very helpful to me when Papa died.

Our neighbor, Ozélie Léger, mother of fifteen, was our postmistress and my idea of a saint. She was my confirmation sponsor. One of her daughters, Rita, also a cousin, was very helpful to me through the years, especially informing me of the missing links in my family history.

Other special people were my cousin Ozélia; my cousin Emery; our pastor Father Albert Brideau, a high-spirited individual, who wrote to me while I was a student in Saint-Jérome, Québec, and I still have the letter, written in French.

My elementary school teachers: Évangéline Léger, Lucie Gallant and Assunta Bourgeois. My wonderful high school teachers: Sister Marie-Géraldine, with whom I corresponded for many years and Sister Aurèle-Marie, with whose help I passed Geometry and accomplished two grades, eleventh and twelfth, in one year.

Senator Aurèle Léger and his lovely wife Albertine were great advisors during my teenage years. Sister Marie-Antonine, ndsc, was my mistress of novices for two years, then Sister Léo-Marie followed in her footsteps and she was a great moral support to me after I left the Novitiate in 1961.

My great friends: Ann Shaw, her sister Therese Berardi, and Beverly-An Burns touched my life in many ways through the years.

Father Daniel Gilmartin, our pastor at St. Brendan Parish, was always there for my family and myself. Father Henry Chambers, who guided me and counseled me in my darkest days during the separation.

My sister-in-law Cécile was always an inspiration to me for all she went through, losing two children in tragic deaths.

My cousin Maryanne was also a role model for me after she became a widow with five young children. My Canadian friends: Anita Pellerin, Gloria Mockler and cousin Germaine with their musical talents and their volunteer work. They were always helping others in some way.

Jocelyne Rapko, my good friend for many years, was a great example to follow. Unfortunately, she succumbed in her fight with cancer at the age of fifty-four, in 1999. Our daughters Lori-Ann and Mary-Beth were friends growing up and their two daughters, Chloe and Tess, are presently friends as well. In later years I met this very special lady, very spiritual and knowledgeable. She taught me so much during our telephone church prayer line conversations through the Christ The King Parish apostolate in Mashpee MA. Alice Melcher was a dear friend. One of her short anecdotes was: "Anger is an acid that consumes its container." Even in her nineties, her voice was strong, assertive but pleasant. I always admired her ladylike manner and her intelligence.

Other individuals who touched my life were: Anna LaBrousse, with whom I shared a long ongoing friendship. Her patience and pleasant disposition have always been impressive to me and my family. She was a great role model to follow, as well. Mary Daly, with her dedication and hard work that made the St. Vincent de Paul Thrift Shop Center a large success and where I volunteered for nine years and loved it.

Pat and Maury, Margaret, Kay, Pat Jackie, Joanne, Dick, Gail, Betty Denise Barbara, Carole,Greta and many more wonderful people made my days easier while living on Cape Cod and volunteering at the St. Vincent de Paul Thrift Shop.

As parishioner at Christ The King Church, I was inspired by Sister Shirley and Sister Dympna, who were great activists in our parish. Betty and June from the prayer line group, Barbara, June R, Peggy and Joanne W were all good friends.

Our pastor Monsignor Daniel Hoye and our three deacons were always impressing me with their performance and their good example.

Another special lady, Pat Davis, who was the director of Volunteer Services at Falmouth Hospital was a pleasure to work with.

In later years, after our return from Mashpee, I was blessed with my relationship with this very special lady Amelia Lombard, Millie, who was under my care for too-short a time. She taught me this little poem that I love:

> When I was young my slippers were red
> I could kick my heels clear over my head.
>
> When I grew older my slippers were blue
> And I could dance the whole night through.
>
> When I got yet older my slippers were black
> I walked to the corner and puffed my way back.
>
> How do I know that my youth has been spent
> Because my get up and go… got up and went.
>
> I get up in the morning and dust my wits
> I pick up the paper and read the Obits.
>
> When I see my name missing I know that I'm not dead,
> So I eat a good breakfast and go back to bed.

It is impossible to name all the kind people who have crossed my path in life and have left their imprint on my heart. I have been so blessed.

CHAPTER 25

Death of Family Members and Close Friends

As part of living, everyone experiences one or more losses in their lifetime.

My dear grandfather, Marcel Léger, died at age eighty, after suffering a stroke, on March 27th, 1948.

My maternal grandparents, Willie and Marie Hébert, whom I never met, died in the diphtheria outbreak in the 1920s.

Several of my siblings died in infancy, before I was born, including a set of twins; as well as Normand and Oscar who died at age eighteen months and five years old. How sad!

My mother, Laudia Léger, died on April 16th, 1941, from pneumonia, at the age of thirty-six.

My father, Amédée Léger, died on May 16th, 1953, at age sixty and six months, from stomach cancer.

My grandmother, Délina Léger, died on December 6th, 1958, at age ninety-one.

My sister, Hermance Arsenault, died on November 29th, 1993, at age sixty, from emphysema. My brother-in-law, André Arsenault, died in July 1998, at age eighty-five.

My brother, Ronald Léger, died on March 25th, 2010, at age seventy-five, after being comatose for two weeks after suffering a bad fall.

Other relatives lost in death through the years were my special aunt and uncle Frank and Sara LeBlanc from Waltham, with whom I lived when I came to this country in 1961.

Phil's aunt and uncle James and Annie Russo from Waltham, whom we visited frequently.

Cousins who passed away in the prime of their life: Leo Brun, age 32, victim of cancer; Reginald and his brother Jean-Paul Brun died in their early forties from cardiac problems and left young families behind. Jean-Paul was married to a former novitiate classmate of mine. Reggie's widow became a very close friend and an inspiration to me. My two nephews Daniel and Gerald Arsenault died in their fifties and early sixties.

Two of my sisters-in-law, Geneva and Georgette, died within seven months while in their early forties and early fifties leaving many children as well.

Linda Richard, Phil's niece also was taken by cancer in her early forties, and Phil's nephew was killed in a tragic motorcycle accident as a teenager. My great-nephew was killed in a motor vehicle crash at age twenty-nine.

Special friends went to their reward too soon: Mary Darling, Fred and Carl LaBrousse, Ralph and Therese Berardi, Antanet Shaw and John Burns.

My nephew Richard (Ricky) Léger, drowned at age seven in 1974; and his sister Joanne perished in a house fire in Florida in 1983 at age nineteen.

So many sad memories. But we must not dwell on the past, for each one of us has a life to live to the fullest, during this short passage here on earth.

CHAPTER 26

The Most Important Person on Earth

The most important person on earth is a mother:

She cannot claim the honor of having built Notre Dame Cathedral.

She needs not.

She has built something more

Magnificent than any cathedral:

The dwelling of an immortal soul;

The tiny perfection of her baby's body.

CHAPTER 27

Priorities

It is illegal to destroy eagle eggs and this act is punishable by a fine up to $250,000 and by up to two years in prison.

It is legal to kill a human being for any reason, by abortion providers funded by taxpayers money.

CHAPTER 28

Letter to Mother

Hello, Mother:

This is your little girl, Dorice Marie, that you left behind in 1941. So long ago. Seventy-seven years to be exact.

I would have loved to have known you, as I know so little about you, only what Papa told me. It appears that you and I have some similar characteristics.

As you know, Grandma Léger took care of us three: Hermance 8, Ronald 6 and myself, thirteen months old. Although already advanced in age, seventy-three years old, she taught us all the important lessons to lead a Christian life, with Dad always at her side helping.

Dad suffered a lot from his stomach cancer for about one year, until his death on May 16th, 1953, at the age of sixty years and six months. I was thirteen at the time. After his death I tended the small village Post Office for two months until it was transferred to our neighbors down the road, the Bourque's house. There was help when I was in school (mail delivery) and I took over after school and on Saturdays. Grandma moved to aunt Lina's house in Shediac; uncle Hypolite, Grandma's brother who lived with us, moved to uncle Léo's house up the road. I went to Hermance's house. She was married to André Arsenault and living near the church in Grande-Digue, where I remained until I was sixteen and a half years old. Grandma survived Grandpa by ten years. He died in March 1948. She died in December 1958, at age ninety-one. While in the Novitiate of the religious order of Our Lady of the Sacred Heart in Memramcook, New

Brunswick, I was allowed to attend the funeral, accompanied by one of our professed sisters.

Hermance died on November 29th, 1993, at age sixty leaving her husband André, seven sons and three daughters.

Ronald died on March 25th, 2010, at age seventy-five after being comatose for two weeks after a bad fall.

I hope you are all together now, in the Heavenly Kingdom.

In January 1957, I left my sister's house to attend a school at Saint-Jérome, Québec, where I studied Home Economics until June with the Sisters of Our Lady of The Good Counsel. I completed one year in six months and loved it.

In June, I returned home and spent the summer at Senator and Mrs. Aurèle Léger's home (you know, Dad's cousin).

In September, I enrolled as a high school student at an all-girl boarding school in Bouctouche, where I graduated after doing eleventh and twelfth grades together, and passing geometry (my nightmare).

In September 1958, I entered the Novitiate where I stayed for two years and five months. On February 4th, 1961, I got out of the Novitiate after I was told it was not my vocation. I returned to my sister's home in Grande-Digue, whose family had increased with an addition of two baby girls while I was away. My sister had ten children. Ronald and his wife Cécile had six children, including twins. It was difficult for me at first to adjust to my new life in the secular world. I got odd jobs; working at the local convenience store. I also was a nanny for the Kennedy family, near Moncton.

In July, I went to the United States with my cousin Emery and his family. I stayed with Ronald, Cécile and newborn baby Diane for a while and worked at different jobs in Waltham MA.

I returned to Canada in November to get my passport, and while there I was in an automobile accident which left me with a cervical fracture which required many months of treatment and much pain.

In September 1962, I married Philbert Bourgeois from your hometown, Shediac Bridge. We lived in Waltham until our third child was born; then along with Marcel 4, Janice 3 and John 17 months, we moved to a five-room ranch house In Franklin MA. Phil worked at General Motors, in Framingham MA and I was a stay-at-home mother for twelve years and our family grew to six children, with Jamie, Mark and Lori-Ann.

In 1973, I graduated from the Henry O. Peabody School of Nursing in Norwood MA and started my nursing career at our local hospital in 1974.

In 1976, when Lori-Ann was three months old, Phil suffered an aortic aneurysm; although he recovered well, he never returned to work. He was disabled at age forty.

Luckily for us, I could pursue my nursing profession full-time and Phil became a very helpful stay-at-home dad.

As a hobby, I started running, and enjoyed it a lot. I participated in many road races, including ten marathons (five prestigious Boston marathons).

In 1996, I met David Darling, my neighbor for twenty-seven years. I was friend with his wife Mary, who died in 1993. Dave and I have been happily married since 1997. He has two sons, John and David, but no grandchildren.

As for myself, I have nine grandchildren and three step-grandchildren by the previous marriages of two of my daughters-in-law now married to my sons Marcel and Mark. I also have four great-grandchildren which include two step-great-grandsons.

I am now retired from nursing since 2002 and have lived on Cape Cod for ten years, where I worked as a homemaker and volunteered.

Mother, it is awkward to call you by that beautiful name, which I have never done before. I hope that this little story of my life will bring us closer to each other when I finally get to know you in Heaven, someday.

Meanwhile, I remain your little girl, who is very anxious to meet you.

With love,

Dorice

P.S. I changed the spelling of my name to Doris when I became an American citizen in 1971.

CHAPTER 29

Children's Mishaps and Injuries

Jamie was the most accident-prone of all his siblings: by age one he already had sutures on his forehead and many more followed. By age six he had already received several minor injuries. It is a wonder that a child abuse investigation was not initiated. Jamie was outgoing and a risk-taker.

Mark sustained a fractured wrist while wrestling with Marcel, who accidentally sat on him.

John fractured his wrist during the last soccer game of the season. Lucky for him it was the last. There were some sprained ankles while playing different sports.

Janice managed to limit her suture quota to one which happened while playing baseball in Grandpa's backyard during a vacation in New Brunswick, Canada.

Other injuries occurred during our vacations: Marcel got a deep laceration on his foot from a piece of glass at the beach, which severed an artery and needed immediate attention with the profuse bleeding. Poor Marcel suffered the rest of our vacation resting on the sofa while his siblings and cousins were out at play. On the same day, there was a need for another trip to the Urgent Care Center as John got hurt while playing baseball. At another Canadian vacation, Marcel got his finger caught in a car door. He was also bitten by the neighbors' dog while retrieving a ball from their backyard.

Jamie had surgery on his fifth finger and developed the chickenpox while having a full arm cast. Oh! How itchy under that cast. Poor Jamie. Mark and Lori-Ann followed suit in contacting the childhood disease and as well the Flynn boys, whom Jamie had cared for recently. A coincidence?

Lori-Ann sustained a fractured toe when Jamie's friend, Richard, fell on her. She was also accidentally poked in the eye and had a near nose fracture when accidentally hit with a shovel by another neighbor, Chris.

Janice, as a child, was often suffering from severe headaches but these were never diagnosed as migraines.

At age seventeen, Lori-Ann spent some time in the emergency department being evaluated with CAT scans to rule out a brain tumor, as she had been suffering from a severe headache for three days. There was a good outcome. Thank God! This took place a few days prior to her trip to France, as a member of her high school exchange program. A few months earlier we had hosted Emilie Truffant, a fifteen-year-old student from France.

CHAPTER 30

Medical History

My past medical history includes:

In 1956, a cyst was removed from my left wrist in a small infirmary in Shediac, New Brunswick, Canada.

In 1977, I had a positive PPD test (a skin test to determine tuberculosis) after, along with other nurses, I was exposed to an infected patient and I had to be on INH (an antibiotic which works by stopping the growth of TB) for one year.

In 1984, the PIE syndrome onset, which translate to: Pulmonary Infiltrate with Eosinophils increase, its modern term Eosinophilic Pneumonia, which has become a chronic lung problem and for which I have been treated by the same pulmonary physician for over thirty years.

In the early 1990s, I had hyperlipidemia, with elevated LDL (bad cholesterol) but high HDL (good cholesterol). In January 1992, gastric distress of four hours duration showed a slight abnormality from a gallbladder ultrasound and upper gastrointestinal series performed and found negative for gallstones; no further problem.

In October 1992, a goiter (a growth on the thyroid gland) caused by a rare infection and hypothyroidism was treated with Inderal and Prednisone for twenty days; problem solved.

Reactive airway disease (exercise induced asthma) was a new diagnosis in 1992.

In 1997, a hysterectomy and bladder suspension surgery was performed.

In 1999, a bunionectomy and hammertoes repair on left foot.

In 2001, a bunionectomy on right foot and a lumpectomy on right breast performed on the same day. The growth was found to be benign.

In 2004, a colonoscopy at Falmouth Hospital found polyps x3 and benign.

In 2006, bunionectomy repeated on right foot. The foot remains problematic today.

On March 11th, 2007, while running on the bike path in Dennis MA, I heard a popping sound and experienced great pain in my right knee which was diagnosed as a torn meniscus with cartilage damage. An arthroscopic surgery ensued on September 10th and it was followed by three Supartz injections and physical therapy under the orthopedist care in Falmouth MA.

In December 2008, a Milford orthopedist was consulted and findings indicated degenerative osteoarthritis and he suggested knee replacement.

In 2009, a second colonoscopy, performed, found one precancerous polyp and it was removed.

In 2010, I was diagnosed with Atrial Fibrillation during a stress test after experiencing chest pain earlier. I started on Warfarin (coumadin) and have been following the atrial fibrillation protocol ever since under the care of my primary care physician,, and that of my cardiologist, and I have been doing well. Atrial fibrillation is a disorder, NOT a disease.

In December 2011, after a near-syncope episode, a near-fainting spell, at Christ The King Church, I was evaluated at Falmouth Hospital and a 24-hour Holter monitor showed no significant findings.

On January 3rd, 2012, a reveal monitor was placed outside my chest to monitor my heart's activity.

On April 12th, 2012, a pacemaker was inserted and set at 70 to 130 to eliminate or at least reduce further near-syncope episodes, which can be hazardous especially while driving on the highway. A pacemaker check is done every six months and it is working well. After five years, Metoprolol was ordered to reduce the rapid heart rate.

ADDENDUM:

According to the Mayo Clinic, atrial fibrillation may manifest these symptoms: decreased blood pressure, lightheadedness, weakness and shortness of breath due to the irregularity and lack of coordination between the two chambers of the heart. Occasionally there could be chest pain or discomfort (angina) but it does not cause a heart attack. With the slowing of the heart pump with the atrial fibrillation, clots may form and the danger of stroke exists and becomes more common as a person ages.

Source: Google Wikipedia

CHAPTER 31

Friends, Family and Coworkers

My family has always been there for me when I was in need. I have made many friends through the years, along the way from Waltham, Franklin, Mashpee and Bellingham. My brother Ronald and I lived close to one another in Waltham and I became reacquainted with some of my old classmates from my hometown and some of my brother's friends.

In the 1960s, Waltham was a little Canada. Once we moved to Franklin, there were more friendships formed through the neighborhood, church and school functions, scouting, sports and other activities.

Our family was involved with church activities such as CCD teaching, and altar service. John, Jamie and Mark served mass.

Some of my coworkers at the hospital became very close friends on and off duty. My long-time friend Louise Nelson Fitzgerald, Sandie, Carol, Maryellen, Ann, Sandy, Joan and our amazing secretary, Anne Bailey on the fourth Floor. It was a joyous atmosphere most of the time. Our holiday parties were also special.

One Christmas party, we went from one club to a coworker's home in Framingham and after disco dancing all night, I got home at 4:00 am with my friend Louise, both sober. That is when I met Louise's future husband Bill (a gem!). Louise and Bill married on June 19th, 1987, at a very beautiful and special celebration. Louise and I share the same birthday, and we are still friends to this day.

In the late 1970s, I met Bill Flynn in the hospital parking lot when he rescued me from my old Nova car trouble. He was the head of the Respiratory Therapy Department. We fast became friends as we shared a common interest in running and we became members of the same running club, The Franklin Bolts.

In 1988, the Fifth Floor at the hospital became my permanent base for the next fourteen years, until my retirement. Roberta, our nurse manager was great to me by accommodating me with extra hours when needed.

My coworkers: Kenneth, Maryellen, Cindy, Sharon, Cherry, Amy, June, Paula, Dee, Charlene, Cheryl, Jeannine, Shirley. Betty, Mary-Beth, and David to name a few, were all friendly to me; as well as other department employees: Bob, Elaine, Veronica, Shawna, and a very special intravenous therapist, Leslie. In later years, Bob, a plumber at the hospital, along with his wife Christine, joined David and me on a Western Caribbean Cruise.

CHAPTER 32

Civic Duty

I was called to serve on a jury case in Dedham District Court but I was not selected for the trial: disappointment.

In 1989, I was summoned by the prosecutor to testify against a neighbouring acquaintance. After this episode, I had no desire to ever appear in court again, but I did on two other occasions.

Christopher, age fifteen, and I actually helped the prosecution by telling the truth. I was the first to take the stand and I was a bit nervous, to say the least. Chris told the court what he witnessed that night from his upstairs bedroom window when Nikki, our black Labrador Retriever, escaped from the house and jumped into the police cruiser. He told the court what he saw when the police officers dragged Michael to the edge of the wooded area in front of our house and were beating him; an altercation from which he suffered a fractured nose. The Prosecution won the case.

I was called to jury duty two more times, once in Falmouth MA and once in Orleans MA, but I did not have to serve.

CHAPTER 33

My Automobiles

My first set of wheels was a Chevrolet Nova 1978, after driving Phil's Chevy Impala 1970 while I was going to nursing school in 1972-1973. In 1981, after our separation, I became the legal owner of the maroon Nova. A couple of years later, I got another Nova, silver in color. I was teased and told that my car was riding sideways on the road.

In 1987, I bought a bronze-colored Chevrolet Cavalier. Jamie's favorite color (NOT). Unfortunately, this vehicle ended up in the automobile graveyard with only 60,000 miles following my defeat in the dispute with the General Motors arbitrator. What a shame!

My next automobile was from South Carolina and it did not have a rear defogger, which is not needed in the South but isn't practical in New England. This 1987 Buick Regal with its eight cylinders was purchased in 1989 and it was too big for me. It was also in need of snow tires for safety reasons on my early morning trips to work.

I kept my navy blue Buick until 1993 when I purchased my first new automobile, a white Chevrolet Lumina, which made many long-distance trips through the years, including trips to Canada. The best asset of this vehicle was the convenience of a very roomy back seat area and a large trunk, which was great during our move to Cape Cod.

After ten years, I gave the Lumina to my son John, when I got my second Buick in 2003. My old silver Buick Century remained my way of transportation until 2016. On March 30th, 2016, I bade goodbye to Old Silver and purchased a silver 2012 Chevy Cruze and crashed it on May 25th. It was totally demolished. Luckily, I sustained only a very badly bruised right leg and a fractured right foot. After eight weeks of wearing the black uncomfortable boot and being unable to drive, on July 30th, I became free again and returned to Imperial Chevrolet in Mendon MA, and purchased a light blue 2014 Chevy Spark.

I loved my little Sparky but my family's opinion differed on safety issues, due to its small size. After seven months, I returned to the same dealer and was assisted by the same salesman, Mike G., who treated me like a favorite customer. I traded Sparky for a 2015 Chevrolet Sonic, in mocha brown. My family and I are very happy with this choice.

CHAPTER 34

Amway Business

In 1992, I became an Amway distributor along with other family members, sponsored by our neighbors and friends, Andrew and Nikki Steinborn, very active and loyal Amway members. I got so excited about that new business and I was certain I was to become very successful and rich, if I followed all the rules and worked hard at showing the Amway plan: recruiting prospects and buying my own products, listening to the promotional tapes (cassette recordings) and attending as many Amway meetings, seminars, rallies and conventions as possible.

Most rallies and conventions were out of state. We drove long distances and at times we flew to distant places such as Atlanta, Georgia; Charlotte, North Carolina; Washington DC; and Baltimore, Maryland. We got caught in a major snowstorm there in March of 1993. The city stood still for one day due to lack of snow equipment. We made it home to Massachusetts safely.

I tried to make the business profitable by traveling on my own, showing the Amway plan to Maine and Cape Cod. I contacted several physicians with my sponsors' help. They were very helpful to me. Three of my children became distributors for some time.

The Steinborns and I went to New Brunswick as well as to Montreal to show the Amway Plan.

Sometimes it was a "No Show". Such fun! My sponsors were a model of patience.

In August 1993, Marcel and I with his two step-children drove to New Brunswick, Canada, on vacation. It was a scary experience driving through the Maine wilderness highways during the night hours and worrying if at any time a moose or a deer would appear in front of our vehicle. My old Buick Regal required eleven quarts of motor oil for the entire trip. We helped a couple from South Carolina who were stranded on the highway. They were very thankful and corresponded with me for some time. We were detained at the Canadian border due to the transport of Amway products but we did not encounter any problem. We had a great time in New Brunswick but on our return home, Marcel lost his wallet, somewhere in Maine. That was a trip never to be forgotten.

That was the last time I saw my sister alive. She died the following November after a long illness. My brother and I were planning to visit her in early December but unfortunately, it was too late.

I received a multitude of messages of sympathy, from all ranks in the business, and from people unknown to me. Some messages were telling me that I was where I needed to be to build a future for myself and my family.

Somehow, all this show of attention did not change my feelings of regret and guilt from not being there for my sister and for being away from my children too frequently to pursue my dream. I finally realized that it was to my advantage and to my family's as well to concentrate more on my guaranteed source of income from the fruit of my labor as a licensed practical nurse at the Milford Regional Hospital.

I met many interesting individuals in my Amway business travels. Some of our inspirational and motivational speakers were: David Thomas, founder of Wendy's Restaurants; country music singer and promoter of patriotic songs Lee Greenwood; retired Four-Star General Colin Powell, an excellent speaker; Barbara Mandrell, a country music singer and a great entertainer. Amway guru Dexter Yager and his wife Birdie were among the great promoters. The Amway co-founders, Richard De Vos and Jay Van Andel made some appearances as well as their family members in the business.

Presently, I still use Amway products but I do not participate in any other aspect of the business.

CHAPTER 35

My Sister Hermance

My sister lived by her own rules. She was steadfast in her loyalties to her family. She gave more than she received from life. I looked up to her.

Hermance married Daniel's father when she was nineteen and André was thirty-nine. I liked my brother-in-law, he was always good to me. They raised ten children: seven sons and three daughters. She was a great worker, fast and strong. She taught herself to cook, sew and tend to farm animals while raising her brood. She was responsible for the upkeep of the farm animals in addition to her family, when her husband was away during the winter, working as a longshoreman in Saint John. In the Summer, he worked on the farm at home.

My sister was a bingo expert. She is the only person I knew who could handle thirty-five bingo cards at once. She spent the last six years of her life on oxygen and in and out of the hospital, where she expired on November 29th, 1993, at age sixty. She was well loved by family and friends and her well-attended funeral attests to that. Her husband survived her by five years.

CHAPTER 36

The 1990s

In 1990, our son John and Juliette (Julie Gralla) were married at Blessed Sacrament Church in Walpole, Massachusetts, on a fine sunny Saturday morning, surrounded by family and friends. It was a special occasion, as we were celebrating our first family wedding. All of John's siblings took part in the wedding party. Nicole, Julie's sister, was maid of honor and Richard Garden was best man. He and his future wife met on that day as they caught the bridal bouquet and the garter. Amazing!

In that same year we welcomed our first grandchild, Angelique Nicole, a beautiful blue-eyed, blond-haired little girl. Shortly afterwards, John and Julie moved to their house on the beach in Warwick, Rhode Island. I was Angelique's first babysitter when her parents went to a movie. I felt so honored. John and Julie had a variety of employments in the early years, including security guard for John and cosmetologist and laboratory technician for Julie. They both went to school at different times.

In 1993, Jacqueline Suzanne arrived, another beautiful bundle of joy. We helped to take care of the girls whenever possible and enjoyed them very much.

In October 1993, Marcel married Marian Hart-Libby, and became Jamie and Lisa's stepfather. Marian's children had already been welcomed to our family for a few years. I taught them both religious doctrine and they received the initial sacraments of the Catholic Faith. They were part of their mother's wedding party and all of Marcel's siblings were as well. It was very festive. Some of our Canadian relatives were present. Angelique, age three, was a flower girl and she danced the night away.

In 1994, Lori-Ann, a junior at Tri-County Vocational School in the Cosmetology program, worked as a hair stylist assistant as a co-op student at Cheri Cheryle Beauty Salon in Medway MA. In December, she obtained her hair stylist license prior to receiving her high school diploma in June 1995, and continued to work at Cheri Cheryle. An appreciative note from a satisfied client was posted in the promotional Hair Salon newsletter. It read:

I recently went to this salon for the first time and saw a stylist named Lori-Ann; she made me feel very comfortable and welcomed as a first time client, but most importantly she really listened to me about my hair and when I left, it was exactly what I wanted.

At this time, all the Bourgeois children had graduated from high school and all were employed.

Marcel was busy working at Good Humor (formerly Sealtest) making delicious ice cream. Janice was still employed by Owens & Minor, in Franklin. John, after several different employments, started his new warehouse career with his sister Janice and Dennis Flinton, Janice's future husband, who was a foreman at the time. Jamie spent four years working at Owens & Minor, before realizing that he could get his plumber's license and make a better living. Thanks to his future wife, Tracy, and her dad, who encouraged him to pursue his plumbing career, he did! with no regrets.

Mark, after spending one year at Northeastern University in Boston, chose to work two or more jobs instead of continuing his education. He worked at Tedeschi's Store in Franklin, and as a UPS night attendant, and was employed by Owens & Minor for a few years as well, until he joined the staff at the Koeller Moeller at their corporate office in Franklin, where he worked until 2005. He was then transferred to Houston, Texas, to become the new warehouse supervisor at a facility newly purchased by John Hamm. It became the new corporate office and the name Koeller was dropped from the company name. Mark worked his way up the ladder to marketing department assistant manager with Ben Orr. Unfortunately, after six years, the company was sold to Eaton, and Mark was in search of new employment.

CHAPTER 37

A Super Busy Year

The year 1996 was an extremely busy year for the Bourgeois clan, with the weddings of three of the siblings, the sale of the family home at 86 Pine Street in Franklin, the Ben Franklin Bank injury, and the meeting of my future husband, David Darling.

On April 27th, Janice and Dennis Flinton were married at St. Joseph's Church in Woonsocket RI. This beautiful day was preceded by a series of unfortunate events. After a fundraiser walk for Multiple Sclerosis, I felt exhausted and feverish with malaise. The following day, I was diagnosed with pneumonia and given the antibiotic Biaxin, to which I had a severe reaction, with a rash and pain all over my body. A few days later, as I was confirming the limousine reservations for the wedding, my Lumina was hit by a dump truck in a parking lot. The passenger door was demolished. The truck driver reported that I collided with his vehicle. How could I possibly hit sideways to cause such damage? It was proven otherwise and the truck company covered the costs of the damages. There was no bodily injury. These happenings were within two weeks of the wedding day.

Janice's and Dennis' special day was beautiful weather-wise. The reception at the Coachmen's Lodge in Bellingham was great with family and friends. The videography and photography, however, left something to be desired. It was strange to see a wedding group photo without the bridal bouquets.

Three months to the day, Lori-Ann and Matthew Zajac got married. July 27th, 1996, was a great mid-summer day at Borderland State Park in Easton MA. To my chagrin, there was no church ceremony. The groom and his groomsmen wore short pants and tuxedos. Very unusual.

Lori-Ann and her future mother-in-law had gotten busy with centerpieces and favors, and her gown alterations as well. Lori-Ann looked gorgeous on her special day as her big sister had, three months earlier. No one would have ever suspected that her beautiful gown was a ten-dollar purchase from The Salvation Army Store.

The frugal wedding was fun and enjoyed by a young crowd. The groom was twenty-two and Lori-Ann would be twenty three weeks later.

On July 29th, 1996, Phil and I sold our five-room ranch home to our son Jamie and his fiancée Tracy. It was a sad day for me as I would have liked to remain in my home longer, but I was convinced that it was for my best interest. The sale of our home went smoothly. Jamie never left home and now was the owner of his childhood home.

On July 30th, I was closing, as planned, on my newly-purchased condominium in Franklin. My new abode was located at 2007 Franklin Crossing Road.

Needless to say, I was nervous on undertaking such an important task on my own. Weeks earlier, I had gotten cold feet and had questioned my decision: starting a new mortgage account, and monthly condominium fees, I found that to be a big responsibility. It was scary.

On the morning of the closing I found out that the funds were not in my bank account yet. I panicked. I was assured that they would be there the next day, not to worry.

At the closing, at the Benjamin Franklin Savings Bank, when I was asked to produce the check for the purchase, my checkbook was nowhere to be found in my handbag; therefore I had to go to my car to look for it.

I took the stairs, as instructed to do. At the bottom of the stairs was a narrow hallway leading to the bank lobby and there was a door which I assumed was an exit to the back parking lot. I turned the doorknob and immediately, without warning, the door fell on me, injuring my left arm. I managed to push the door against the wall and left. The adrenaline was flowing high. I made it to the car, retrieved my checkbook, thank God! and returned to complete the mortgage transaction.

At the conclusion of the closing, I left without speaking to anyone. This was probably a mistake on my part. I was baffled at the fact that an unattached door (an illusory exit) would not have a warning sign displayed as there was construction activity in progress, but not at the immediate time of the incident.

As the day went on the pain, swelling and bruising increased. Having difficulty performing my nurse's duties, I needed medical attention and suffered through neurological testing, imaging, physical therapy and loss of wages.

To my family and friends' suggestion, including that of my nurse manager and some of my coworkers, I got legal assistance, which helped me through this ordeal. After two years of diligent work, and a private court session, the battle was over. The Benjamin Franklin Savings Bank reached a settlement in my favor. On November 13th, 1998, I received a check to the amount sufficient to compensate for my pain and suffering and loss of wages It was worth the wait.

I recovered completely from my injury and after seven weeks of treatment, I resumed my normal living.

In June 1996, I met my husband to be, David Darling, at our parish's beloved pastor Father Daniel Gilmartin's retirement party. Dave had been our neighbor for twenty-seven years along with his wife, my friend Mary, who had died three years earlier. David joined my friends the Berardis and myself, at our table. We enjoyed casual conversation. David left early as he had to work in early morning at his landscaping business.

The following evening, there was a message from him on my answering machine. After a couple of days of playing telephone tag, we finally had a long telephone conversation, with the main topic: religion, a common interest as we both had been religious education teachers at St. Brendan Parish. A date was set to see a movie in Framingham the following

Saturday evening. We both enjoyed the movie Flirting with Disaster, and each other's company, on that warm rainy June night. David is a gentleman, sometimes overly courteous, and he always lets ladies walk before him. He told me he would never walk in front of a woman. As I am an independent person, I told him it was not necessary for him to open my car door. But I loved the attention, especially when on our first date he presented me a red rose.

His two sons, John and David, were familiar with my sons but they were not close friends. David Jr. had been in my CCD class, and both David's boys were altar servers as three of my sons were. Our sons named John graduated together from Franklin High School in 1985.

On September 28th, 1996, the third wedding of the year: Jamie and Tracy's special day and it was a beauty. It was our new pastor Father David Mullen's first wedding in our parish; he performed a great ceremony. We were informed however that future weddings would be scheduled at a different time, not to interfere with Saturday afternoon devotions. To this day that rule still applies. The wedding reception at a nearby Elks Hall was a fun event and was well attended. Upon their return from their Cruise Honeymoon, Jamie and Tracy enjoyed their newly renovated home, courtesy of Tracy's dad and his carpentry expertise.

CHAPTER 38

Old Home, New Home

I loved my new home, my condominium at 2007 Franklin Crossing Road, but it was an adjustment for me with the transition from a ranch house with a good sized fenced-in yard, a spacious driveway, friendly neighbors, close to my workplace, from such amenities to a second-floor condominium unit.

I had left behind at the ranch house my cat Spunki, with cat-friendly Tuchie. After about a week, however, Spunki was miserable and moved in with me. The move to my condo was very challenging for Spunki as he was restricted to indoor living after being an outdoor cat for years, free to hunt as he pleased. After one year of sharing our new abode, Spunki and I welcomed David in August 1997.

Among the new friends made at our new home was this special lady, Dorothy Jean Reed, who became like a mother to me. I loved to stop and chat with her every day, bringing in her mail. Eventually I became her house cleaner. Some of my grandchildren became fond of her as well. She was originally from the great State of Vermont but she had moved to several States with her husband's employment. Her daughter Linda remains a friend and resides in our neighborhood. Mrs. Reed always remembered the important dates in my life with a written message or a telephone call. Her ninetieth birthday party was very special. I continued to visit her years later even after we moved to Mashpee. She was living at the Forge Hill Assisted Living Facility in Franklin, where she had moved from our condominium complex. At age ninety-two, she returned to her Creator in May 2007. She is sadly missed.

Holiday celebrations and special events were frequent at my condominium. It was during this time that the younger generation, in my opinion, became closer to each other. I reduced my working hours, which freed more available time for babysitting my grandchildren. My condominium was a corner unit and had a huge bedroom (20x20 square feet). It was so convenient for Christmas present opening sessions with the grandchildren. Such celebrations as birthdays, Thanksgiving, Christmas, Easter, Mother's Day, Engagement Day (Dave and I) took place there. This home welcomed many old friends. It served as my center of recuperation for two foot surgeries, when it was a challenge to get down a flight of stairs on crutches; therefore, I used my derriere to slide my way down. There are many good memories of the six years spent at Franklin Crossing Road.

Summers of 1996 and 1997: David was busy with his groundskeeper foreman job with the town of Wellesley and his own landscaping business. myself, I kept busy with my nursing schedule at the hospital and my part-time house cleaning business.

We were seeing each other mostly on my weekend off (every other week). We stayed locally, enjoying the Fourth of July celebrations in Franklin, a four-day affair, and the St. Rocco Festival. We went to movies, we went bowling and we attended Church together. During our first summer of courtship, David vacationed on Cape Cod and he was joined there by his son John and wife Laura. We spent a day on Martha's Vineyard with his other son David and some of his friends. We visited the famous mansions of Newport, Rhode Island. We enjoyed the Cliff Boardwalk, the Kite Park, the restaurants, the shops and a relaxing boat ride on a beautiful Sunday afternoon. We toured Nantucket Island, which was radiant with the most amazing natural floral displays I had ever seen. I was very interested in photography at the time. The panoramic photo era. A pleasant Sunday afternoon was spent in Plymouth MA enjoying sites such as The Rock and The Mayflower, and a picnic on the grounds. We both shared an interest in beautiful landscape and historical buildings, especially old churches. We spent much time visiting John and Laura in Nashua, New Hampshire, where we did some hiking on small mountains such as Pack Monadnock (1.6 mile). Once at the top, we could see the Boston skyline. Those are great memories.

John and Laura were always so hospitable and introduced us to so many new places and things to do, such as going to farm stands, picking apples, going to movies or watching videos at their home. They also had a good choice of restaurants; Timeless, The Cracker Barrel and Buckley's, among my favorites.

David Jr and girlfriend Tina, had a beautiful home built in East Bridgewater after selling the Darling family home in Franklin; where they and Jamie's family were neighbours for a few years.

I felt the acceptance in the Darling family and the friendship has blossomed through the years. As we visited my relatives, David was very well accepted by all my children and a new friendship was born between David and Phil. HOW GREAT IS THAT! He also scored points with my brother Ron, which was a good thing for me.

CHAPTER 39

Mementos

I have always been a KEEPER: letters, greeting cards, notes, pictures and newspaper clippings; everything is a souvenir of a special event in the past or present and all are important to me.

That explains how devastated I was when a trunk filled with my personal treasures disappeared from our homestead when I was thirteen years old. I still miss my school report cards, scrapbooks and other childhood memories.

Through the years, I have collected scores of papers, all precious to me, whether they may be philosophical documents, scripture passages, or simply a young adult's or a child's drawing or a small note...

Here are samples of such literary trophies:

My report card from Saint-Jérome, Québec, upon completion of the first year of the Home Economics course in 1957.

My 1958 Junior Matriculation Exam and Certificate, as well as my High School Graduation Program.

My Novitiate group photo.

My Henry O. Peabody School of Nursing diploma from 1973.

A copy of the letter of confirmation to the John F. Kennedy Elementary School in Franklin, for initiating the legislative bill to make the ladybug the official State of Massachusetts insect in 1974.

Muscular Dystrophy Telethon (1981). My childhood classmate, Paul Bourgeois' letter.

Letters from sponsored Mexican boys.

In 1968, Mrs. Ethel Kennedy's note of acknowledgement of my expression of sympathy on the loss of her beloved husband Robert, whom I admired, and in whose honor I would later write the song The Man With Charisma. Ethel Kennedy's note read:

We are consoled that you share our sorrow and the love he gave was returned in full measure. Blessed are they who mourn for they may be comforted. Blessed are they who hunger and thirst for justice, for they may be fulfilled. Blessed be the Peacemakers for they shall be called the Children of GOD. Matthew V.3

Ethel Kennedy

In 1969, The Man With Charisma was written. Here are the words:

Chorus

Oh, he was with Charisma,
The pride of America;
For he loved his life quite fully,
Working for peace and unity.

Recitation

He stood silent, behind his slain brother's grave,
Staring but still teaching us to be brave.
His bleeding heart was suffering because
O the pitiful state of our country.
What would become now
Of civil rights and anti-poverty?
He was a valiant knight
And a great nature lover;

He learned early in life
That he who fights
Does not always conquer.

God was his true source of strength and courage
And along with his friend Martin Luther,
He tried to conserve our beautiful heritage.
Then in early June 1968, in the State of California,
A sniper's bullet terminated a life dedicated to the welfare
Of the poor people of America
And thus by far
Extinguished the last light of hope of the ghetto residents.

The Senator's death saddened many hearts around the world,
But mostly those of the United States' Black citizens.
May his obsession for peace be asserted
By the ceasefire and may our lives reflect a sparkle of his burning desire.
Let us hope that all Americans will share his beliefs...
May the soul of Robert F. Kennedy rest in peace.

Unfortunately, I was unable to publish this song, but I did receive three promotional records (45s) and a certificate for registration to obtain the copyright of the song, which I never did obtain; but I still have the records.

December 1973 One of the most important letters I ever received was from:

> The Massachusetts Board Of Nursing
> State Board Test Pool Examination
> Practical Nurse Form 873
> Date of Examination: November 20, 1973
> Date of report: December 20, 1973
> Bourgeois Doris M. Mrs.
> Candidate Number 0961
> 86 Pine Street
> Franklin MA 02038
> 1973 Graduate of Henry O. Peabody - Girls Norwood MA

Score 523 Pass 350 Passed.

Nothing exceptional to brag about. BUT I DID IT!

A very short but special note from my brother, thanking me for a birthday gift: a musical water fountain.

Doris, thank you for the gift and everything. I listen to it every night. It is relaxing. Love, Ronnie

This clipping was sent to me from San Diego CA, honoring my best friend Therese.

OUR OWN BLITHE SPIRIT FROM BOSTON

———————◆•◆•◆———————

Therese Berardi, affectionately called "Mother Therese" by the home office staff, is the national spokeswoman for Private Ledger.

Callers who reach Private Ledger Headquarters San Diego are surprised and charmed to be greeted by a warm, friendly Massachusetts accent and they are in good hands because Therese Berardi is more than a receptionist, she is an expert at helping people.

As everyone who has ever called knows, Therese connects you to the right person even when you had no idea who you needed to talk to.

Our blithe spirit came to us three years ago from the Boston area, where she and husband Ralph had raised five children. Therese had been head receptionist at the Zayre Corporation, but those Eastern winters and most importantly, the presence of children and grandchildren in California made the migration easy. "Two of my three grandchildren are native Californians."

We think that Therese's attitude about her role at Private Ledger makes her a star performer. In her own words: "I care about people and because of that, two things are important to me: treating every caller and visitor well and being a good receptionist."

I saved newspaper clippings of events such as Queen Elizabeth II's coronation in the mid-fifties; President John F. Kennedy's assassination as well as the assassination of his brother Robert and of Martin Luther King Jr.; Mother Teresa's demise; Princess Diana's tragic death, which happened five days after David and I left Paris.

The massive accumulation of newsworthy articles is a reminder of my interest in current events (important ones) as well as of my being a pack rat as my son Jamie would say.

CHAPTER 40

Anecdotes

Once, when Mark was about fourteen, he decided to do laundry and as it was just before the start of a new school year, he was breaking-in his new denim jacket. But while using bleach on the whites, some splashed on his jacket... DISASTER! For Mark, as his jacket became a very pretty blue and white spotted jacket. But it became Lori-Ann's favorite. It was so original that it was the envy of her friends. She wore it on our trip to Europe and it was noticed. Mark's mistake was his loss and Lori-Ann's gain, that time. Poor Mark!

Here are a few short notes from David to me:

> Dear Mother: When will I get a blanket and socks to wear to bed at night? Please meow me a lullaby too before I go to sleep.
>
> Love,
>
> Spunki

Dear Human Mommy:

> You are the nicest master a cat could have.
>
> Love,
>
> Spunki

P.S. I guess you never knew I could write English.

David has a great sense of humour. He has provided us with a few moments of merriment. Janice and Brianna laughed all the way from Mashpee to the Bourne Bridge one day when the cornbread with butter in a plastic bag, given to them by an insisting David, was dripping profusely.

One Summer evening while Lori-Ann and her family were visiting, frisky Spunki was outside past his 8:00 pm curfew. I was therefore frantically calling to him and searching the backyard for my beloved pet, so I called David for help. He nonchalantly pulled the bedroom window shades down and said: "I think you're nuts. I think you're nuts". Do you think I got the message? Well, everyone had a good laugh and still talk about it today.

A precious gift: The bird on the cross: every morning upon my awakening, I look out my window and there he is: my feathered friend, Mr. Bluebird, perched on top of my beloved St. Brendan Church replica birdhouse, courtesy of my daughter Lori-Ann and her family. What a thoughtful gift!

CHAPTER 41

1997

On June 14th, 1997, Mark Jason and Melissa G. Kerr tied the knot after four years of courtship, which had begun when as teenagers they were coworkers at a Pizza restaurant in Franklin.

It was a beautiful wedding day, only to be darkened unfortunately by two unexpected happenings: first, Margot, Melissa's mom, fell in the church while arranging flowers and sustained facial abrasions but thankfully was not otherwise indisposed. And then our ride in the jeep, Margot and I, going to the reception, left my hairdo in a state that left much to be desired and the subject of conversation. Speed and windy conditions were responsible.

A series of unfortunate events had preceded this wedding and, unfortunately, Mark and Melissa's marriage lasted but a short time.

Two months and two days later, on August 16th, 1997, David Darling and I were married at St. Brendan Church in North Bellingham by Father Daniel Gilmartin, who came out of retirement to bless our union.

My four sons gave me away and my two daughters were my matrons of honor. David Jr. was Dave's best man. His other son John and his wife Laura were also present, but not in the wedding party. Our altar servers were Mary Beth Rapko, a family friend, and Patrick Fitzgerald, my former CCD student and neighbor. Mark and Lori-Ann did the readings including Footprints at the end of the mass.

It was an exceptionally hot day with temperatures in the upper nineties. Janice, in her fourth month of pregnancy, felt the discomfort in the non air-conditioned church. The choir was at its best in honor of its member David.

In addition to family members, a few friends and coworkers were present as well as parishioners, as the church is a public place of worship.

Following the photography session outside the church with our family friend, photographer Jonathan Blaisdell, we proceeded to our lovely reception at Florentina's, a small restaurant in Franklin. Our invited guests were handpicked. In addition to family members, our Pastor and the photographer were included. My two granddaughters, Angelique then age seven, and Jacqueline, age four and my grandson Matthew, nineteen months, were present.

After a perfect afternoon - I was so happy! - we headed to Boston and noticed from the limousine window that the temperature had risen to 97 degrees Fahrenheit.

The following morning, we departed on our ten-day tour of Europe with Cosmo Travel. We arrived at Heathrow Airport in the late evening. It was a long flight and when we finally reached the Hotel Royal Scot at 11:00 pm, we were exhausted.

On August 18th, we got our information and caught up with the tour already in progress. The visit to Windsor Castle was very interesting with its history and beautiful scenery. We had a photo taken with the Royal Guard. We then went to Piccadily Square, which reminded us of Faneuil Hall in Boston, and from there we went to the Underground Train and enjoyed a great ride.

August 19th My thoughts were at home with Lori-Ann on her twenty-first birthday. We left England for Brussels by the Channel Tunnel, a tunnel in part under the English Channel that runs over two hundred feet below sea level. What an experience that was, to cross from England to Calais, France, a forty-eight-mile distance, in thirty minutes.

After a stopover in France, we proceeded to Belgium, where we met with our tour guide Benny and our coach driver Marcel. On a long walk that evening we sampled some Painted Desert Soup, spicy but good, at the Firebird Café, an American-owned restaurant.

August 20th A tour of lovely Brussels with its historical buildings, monuments and churches. We visited chocolate and lace factories, then headed to the Netherlands. We spent some time at The Hague, which is the government center in Holland. We saw the town hall, museums and Queen Josephine Beatrix's palace. We peeked in her office through an opened window... Fun! We met Americans from Miami, Florida, at dinner.

August 21st We had an early morning jog and Dave did well. The day was a touring day and we visited a diamond factory, a cheese farm and a clog factory. We saw many windmills and leaning houses along the Canal route. A five-foot wide house was quite a spectacle.

August 22nd En route to Bonn, Germany. We visited museums, the Market Square, churches, all very impressive, including Beethoven's birthplace. The Black Forest was thick, dark with a winding road, a little gloomy.

We were then on our way to Koblenz, to our small quaint Zur Kripp Hotel, a family-owned business where Sasha did everything. In that hotel was the tiniest bathroom ever seen. Our room was very noisy at night indeed, as the train sped by our bedroom window all night long. BUT, the food was good.

August 23rd My son Marcel's thirty-fourth birthday. We left Koblenz to meet with the ferry for the River Rhine Cruise. It was a fantastic journey along the river with views of countless castles, crops and vineyards where farmers were working on steep hills with their spike shoes. We visited a cuckoo clock store and had a factory demonstration.

The Rhine River Cruise was so special that we must have been hypnotized as we were left on the ship with Benny, who was aware that two people were not accounted for. Therefore, like a good shepherd, he stayed behind with us. We were picked up at the next port. Although it was an embarrassing moment, we were warmly welcomed by our fellow travelers.

A typical German meal consisted of bratwurst, potato salad, and Fanta (a very popular soft drink in Europe at that time).

We visited a biergarten. Yes, I tasted the German beer… not for me.

The city of Trier had beautiful grounds and Gothic churches but all churches and stores close down at 4:00 pm on Saturdays. We were unable to attend mass. We were in the Porta Nigra (Black Gate) district, which has a lot of history. We arrived at our TEAM Hotel in the early evening had a great dinner. There was an entertainment night at the discotheque nearby; we danced the night away to good German music.

August 24th After a short jog in the early morning we left for Luxembourg with our tour bus. Luxembourg is a small country with beautiful gardens, museums and valleys. We crossed the French border without any check on our passport. We ate lunch in Verdun in Alsace and enjoyed raspberry cheesecake. So sweet!

We were then on our way to the Campanile Hotel. In a suburb of Paris, at Duverney, we visited a champagne factory. Interesting and cold.

Amazingly for a major city, the traffic was mild. Our Campanile Hotel was very nice. How exciting! We were in Paris.

BIG EVENT: World Youth Day. Pope John Paul II had left the Sacré Coeur Church a short time prior. We could still feel the pope's presence. Young adults from one hundred and forty countries from around the world had been where we stood. What a privilege to be there. The Sacré Coeur Church is renowned for its majestic pillars and the gargoyles with which it is adorned. As we walked away, we could hear prayers recited in that gigantic church.

Our seven-course dinner at Restaurant Saint Germain, which featured French onion soup and canard à l'orange was not what we expected. There was a toast in our honor and a dance for us newlyweds. A late and fun night ensued.

August 25th Tired, no jogging today. We toured parks and monuments in the morning: Champs-Elysées, Arc de Triomphe and Tour Eiffel. After lunch, afternoon shopping with Dave. We took the metro back to the hotel and had a two-hour rest. We were later picked up by the coach for our big night on the town… at the Paradis Latin for a French Cabaret Show. The music, costumes, choreography, the whole atmosphere was fantastic. One singer was from New York and had a great voice. The American National Anthem made us feel good. We returned to the hotel at half past midnight.

August 26th We jogged over two miles, had breakfast, then, after the etiquette rules were taken care of regarding monies exchanged and tips, we boarded a shuttle bus to the Charles de Gaulle Airport. At 1:15 pm, we were en route to America.

Our return flight went smoothly, our arrival in Boston, and the shuttle bus to Framingham, where we were being picked up by Dave's brother Dan, all went as planned.

It is to be noted that on August 31st, five days after we left Paris, Princess Diana was tragically killed in a motor vehicle accident in Paris… How sad!

On September 13th, 1997, our delayed wedding reception took place at the Elks Hall, on Pond Street in Franklin MA. We were surrounded by over eighty invited guests, and we were greeted by our disc jockey, who played the old favorites of the 50s, 60s, 70s, 80s and 90s at our request. Our theme song was "I will always be right there" by Bryan Adams. There was also karaoke for many to enjoy.

My Franklin condominium became our home for the next five years.

1998

In June 1998, we planned a trip to New Brunswick, Canada, for my fortieth high school class reunion at the all-girls boarding school where I graduated in 1958. In mid-June, I realized that my certificate of naturalization was nowhere to be found. After my initial panic attack subsided, the department of Immigration and Naturalization Services was contacted pronto.

Not knowing how to cross the Canadian border legally, I went to the Franklin Town Hall and I was given a card as proof of citizenship, with right to vote. Well, that little card sufficed and David and I enjoyed a week in New Brunswick in celebration of my high school class reunion. It was a well-organized event with my friends Anita Pellerin and Gloria Mockler in charge. Several of our novitiate colleagues and some of our teachers were present. It was so wonderful to see everyone, after so many years.

We spent a very pleasant and relaxing day on Prince Edward Island after crossing on the nearly nine-mile-long newly opened Confederation Bridge. That was a great experience.

There was no problem at the American border upon our return. After several attempts to replace my lost document, I was told the process would take about one year. I was impatient and several letters were exchanged between the INS and myself proved to be futile, even with contacts to the offices of Senator Ted Kennedy and John Kerry from whom there was no response. On April 20th, 2002, I received my long-awaited certificate, almost four years later.

In 1998, I reduced my working hours at the hospital and started my own house-cleaning business. A newspaper advertisement resulted in two replies and these were limited to bathroom cleaning only. But I persevered. My clientele expanded to six by the year 2000 and I reduced my nursing hours to twenty-four hours a week. Most of my clients were from my hometown except the Mitchells in Holliston and the circa 1754 Baldessari's home in Walpole MA. In 2001 I added the McKittrick's beautiful home in Mendon to make my circle of seven. I kept that group of clients until my 2002 retirement from the hospital. I have fond memories of all my clients and I have kept contact with some of them to this day.

I continued cleaning the McKittrick's home, eighty miles away, while living on Cape Cod, until 2005. Martha Stewart had a prominent place in that home and some of my friends called it "the Martha Stewart house".

CHAPTER 43

Cape Cod

In April 2002, prior to moving to Cape Cod, I rented my Franklin condominium to a young father and his twelve-year-old daughter. Unfortunately, due to circumstances beyond their control, they left before the contract expired. That was a financial loss for me. My rental experience was a headache for the last three months prior to their departure. The condominium was sold in May 2003 with a good profit.

In May 2002, Dave and I moved to Mashpee, Cape Cod, to our new home that we had purchased in July 2001. We were actually in moving mode for ten months.

I helped my dear friend Mrs. Reed until she moved to an assisted living facility in the summer of 2002.

After moving to Mashpee, I continued to clean homes. I got more clients. And I got involved in volunteering at several facilities such as the Falmouth Hospital, working in the dietary department, visiting patients regarding their diets and their meal menus, which I enjoyed very much. I also helped with clerical data with the Surgical Day Unit.

Helping out at the Mashpee Rehabilitation Center, in the activities department, was fascinating, playing games with the residents, especially the WORD game, which was fun. It was amazing to me how those elderly clients exhibited such great knowledge of vocabulary. I also volunteered at the Christ The King church library and at a small clinic at the Mashpee Commons for a short time. Working as a receptionist at the C-Lab Center in Mashpee was also a very interesting experience, while meeting many wonderful people.

I also volunteered at the St. Vincent de Paul Clothing Center, sponsored by Christ The King Church, for nine years and many friendships were formed among my coworkers (my fellow volunteers) and I still cherish these friendships today.

David and I became Friends of The Library and helped to raise funds with our weekly book sales to build a large state-of the-art library near the Commons.

My first self-employment was shortly after moving to Mashpee in July 2002. I became a part-time caretaker to this lovely, intelligent, wheelchair-bound and oxygen-dependant lady in Falmouth MA. Marianne Borchelt had been an herb culturist, gathering herbs from her own backyard. She was an interesting conversationalist. I learned from her wise advice. Unfortunately, this assignment came to an end after five short months. Mrs. Borchelt went to her eternal reward on December 12th, 2002.

Meanwhile, my cleaning business grew and some one-time special assignments happened periodically. One such occasion was when Mr. J. Stanley, a deacon at The Lady of Victory Church in Centerville, wanted to surprise his wife for Mother's Day with the gift of a clean house. How nice! Later on, I assisted with their daughter's pre-nuptial house preparation. Deacon Stanley also introduced me to his friend Mr. Cousins, who was moving. Not only did I clean his condominium but I brought home a carload of leftovers. Everything had to be out of the unit by the next day. David did not always appreciate the extras brought home.

Cleaning one home prior to a wedding proved to be quite a challenge getting around boxes of food and liquor and too many early house guests.

An interesting assignment was when I helped a friend of a friend from church who needed major home renovations and unbeknown to me, Janice Lundgren had purchased her home from a very popular young artist and rock/pop/folk singer-songwriter in Mashpee. To my great surprise, I got busy packing Cyndi Lauper's paintings and white dishes. That experience of mine soon became a conversation topic in my family. Cyndi Lauper was one of Jamie's favorite artists.

The Walshes, the Palumbos, the Sullivans, the Englishes, Peggy and Alice kept me busy for many years.

The Walsh's beautiful twenty-three room house was always organized and tidy. I often wondered why they needed me. I got to know their lovely family and even their grandchildren by name. Their main residence was in Boston, where they were friends with well-known city mayor Thomas Menino. Karylann and I still keep in touch today.

The Sullivan's household was at times a challenge to clean, as the twenty-two rooms were fully occupied with either athletic equipment, musical instruments or a variety of up-to-date footwear. Their two large dogs, Grady and Roxanne (who was petrified of my mop), were friendly to me once I was inside the house but first, I had to bypass Grady.

Linda, called Missy by her mother, was a highly energetic and athletic young lady who was also very generous. She and her three smart and handsome sons were like family to me. Linda's mom, Peggy, lived in a charming little cottage on the premises. Her house was a breeze to clean, and her advice was always welcome. Our friendship remains today.

I cherish the fond memories of my numerous Cape Cod friends. I love to visit as often as I possibly can. The eighty-mile trek is always an exciting trip to me.

Some of the Cape Cod attractions that I still miss are:

The Heritage Museum and Gardens in Sandwich.

The Mashpee and Falmouth harbors with their multitude of varieties of ships: fishing, speed and sail boats.

Woods Hole, the site of the start of famous road races, with shops on the water's edge and one of our favorite eateries, PIE IN THE SKY.

The Islands: Martha's Vineyard and Nantucket are lovely places to visit, especially in the Summer.

Osterville offered a very attractive scene to the viewer. Although I am not a swimmer or a beach lover, I enjoyed walking, or running, by the ocean.

The many sightseeing excursions brought us to visit the numerous beautiful lighthouses throughout Cape Cod. To name a few:

The Nobska Point Light, built in 1829, and located in the little town of Woods Hole.

The Sandy Neck Lighthouse, built in 1826, and located in West Barnstable.

Bishops and Clerks Light, built in 1858, and located in Hyannis.

The Hyannis Harbor Light, built in 1849.

The Point Gammon Lighthouse, built in 1816, and located in Yarmouth.

The West Dennis Lighthouse, built in 1856.

The Stage Harbor Light, built in 1880, and located in Chatham.

Another lighthouse in Chatham, built in 1808.

The Nauset Light, built in 1838, and located in Eastham.

The Mayo Beach Light, built in 1837, and located in Wellfleet.

The Highland Light, built in 1797, and located in Truro.

The Race Point Light, built in 1816, and located in Truro also.

Those were interesting historic sites as well as Sandwich, the oldest town on Cape Cod, incorporated in 1638. This historic town is graced with picturesque homes such as the Newcomb Tavern, a well-known Tory establishment. My friend Cindy 's ancestry leads to the Newcomb family.

Sandwich is also the home of the First Parish Meeting House; the Glass Museum, where we attended a glassblowing demonstration with John and Laura and found it fascinating; The Hoxie House; The Green Briar Nature Center; The Dexter Grist Mill; and The Heritage Museum and Gardens with its collection of thousands of rhododendrons as well as over a thousand varieties of shrubs and herbs, galleries for American Folk Art, a vintage carousel, classic automobiles, children's activities such as a maize, a playground, and a stage for plays. The boardwalk, about 1350 feet in length, was always fun to stroll across the Mill Creek and through the Marsh heading to Town Beach on Cape Cod Bay.

The Cape Cod Baseball League started out in Sandwich. The Otis Air Force Base is a very busy place and has hosted Air Shows at times. The Dan'L Webster Inn lives up to its great reputation for hospitality and great food. Sandwich is also the birthplace of Thomas Burgess, a naturalist and the author of the classic Peter Rabbit.

The town of Mashpee, home of the federally recognized Wampanoag Tribe, was founded in the year 1870. Its population of 1,400 plus is comprised of several nationalities with Irish being more prominent. The oldest Indian Meeting House in the Country was practically in our backyard, next to the Old Indian Cemetery, which was one of my running haunts and where I befriended L Potter, a member of the Wampanoag First Nation and cemetery caretaker.

Mashpee has a few swimming holes of its own as well: Southcape Beach, Lake Wakeby, and Mashpee Neck. The Mashpee Commons is well known for its high-end quality shopping as well as for its fine restaurants appreciated by a throng of tourists in Summertime. The Polar Cave # 1 Ice Cream Parlor on the Cape, Brianna's all-time favorite, was a short drive from our home. I feel privileged to have experienced and enjoyed living there for ten years. I miss that little town.

Yarmouth had our favorite mini-golf courses. Cotuit had the Cape Cod League Park where some of our Red Sox players have started their playing career, such as Carl Yastrzemski, Tony Conigliaro, Dustin Pedroia and Jacoby Ellsbury, to name a few.

Hyannis is known for The John F. Kennedy Museum and The Kennedy Family Compound.

Eastham also had its charms and there we visited a relative and enjoyed walks along the beach and fine meals at its restaurants.

Orleans was where I was called to jury duty once. Along Route 6A, you can find many specialty shops with a lot of surprises.

CHAPTER 44

Christ The King Parish

I am very grateful to have been a parishioner for ten years at this beautiful church in the center of Mashpee MA.

Christ The King Church was founded by Monsignor Ronald Tosti in 1984. The parish evolved from a small chapel on the grounds where presently sits The St. Vincent de Paul Clothing Center in Cotuit. The church grounds house the beautiful large church itself and the St. Jude Chapel, which was my favorite corner to pray. The chapel's stained glass windows, second only to St. Brendan Church's windows, were a beauty. The Chapel was moved from Cotuit, three miles away, after the new church was built near the Mashpee Commons.

The church hall is also impressive with its several classrooms for multiple uses, a gift shop, a kitchen, an auditorium and a library, where I volunteered for some time and brought Brianna with me to help at times. The church grounds are very pleasant with large flower gardens, a gazebo, a grotto and a small playground which was very inviting to grandchildren. Numerous organizations were part of CTK parish, such as: The Knights of Columbus, the Women's Club, the 50+ Club, CCD, RCIA, Boy Scouts, AA, Alanon, and the Food Pantry, where Dave volunteered for a few years. An organized exercise class kept many ladies in good physical fitness, thanks to June Robillard's great effort.

The MOM's program, in which I took part in 2005, was another enrichment ministry for women that I enjoyed very much. I was involved with the Prayer Line that accepts prayer requests for special intentions, either by telephone or by computer. I still call-in prayer requests as needed. Sister

Dympna and Sister Shirley were devoted assets to our parish and leaders of Faith Sharing and Renew programs.

Monsignor Tosti's good taste and his Italian heritage showed through in his love of good food, his love of fine music, being a talented pianist, and his artistic disposition proved true in the most exquisite work of art which became Christ The King Church. It was dubbed "The Cathedral" under his direction.

One bizarre rule, which puzzled Dave and me, was Monsignor Tosti's desire to keep the parishioners close to the altar by closing the back pews with a thick green rope. A rope that I would remove to sit wherever I pleased at daily mass. More proof of my non conformity to rules, which I do observe if they are sensible.

Monsignor Tosti had the pleasure and honor of burning the sixteen-year, $8.1- million mortgage, which had been financed by the diocese of Fall River, which encompasses over one hundred parishes in Southeastern Massachusetts and twenty-two on Cape Cod and the Islands. That very special celebration took place on November 20th, 2005, close to the solemnity of Christ The King's Feast Day.

In 2006, Monsignor Tosti retired from our parish, but he continued to minister at surrounding parishes and to enjoy his Rose Medallion Collection, in his new home in Cotuit. He led several guided tours in Italy with parishioners and other tourists. One of those special events was the elevation to cardinal of our beloved Sean Cardinal O'Malley, who had been the Fall River bishop previously.

In 2006, the parish welcomed Monsignor Daniel Hoye to shepherd us. He was soft-spoken, reserved, had a good sense of humor and, with eight siblings (seven brothers and one lonely sister), he could relate to family matters easily. He made his residence at the parish rectory and although being a Monsignor, he was never seen wearing his purple sash. A humble man. His first order of business on arrival was to remove the GREEN ROPE. My kind of man!

CTK had a large staff which included three permanent deacons, each with individual duties, and a well-run office thanks to the expertise of several ladies. Volunteers were plentiful and senior citizens were serving daily mass, to my amazement! My friends Barbara, Peggy and Betty were among them. The Sunday 8:30 am mass was the children's mass, where the celebrant or the deacon sits and discusses the Gospel theme with the children. My granddaughter Brianna used to participate in the ritual and loved it. At the end of the mass, the children go to the celebrant or the deacon for a blessing. Sometimes small tykes are carried by their older siblings, which always impressed me. The practice was initiated by a former parishioner who later became a priest and who helped at CTK at times. The large Christ The King compound still impresses me and I visit every time I come to Mashpee.

CHAPTER 45

Income Tax 2003

On March 1ˢᵗ, 2004, I filed my taxes with H&R Block in Franklin MA, where I had been going for several years with the same preparer, Miss Connie She had always been knowledgeable and helpful, therefore I requested her services year after year.

This year was different, as I had sold my condominium in May of 2003. I was told I had to pay the Internal Revenue Service the sum of thirteen thousand and forty dollars in federal taxes and five thousand four hundred and seventy-two dollars in State taxes. I was shocked at first, and tried to digest the bad news all the way home to Mashpee.

Even though Connie had apologized to me for my disappointment and had assured me the reason was that I had rented my condominium for one year prior to selling it, I was doubtful. Therefore, after a discussion, Dave and I decided to have a second opinion at another H&R Block office in Mashpee. There, M K reviewed my 2003 taxes and informed me that I was exempt according to a new tax reform which stated that if you lived in the said dwelling for two of the last five years at the time of the sale, you are exempt of the capital gains tax. After much work, he concluded that I did qualify for that exemption.

My tax papers along with schedule D were sent to the Massachusetts Department of Revenue in Boston. The correspondence between the IRS and the Massachusetts Department was intense from April to July of 2004. During that period of time, I was charged interest and a penalty was added which amounted to fourteen thousand three hundred and sixty-three dollars due to the IRS and five thousand four hundred and seventy-two dollars to the Commonwealth of Massachusetts as of June 17ᵗʰ, 2004.

On June 30th, the abatement was approved. What a relief! Many prayers had been said. On July 12th, I received the revision of account and was refunded $1,315.00 from the IRS and shortly afterwards I received a refund from the State department for $155.00. The nightmare was over! Obviously, Ms.Connie was not aware of the new law passed in Massachusetts.

My friend Margaret, and myself informed a mutual friend, Kay, and with her new awareness, she saved herself thousands also. How nice!

CHAPTER 46

Grandchildren

Angelique Nicole, a beautiful blond, blue-eyed infant, born to John and Juliette, was a precious gift which brought great joy to our family. The Bourgeois children became proud aunts and uncles and I, an exhilarated grandmother. I became Mammy "B".

Angelique was an inquisitive child. At age three, she was giving her Papa Bourgeois directions to her maternal grandmother's house in Walpole MA, from Franklin, a distance of about twelve miles. She loved the movie Home Alone, which she watched repeatedly. She attended preschool at The Blessed Sacrament School in Walpole where her maternal grandmother, Suzanne Gralla, was a teacher for many years.

Angelique became a big sister to Jacqueline Suzanne in May 1993. Little Jackie was a blue-eyed brunette with chubby cheeks and a contagious smile. She followed in her sister's footsteps to Catholic school. We were very proud of our two lovely granddaughters learning so well and participating in school activities such as plays, concerts and recitals. They both made their First Communion at the Blessed Sacrament Church. Angelique was very artistic, loved poetry, drawing and painting; while Jackie was more active in sports and later became a cheerleader in high school.

Their childhood was affected by their parents' 'troubled marriage', which ended in divorce in 1995. Their maternal grandmother became their guardian, as their mother had health issues. Their dad, my son John, had visiting rights and that is when the girls were visiting our family. Their adolescent years were very difficult and unfortunately a good part of those years were spent away from our family. Although we corresponded, we missed them terribly. Here are some excerpts of their letters:

Dear Mame "B",

> I know you are Mame "D" but to me you will always be Mame "B". I was very excited to hear from you. I was worried I was not going to receive a letter from you. My dad wants to set up a visit with me soon. I can't wait. Can you possibly send me a long distance phone card so I can call him.

> Can you also send me Harry Potter stickers, please.

> My school subjects are: literature, history, psychology, math, English and biology. I can only do my art in my room. I play board games and we have outside activities, and we go on day trips.

> Please write back and tell everyone I love them.

> Love, always,

> Angelique xoxo

Dear Mame "B" and Papa Dave,

> How is everyone? I'm doing great in my new semi-independent placement. I got my report card from my other school in North Smithfield and I thought I would share with you.

> Well, I hope your summer is going well. Stay cool!

> Happy Fourth of July!

> Love

> Jackie xoxo

Report card Academic Year 2006 - 2007

—————◆•◆•◆—————

Language Arts	Final 77
Literature	Final 81
Geography	Final 77
Math	Final 80
General Science	Final 95
Physical Education	Final 91
Skills Development	Final 94
Health	Final 97

The teacher's comments were as follows: An outstanding student with an excellent attitude and well motivated. Jackie, you made us proud! And after a few years of separation, my two granddaughters were finally back in our family to stay and for us to enjoy their presence among us.

IT'S A BOY! On January 30th, 1996, my first grandson, Matthew William Zajac, was born to Lori-Ann and Matt, at 10:15 pm at Milford Hospital, weighing in at seven pounds thirteen ounces and twenty inches long. Very cute with black hair, blue eyes, rosy cheeks, round face and healthy. I got to hold him the next morning. What a thrill!

Matthew was a fast learner, a poor eater and very attached to his mother and paternal Nanna but disliked me, for whatever reason. I firmly believe that by age four, Matthew really thought his name was BATMAN. A telephone message said he was out fighting the CRINIMALS... He was a good student from preschool on, with several little girlfriends.

In fifth grade, he sent me the following letter.

May 14th, 2005

Dear Doris Darling:

Our class read a book called Flat Stanley; it is about a boy who became flat. He wanted to visit his friend in California, but it was too expensive to fly or take the train so Stanley decided to mail himself.

Our class made some Flat Stanleys and wrote about their adventures with us. We are now sending Flat Stanley to you; so please write about your adventures with him and after that is done, mail him, along with your journal entry, back to me, at this address.

Matthew Zajac.
Davis Thayer School.
137 West Central Street.
Franklin, MA. 02038.

Please mail them back by June 13th so we get them back before school is over.

Love,

Matt Zajac

Matthew loved to play Batman games with his uncle Marcel. As he got older he became friendlier towards me. He actually became a sports active teenager, playing baseball and football and enjoying it. He performed in many plays while attending The School of Performing Arts in Franklin as a young boy and his love of music, and a lot of practice as well, resulted in Matthew becoming a great drummer with his own band and in demand by other music groups.

Matthew is presently attending Berklee School of Music in Boston and has spent a semester in Spain this past year. Matthew and I are as close as we should be at this time and I am grateful for that. Whenever we see each other, he always expresses his love for me.

An interesting incident took place while Matthew was in Spain: he found out by accident that his roommate was a fellow classmate in kindergarten in Hopedale, years ago. This Berklee student, whose birthday is April first, received an empty box, an April Fool's prank, on his birthday from Matthew (his mom, Lori-Ann's trick, I'm sure). What a strange coincidence to reunite this way, so far from home.

CHAPTER 47

My Journey with Flat Stanley

I met Flat Stanley on May 23rd, 2005, a Monday, when he arrived at my door in Mashpee MA. We started our journey on the following day on our way to Falmouth. Our first stop: St. Anthony's Church. He waited for me on the front seat of my car, patiently, without complaints, even for long periods of time as I volunteered at the hospital or was busy cleaning my clients' homes.

On the next day we left our driveway at 5:45 am and drove to Franklin MA. I pointed out to him his birthplace: Davis Thayer Elementary School on West Central Street. He waited, and took a nap while I attended mass at St. Mary's Church. Afterwards, we proceeded towards Mendon MA to 95 Hartford Avenue where I worked for four hours house cleaning.

At 12:30 pm we headed for Medway, after a stop at Cumberland Farms in Bellingham for automobile fuel and the local newspaper, to keep up with the old neighborhood news. We visited at the Zajac's house for a while and started our return trip home. Flat Stanley made friends with my thirteen-year-old cat Spunki and with David.

On the following days we had a similar schedule except at different homes. Afternoons were quiet, keeping each other company at home. Flat Stanley was my co-pilot and accompanied me with all my errands.

On Friday evening, May 27th, my seven-year-old granddaughter Brianna arrived for the weekend. The two soon became friends.

Saturday, May 28th was a beautiful sunny day and most of it was spent outdoors in our backyard and in our flower garden. We went out to lunch and after a trip to the store, we watched the movie The Music Man. Flat Stanley was present at all events.

Sunday, May 29th After church, Brianna and I went for a jog and a scooter excursion. You guessed it, Flat Stanley came along. Later on, we gathered seashells and special rocks at the beach. In the evening we watched the conclusion of The Music Man movie.

Monday May 30th, Memorial Day We went to mass and the grocery store, played basketball in the backyard, and had a barbeque in the afternoon. Stanley met Brianna's mom Janice and we took photos. We had a good time.

On Tuesday May 31st, Stanley and I went to church, the post office and to the Stop and Shop. Stanley stayed in the car and rested for his busy morning ahead at the St. Vincent de Paul Thrift Shop in Cotuit. Flat Stanley was introduced to all my lovely volunteer coworkers. Carol had already participated in the Flat Stanley saga, two years earlier. We had a great time there; especially operating the cash register. Fun! We had a much needed rest upon our return home.

On Wednesday June 1st, we went to Cotuit to clean the Sullivans' home for five and a half hours. Stanley had a very long rest in the car.

On Thursday, June 2nd, we ran errands, then spent some time sitting on the bench in the flower garden. I planted some salvias and Spunki kept Stanley company for a while.

On June 3rd, to church, the library, the supermarket, then to the Indian Historic Cemetery where I jogged briefly. In the evening at home we relaxed, watching television and I used the telephone and the computer while Stanley rested near me.

On Saturday June 4th, we went to church, did errands, washed my car, then I took Stanley for a ride to measure how far I had run earlier on that very humid 80 F day. It was 7.4 miles. Stanley seemed pleased. In the evening, Stanley rested while Dave and I watched the movie South Pacific.

June 5th, another beautiful day. After church, Stanley kept me company in the backyard while I read and enjoyed the birds, the butterflies and the beautiful flowers, spending a quiet afternoon. After dinner, we went out for a ride to Cotuit and enjoyed an ice cream cone. Upon our return home, Stanley rested while I wrote in my journal.

On Monday June 6th, we went to Falmouth, attended mass, and did my volunteer assignment at the hospital. Stanley seemed to enjoy the comfort of my Buick Century, for he never complained. After a short stop at CVS to pick up photos, Stanley rested in my bedroom. Later on, while sitting on the stone wall, he watched me sweep the driveway.

On Tuesday June 7th, Stanley and I left Mashpee early, at 5:40 am, and arrived in Franklin at 6:40 am, when we started our day's agenda; first, mass at St. Mary's, to Franklin, then to Mendon, where I ran before starting my cleaning work at "the Martha Stewart house", as called by my friends Mrs. Reed and her daughter Linda. Stanley waited patiently in the car for four hours. We ran errands on our way home: at Walmart, Barnes & Noble, Olympia Sports and the gas station. After visiting with my good friend Mrs. Reed, we were en route to Mashpee. It was a quiet evening, and Stanley slept in our bedroom for the first time.

Wednesday June 8th, to early mass at St. Anthony's in East Falmouth prior to house cleaning until noon.

Thursday June 9th was a sad day for Stanley and me, as we had to part ways. After sixteen days together on our adventure on Cape Cod, I brought Flat Stanley to his friend, my grandson Matthew Zajac, at his school in Franklin.

I cherish Flat Stanley's photo, which is a reminder of the good times we shared in early Summer 2005.

CHAPTER 48

More Grandchildren

On February 5th, 1998, I became a fourth-time grandmother, this time to beautiful curly-dark brown-haired Brianna Nicole, born to Dennis and Janice Flinton. Although I had just been told that I had pneumonia, I gowned and, wearing a face mask, I went to visit my daughter and her new baby at Milford Hospital.

Brianna was a charming baby and from the time she was seven weeks old, while her mother worked, her maternal grandfather, Pépère, was her caretaker, until she started school. I helped out on my days off from work. As she got a little older, there were always some interesting events happening with Brianna. She loved animals and had many pets: cats, rabbits, birds, hamsters. She loved to visit David Jr.'s Doberman Pinscher on Pine Street in Franklin.

Once, at age two, when waking up from a nap at our condominium in Franklin, Brianna became terrified at the appearance of a rainbow on the bedroom wall from the sun's reflection.

At the Southwick Zoo in Mendon, Brianna had the visitors laughing at the sight of that little girl chasing a chicken that had escaped from its pen. She also entertained the tourists on the horse and buggy ride, at Acadia Park while visiting in Bar Harbor, Maine and where she fed nuts to a chipmunk when the little critter had entered our motel room.

Brianna spent much time visiting us in Mashpee and it was always a pleasure to have her visit. We always enjoyed reading, playing board games, going to the Children's Museum, the library, the church's playground, to the beach and ice skating in Bourne. Another memorable day was in 2006 at Brianna's First Holy Communion at St. Brendan Church.

Brianna had been dancing since the age of three and loved it. In later years she was doing acrobatics as well. At age seventeen, she received a well-deserved $3,000.00 scholarship for her efforts and she made us happy and proud.

On November 4th, 1998, we welcomed my fifth grandchild and second grandson born at Newton Wellesley Hospital to Jamie and Tracy Bourgeois. Connor Richard was a precious handsome baby and he remains just as sweet to this day, as a very intelligent and quiet young man. I cherish the time spent with him, especially one Sunday afternoon, playing with him for hours at my condominium in Franklin, when he was about two. I also recall his first visit to our new home in Mashpee, where he joined his cousins in a game on the patio and seemed to have so much fun. Unfortunately, we missed his First Communion, which was at St. Mary's Church in Franklin, as we were away in Texas to attend his uncle Mark's wedding in April 2007.

Connor was always a quiet and polite boy as well as a good student. We watched him play soccer, baseball and football. During one game in Falmouth, he got injured. Connor found his true sports calling when he started a swimming program. He had been practicing in his maternal grandparents swimming pool since he was a toddler. Both his parents are good swimmers and, no doubt, he was gifted with that talent since birth. He became a fierce strong competitive swimmer. At the present time, Connor ranks eleventh among competing high school boys. My handsome grandson is a responsible teenager and a junior automobile operator, who works as a lifeguard at a swimming club. Recently, by his quick action, he saved the life of a two-year-old girl. Great job, Connor! my second grandson will attend a very prestigious engineering school, the Worcester Polytechnic Institute, in the fall. We have enjoyed his swimming competitions as he has mastered the sport and always make us proud.

Cousins Brianna and Connor are nine months apart in age and have become closer to each other in their teens.

On November 20th, 1999, Tyler Perry came into this world singing, and there is no stopping him. Parents Matt and Lori-Ann and big brother Matthew welcomed him in the little nearby town of Hopedale. When Tyler was a little over one year old, the family moved to Franklin, close by to my condominium at Franklin Crossing. Tyler and I bonded as we spent more time together.

Tyler developed a haemangioma, a red strawberry birthmark, located between his eyebrows. That did not diminish the looks of his beautiful angelic face with his blond curls and attractive green eyes. Tyler and I had great times together, taking walks, playing games and reading books. His favorite book as a child was Goodnight Moon. He loved music at a very young age and amazingly, could memorize songs quickly. Tyler was three and a half years old when Dave and I moved to Mashpee. He would complain to his mom: "Mammy's house is just too far."

Our grandson had a big interest in light switches and loved to turn them on and off. Once when visiting us in Mashpee, and while riding on Dave's shoulders, Tyler passed by the furnace switch up high on the wall, and, you guessed it! the house chilled out with cold shower results. Lori-Ann unraveled the mystery. We always had a good supply of fresh blueberries on hand for Tyler's visit, as he loved that little fruit.

Tyler attended pre-school at Tri-County Vocational School; where his mother was an alumni. He was privileged to attend kindergarten at the Red Brick School, one of Franklin's treasures. Tyler learned to read before going to school, and made his musical debut at the Davis Thayer School talent show, of which his mom was co-chair, when he sang This is Halloween at the age of six.

He played the piano, the guitar and the drum at a young age. At about age nine, Tyler's exclamation of gratitude to his mom was very impressive to me. He said: "Mom, thank you for taking me trick and treating. I know you were cold and tired (Lori-Ann was in her first trimester of pregnancy) and you do not even want me to have all this candy because it makes me too hyper, but you took me anyways and I had a great time". WHAT A KID!

Tyler has been entertaining us at the gazebo at the Franklin Commons during the July Fourth celebrations, which last four days, since the age of twelve. Besides playing several musical instruments, he writes his own lyrics to songs and piano pieces. He has already recorded three compact discs and composed many songs. Presently a senior at Franklin High School, he envisions a career in music after college.

It was not until six and a half years later that we had the joy of welcoming our fourth granddaughter and seventh grandchild. On May 3rd, 2006, Sydney Claire, Jamie and Tracy's daughter, arrived as a healthy beautiful brunette;a bundle of joy and her daddy's delight.

Sydney was always so dainty-looking and so photogenic; numerous photos are proof of that. Sydney was so generous, even as young as two years old, she would serve us pizza and French fries with her little fingers, while daddy was in charge of lunch and mommy was at work.

She started dancing lessons at about age three and it was always a pleasure to attend her recitals in the spring and we enjoyed The Nutcracker performance at Christmastime. In her earlier years at elementary school, she told me she loved "The Ladybug School" (John F. Kennedy, in Franklin). She was a good student and also played the recorder in music class. She had already attended concerts with her mom and some friends.

Sydney loves clothes and preteen television shows; she loves to decorate her very nice, neat and girly bedroom. She loves arts and crafts and has produced beautiful items in that category. She learned to swim at a very young age and, following in her big brother's footsteps, has become a good competitor as well. We have witnessed some of her achievements, which have earned her awards at her swim meets. I cherish the time we spent together on a beautiful Summer Sunday morning at our townhouse in Bellingham. Sydney is caring and protective of her younger cousins at family gatherings. She is funny and her contagious laugh in excitement shows what a healthy and happy girl is my granddaughter. She has many friends and is fun to be around.

On October 17th, 2007, Sophia Anne was born to Mark and Kristine in Houston, Texas. We received lots of photos prior to our first visit to meet our eighth grandchild and fifth granddaughter. This beautiful child was five months old and living in Angleton, Texas, when we first saw her. We spent a fabulous week enjoying our precious baby. It was amazing to watch her sucking her two middle fingers and smiling so readily and cuddling with Lord Nibbler Bourgeois, the handsome black and white family cat. Sophia was tiny at birth weighing only five pounds and ten ounces (two ounces more than her daddy did at birth). She was a very calm and patient baby as we went on several excursions during our too short visit. Great memories remain with us of the wonderful time we had.

The following August we had the honor of entertaining Sophia and her parents in our home in Mashpee, where we enjoyed the beach, family gatherings, backyard cookouts, and even spent a day at the Boston Museum of Science with many family members and some friends. Sophia was the center of attention as the youngest family member.

Sophia celebrated her fourth birthday in California while visiting her maternal grandparents; her fifth birthday was celebrated in Massachusetts; and her eighth birthday in Kansas where she was in her aunt's wedding party. Lucky little traveler.

Our granddaughter introduced us to Frozen as she demonstrated her knowledge of the popular song Let it go. Her choreography was pretty good for a six-year-old. We watched the movie Frozen with her in our motel room while visiting in 2014.

Sophia is very intelligent, energetic and expressive. She loves school and is a good student, she enjoys girl scout activities (she is a top cookie salesperson). I have great pleasure preparing and sending her birthday and Christmas packages. In spite of the great distance that separates us, we feel close to our sweet and affectionate granddaughter, who loves to

receive colorful autumn leaves from us. I love our telephone chats, which are too infrequent lately due to our busy schedule.

On April 20th, 2009, during the Boston Marathon, a little princess was born to Matt and Lori-Ann at Milford Hospital. To her thirteen-year-old brother Matthew and to nine-year-old Tyler, she was their little princess and they still treat her that way today. Tiny Chloe Jane, with brown hair and hazel eyes, was a precious addition to the Zajac family, which is close-knit and loving. Chloe was a pleasant and smiling baby, her daddy's pride and joy, and still is today. Tyler was always possessive of his little sister. Whenever I was holding her, he wanted to take her from me.

At six weeks, Chloe paid her first visit to Grandma's house in Mashpee and she stayed overnight as mommy had a social engagement. She was good and slept well. Many more visits followed and smiley Chloe was always a ray of sunshine. We enjoyed The Wiggles Show at the Melody Tent in Hyannis MA to celebrate her second birthday. Chloe developed her knowledge of the fashion world at a very young age and learned how to manipulate her mom to let her wear her chosen outfits, even before her pre-school classes at Tri-County Vocational School. Chloe became a whiz at making puzzles. She informed me that she would teach me how to make puzzles.

Chloe and Daphne are soul mates, knowing each other since infancy. They take dance and acting classes together and Chloe performed in several plays and talent shows with singing solos already and she exhibits her musical talents in the form of dance. Following in her mother's footsteps, she is already a good gymnast. Chloe entertains us during her sleepovers at our home, which is always a welcome event for David and me. Her extremely agile and miniscule stature is like a butterfly, gracefully fluttering around. She is very close to her Nanna who spends much time with her while her mother works. She idolizes her family and loves to be home. She enjoys a multitude of friends and is fun to be around.

CHAPTER 49

Brother Ron

My brother was five years my elder and always gave me advice, whether good or bad. Through the years Ron kept me informed on our family history and passed on many facts unknown to me; he also was blessed with a good memory. He kept in contact with different Canadian relatives other than the ones I was in contact with; therefore more family history information was available to me He could sing, he taught himself to play the guitar and imitate people's voices; he was an entertainer Ron played sports: baseball and hockey..He got his driver's licence at age seventeen and also enlisted into the Canadian Army at that age, after forging our dad's signature on the application. It was during peacetime and he was stationed in Germany. Upon his return he gave me my first wrist watch, which I still have.

After the Army, Ron worked in Ontario, Canada, for some time and for the Canadian Telegraph Company in the province of Quebec. He was a talented woodworker, without any training. He built a canoe, and a violin which played, among many other things. He did some drawings, including a replica of our old homestead in Saint-Marcel, New Brunswick.

He loved to fish and hunt and was called "Frenchie" among his many friends. Ron's best deed was to take Cécile Richard, my wonderful sister-in-law, as his wife. They had six children, including a set of twins. They suffered two tragic losses: the first when their little boy Ricky drowned at age seven and nine years later, when their nineteen-year-old daughter Joanne died in a fire.

Ronald was my worst critic but also my best cheerleader when it came to my running accomplishments, according to his daughter Nancy.

Ronald went to his eternal reward at age seventy-five. May God rest his soul. I miss my brother.

CHAPTER 50

Tidbits

Here are some important messages found among my SOUVENIRS. Some are from my children, others from friends, acquaintances or anonymous authors.

A note from Janice on Mother's Day read:

> Mom, sit down and enjoy.
>
> Let Calgon take you away to what you have never experienced before.
>
> Relax, read and enjoy.
>
> I hope you do it tonight, when you want to relax.
>
> Love,
>
> Janice

A Happy Mother's Day card from Jamie and Mark:

> Dear Mom:
>
> This container will not even begin to fill the love and the light you bring to us every day. To you, I present this token of my gratitude for the most precious gift of all. We love you.
>
> Jamie and Mark

A note to Jamie from Mark after he learned that new suits and dress shirts were being ordered for himself and Jamie:

Jamie: measure your neck; Mom wants to make sure the noose fits properly; no slip = quick death.

From Mark J.:

> Hi Mom, I came to pick up my clothes; thank you…
>
> I read your notes, I think you're tapped; but I love ya,
>
> > > Mark

> Happy Birthday Mommy!
>
> Roses are red, violets are blue
>
> There's no other mom as special as You.
>
> > > Love,
>
> > > Lori-Ann

On May 9th, 1982, for Mother's Day, I received this special card:

> As I grow up and years go by,
>
> You will look at this gift and say: "Oh My",
>
> Could this handprint have belonged to me?
>
> For now I am all grown up, you see.

Thank you for the things you do

And always remember I love you.

Love,

Lori-Ann

This little Get Well note from one of my religion students read:

Please get well NOW!

I hope you get BETTER.

John Griffin

Just a note:

Dear Grandma: Hello there! How are you? I hope you're good. Okay, I'm going to go now. I love you.

Your favorite granddaughter,

Brianna,

xxoo

Here are thoughts to live by that impress me:

I am too blessed to be stressed!

The shortest distance between a problem and a solution is the distance between your knees and the floor.

The one who kneels to the Lord can stand up to anything.

You cannot change the past But you can ruin the present by worrying about the future.

Yesterday is history, tomorrow is a mystery, today is a gift; that is why it is called the PRESENT.

FAIL means: First Attempt In Learning. GREAT PHRASE!

Pets are like small children. They do not care how much money you have, what you wear or where you live; they truly love you for You.

HELLO: Have you ever thought what the word stands for? Do you know that a simple hello can be a sweet one. Read on:

The word H E L L O means:

H = How are you?

E = Everything all right?

L = Like to hear from you.

L = Love to see you soon.

O = On my mind.

Do you know that

When you carry the Bible, Satan has a headache;

When you open it, he collapses;

When he sees you read it, he faints.

Let's read the Bible every day, so he keeps on fainting.

Maybe someday, he will have a stroke and never wake up.

And did you know that when you are about to pass this on,

The devil will discourage you, but pass it on anyway.

Author unknown

The Jelly Bean Prayer

———————•⬦•———————

Red is for the blood He gave.

Green is for the grass He made.

Yellow is for the sun, so bright.

Orange is for the edge of night.

Blue is for the sins we made.

White is for the grace He gave.

Purple is for His hour of sorrow.

Pink is for our new tomorrow.

A bag full of jelly beans, colorful and sweet

Is a prayer, is a promise and a special treat.

Happy Easter!

Charlene Dickerson

Good Bread is the most fundamental and satisfying of all foods

And Good Bread with fresh Butter is the greatest of feasts.

James Beard

Live in the Sunshine, Swim the sea, Drink the wild air

Ralph Waldo Emerson

From an anonymous author:

If God brings you to it, He will bring you through it.

Here is a similar good message:

In happy moments, praise God

In difficult moments, seek God

In painful moments, trust God

Every moment, thank God.

Author anonymous

When I stand before God at the end of my life, I would hope that I would not have a single bit of talent left and could say: "I used everything you gave me".

Erma Bombeck

If the grass looks greener on the other side, stop staring, stop comparing, stop complaining AND start watering the grass you are standing on.

Author unknown

I can be bitter

Or I can be better;

The choice is mine.

Only one little letter

I make the choice.

Kathy Lee Gifford song

So often children are punished for being human… Children are not allowed to have grumpy moods, bad attitudes, disrespectful tones or bad days. Yet we, adults have them all the time. None of us is perfect and we must stop holding children to a higher standard of perfection than we can attain ourselves.

Positive Parenting Toddlers and Beyond

Here are some famous quotes filed in my memory:

After all, it is not the years in your life that count BUT the life in your years.

We are not human beings with spiritual experiences; we are spiritual beings with human experiences.

What we do in life echoes in Eternity.

THE BEST SINGLES AD EVER!!!

———————◆•◆◆•◆———————

Single black female, seeks male companionship; ethnicity unimportant.

I'm a very good girl who loves to play.

I love long walks in the woods, riding in your pickup truck, hunting, camping and fishing trips, cozy nights lying by the fire.

Candlelight dinners will have me eating out of your hand.

I'll be at the front door when you get home from work, wearing only what nature gave me.

Call 404 875-6420 and ask for Annie…

I'll be waiting.

Over 150 men got talking to the Atlanta Humane Society.

CHAPTER 51

Friends

As we go through this life, we will make many friends. Some we will know for only a short while. Others, we will always have close to us, to share our daily lives; others we won't see so often. Yet, we'll think of them just the same, whether they're near or far, long or short friendships are important to have. Friends are the best there is in life.

Here is an excerpt of a letter sent to me by a long-time and dear friend of mine:

July 16th, 2007

Dear Doris:

Thank you for the wonderful birthday card and the "Hats Off to Tea" book. I so enjoyed the words on your beautiful card and the card illustration.

The friendship we share is a unique blessing and I am truly grateful for it.

When I received the "Hats Off to Tea" book, I fixed myself a cup of tea and wished you were here with me.

Then, I read the book. It is a book I will go back to many times. It is filled with information and it will serve as a fine reference book. It discusses the history of Tea, gives recipes of desserts that can be made and used at tea time, how to make a proper cup of tea and what to wear at a tea party, to mention a few topics.

The illustrations are cleverly done and reading it makes me feel happy.

Love,

Janet

My friend Therese Berardi always reminded to Live One Day At A Time and, to this day, I still miss her voice singing Happy Birthday to me every year, on the telephone and hearing her respond to "I love you" with her typical "I love you more."

Friendships have always been very important to me.

CHAPTER 52

Trips

In June 1998, Dave and I went to New Brunswick, Canada, to my fortieth high school reunion. We also went to Prince Edward Island. It was Dave's first time to my native country, and we had a great time.

In April 1999 we went on a Western Caribbean Cruise with some friends from David's high school. We enjoyed visiting The Grand Cayman Island, Cozumel, Cancun and Mexico City. It was a memorable voyage, with wonderful people. I especially loved the shows. One of the performers was from Massachusetts, which made it special as our group became friends with Mr. Perry.

In May 2000, Dave and I took a short trip to the Berkshires, in Western Massachusetts. We visited the interesting towns of Lee, Amherst and Stockbridge, where we visited the Norman Rockwell Museum. A great place.

We stayed at the Rockwell Walker House, a bed-and-breakfast, in Lenox, where we met Peggy's cats named Bean and Alphonso.

In July 2000, we visited the Tall Ships in Boston Harbor. It was fascinating to see so many ships docked together; the biggest, a Russian vessel 520 feet long. Sailors gave us a tour of American Warships, which was impressive.

On July 4th, we went to Boston with Dave's brother Dan and his wife Helen to watch the Boston Pops and the fireworks. It was an interesting evening.

On August 12th, Dave's birthday, we took the train from Franklin to Boston South Station; then walked to the Esplanade on the Charles River and to the Hatch Shell where we saw The Temptations Show, the old version, on a beautiful Summer evening.

In July 2001, we purchased our home in Mashpee therefore, for the next ten months, we traveled to Cape Cod every other weekend on my time off from work.

In August 2002, we visited Provincetown and stopped in Truro on the way while we toured the Highland Lighthouse and Museum. We walked along the beach and dined by the water. A very lovely day!

We had several trips to New Hampshire, Dave's son and daughter-in-law's home. On one occasion, we visited my elderly uncle Jim who resided in Salem, New Hampshire, at the time. His alertness and his outlook on life at age ninety-seven were quite impressive.

In August 2003, we drove to Bar Harbor, Maine, with Janice, Dennis and Brianna who was age five and a half. She rode with Dave and me and slept most of the long trip. We visited a fish hatchery on the way: she and her dad love fishing. We went to Acadia Park but we were unable to view Cadillac Mountain due to thick fog, but we saw a deer and we had a great vacation in Northern Maine that Summer.

In August 2004, we made a second visit to New Brunswick. We stayed at the Four Seas in Shediac and visited family and friends and had a great time again.

While we were parishioners at Christ the King in Mashpee, we belonged to the 50+ Club and made many trips with this group of wonderful people. We tremendously enjoyed two trips in particular.

On October 4th, 2004, we boarded the bus for our four-day tour of Lancaster County, Pennsylvania. This proved to be a marvelous trip. We visited Amish villages, learning about the culture of the Amish, which we found very interesting. We also visited Gettysburg, with all its military history such as the monuments, The Union Generals, The Gettysburg National Military Park and several other Gettysburg historical sites. In Strasburg

PA, at the Millenium Theatre, we witness the most amazing performance of NOAH, The Musical with live animals. We visited The Longwood Gardens as well as a winery in Pennsylvania. Hershey, the sweetest place on earth, was appealing to our taste buds. It was a memorable trip.

On April 2nd, 2005, we started on another journey to Washington DC with the 50+ Club, via Fox Tours, in their luxurious Silver Fox motor coach. We had a narrated tour of Washington which included The Capitol, Embassy Row and a view of the White House. We visited the Vietnam Veterans and Korean War Veterans Memorials as well as the new FDR and WWII Memorials, and the new Women in Service Memorial.

We spent some time at The Smithsonian Institution which displayed the American Indian Museum and the Air and Space Museum, which contains Lindbergh's Spirit Of St. Louis, the first airplane to fly the Atlantic Ocean. At the Museum of Natural History, we admired the Hope Diamond and other unique collections. We visited Arlington Cemetery, with a narrated tour. The Eternal Flame at John F. Kennedy's resting place where he lies along with his wife Jackie and two infant children. It was very impressive to me. At the tomb of the Unknown Soldier, we witnessed the changing of the guard, a somber ritual, especially in the rain. We had an illuminated tour of Washington DC, featuring the Presidential Monuments, the Lincoln Memorial, the Library of Congress, the Embassies with their respective flags, agricultural, architectural and art museums. We attended mass at the prestigious Basilica of the Immaculate Conception Shrine then proceeded to Philadelphia, where we visited the National Constitution Center, the Liberty Bell and Independence Hall.

After a delay, due to a long line at the Statue of Liberty, we missed the ferry and therefore were unable to visit the Statue, but Ellis Island was intriguing to me. Upon returning to Battery Park in Manhattan, we passed by Ground Zero, Rockefeller Center and St. Patrick Cathedral on Fifth Avenue and then enjoyed dinner at the El Dorado Restaurant in Tarrytown, New York. We stayed at another luxurious hotel, the Hyatt on the Hudson. We returned home on May 2nd from a wonderful and inspiring trip to Washington DC, to Philadelphia and to New York.

In the spring of 2005, Mark J. was recruited by a representative of Moeller Electric from Houston, Texas, after a visit to their corporate office in Franklin MA. Mark was offered a position as their new warehouse supervisor in Houston. He happily accepted and prepared himself for the big move. On Father's Day, we enjoyed a PawSox baseball game, the Boston Red Sox farm team, as a family, which was a lot of fun. Shortly afterwards, we surprised Mark with a farewell party in his honor, at the Legion Hall in Medway. I presented him with his finally completed Baby Book, and he was given a digital camera and a briefcase. It was a bittersweet time for me as my youngest son, Little Marky, was moving so far away. On June 29th, Mark and I met for dinner in Medway, and I drove home, by myself, with a heavy heart.

Mark left for Houston on July 1st with his old Pontiac Grand Prix loaded to the maximum. Like a good son, he called me every evening to report on his daily trek, which I appreciated immensely. He arrived safely to the Holiday Inn Express Hotel on July 4th. Praise the Lord! My prayers were answered. Now he had to get used to temperatures of 100 degrees plus. Shortly after his arrival in Houston, Hurricane Rita hit the area. Mark slept through it. We were in Kennebunk, Maine, when we heard that Houston was ok.

We attended David's nephew's wedding in Grand Rapids, Michigan, later in the month and later on, we returned to the Berkshires, in Western Massachusetts, to Great Barrington, a nice area to visit.

We enjoyed frequent, short trips during the Summer and early Autumn.

CHAPTER 53

2005 ~ 2006

May 2005 was the completion of the MOM's program at Christ The King parish. I received a Serenity Certificate. It was a splendid evening; but it was saddened by the fact that a group of very special ladies had to separate. Jamie was hospitalized at a Boston hospital with an infected hand, caused by a wood splinter, which occurred at his plumbing work. No surgery was required.

Spring was always enjoyable for us with gardening and the planting of shrubs and flowers but this spring saw the creation of a brick patio by David. With bird feeders, a bird bath, benches, a hammock and pretty flowers, our backyard was inviting to all, including humming birds, squirrels and Spunki. Family and friends were always welcome and the children enjoyed different activities, such as basketball, baseball, and hide and seek.

In early July is the Tribal Wampanoag POW WOW, a traditional First American Culture Festival. John, Paula and her three daughters had a great time dancing with the Indians in their very colorful tribal garments. July Fourth is always a big celebration in Franklin MA.,which usually lasts four to five days,and we are faithful attendees.

Later in July, we enjoyed the Barnstable County Fair at the fairgrounds in Falmouth, a carnival-style country fair with well-known artists as entertainers.

Our friends the Bourbeaus spent a couple of days with us, which was a relaxing time as we all share the same lifestyle. We spent time in our backyard, enjoyed dinner at a favorite restaurant, followed by a long walk near the wharf in Sandwich. Our visit concluded with the morning mass at Christ the King on their way home.

The following day, we boarded an airplane to Grand Rapids, Michigan, to attend David's nephew's wedding in the company of David Jr. and Tina. Mike and Molly's wedding was wonderful, but the weekend just flew by. The flight home was good.

During the Summer months, Wednesday evening was Concert Night at the Mashpee Commons. We were there, often times with Brianna. These are precious memories.

August is always a busy month due to several family birthdays and our wedding anniversary and we faithfully go on vacation in mid-month and visit our friends the Berardis in Leominster and my cousin Helen in Kennebunk, Maine. We enjoyed the grandchildren who love to spend time at the Southcape Beach, either swimming, picking up shells or finding odd shaped stones, Brianna's favorite activity.

The Mashpee Commons is a popular tourist attraction for its high-end trendy novelty shops. After Labor Day, Cape Cod residents regain their towns for most of the tourists are gone, until next Summer. Mashpee is a great little town to live in.

On November 27th, at the Ma Glockner Restaurant in Bellingham, we held a baby shower for Lisa Libby Birren. It was a beautiful event. Lisa was expecting a boy, and the writing on the cake read: "Twinkle, Twinkle, Little Star. The arrival of Nicholas is not very far". This was the proud maternal grandmother, Marian's creation. Impressive!

On my return home, about eight miles from the Bourne Bridge, a very nice police officer with the cruiser's blue flashers on told me to: Slow Down and drive safely home, which I did.

Christmas 2005 was celebrated in Mashpee, with all family members present except Mark.

In March 2006, David and I took our first trip to Texas to visit Mark. He met us at Bush International Airport in Houston. After checking in at the Holiday Inn Express, we visited Mark's apartment nearby, and we took a walk around the grounds on a fair day. Later, we met Kristine and her son Dylan and their little dog Molly. It was "like at first sight" for me regarding Kristine. She was very friendly and talkative, and that suits me. I was so happy to see my son, even though it had been only a few months.

We enjoyed Chinese food in a restaurant near our hotel that evening. The next morning, David and I ventured ourselves to the Super Food Market located about half a mile away, along a highway with very dangerous intersections. Mark was appalled at our risky adventure, but proud of our bravery. Houston has seven and nine lanes on highways, in some areas. We also learned that there is a street in Houston named "Bourgeois".

The next day we had a two-hour ride to Galveston,Texas in Kristine's Pathfinder. It was a fun day. We saw Moody Gardens, which were very interesting. We had a boat ride on a gorgeous day and we saw an IMAX 3D The Spongebob Movie. Dylan, a polite twelve-year-old, loves all fishes but he especially likes sharks. I experienced Mexican food for the first time... ok.

Sunday mass at St. John Neumann Church, a beautiful modern church, was a great pleasure. Late afternoon, we headed for Angleton to Kristine's house, where Chef Kris treated us to a TurDuckHen dinner with roasted potatoes, broccoli and a salad. TurDuckHen is a combination of turkey, duck and hen, a very unusual dish but it was good. For dessert, we had Mark's favorite: cheesecake.

Mark worked in Houston, an hour away from Angleton, and Kristine worked in Freeport, a nearby seaport where "The Coast is Clear" is their motto. As we visited her workplace, I was amazed at such enormous loads of imported bananas in their warehouse.

As it was school break, the Houston Zoo was overly crowded, but we enjoyed the animals and learned that an okapi is part giraffe and part zebra. I personally loved to meet the penguins for the first time.

We attended a basketball game between the Rockets and the New Jersey Nets at the Toyota Center downtown Houston. The latter won. It was my first attendance to a professional basketball game and I loved it. The tickets were courtesy of Mark's employer, Mr. Hamm.

We visited Mark's workplace as well and we were introduced to his supervisors, coworkers, and employees in the warehouse (whom Kristine calls Mark's minions). Karen, a coworker we had met on Cape Cod, affectionately remembered the Polar Cave Ice Cream Parlor in Mashpee. How sweet! We met Moller's CEO, Mr. J. Hamm, and other employees.

Regina, the receptionist at the Holiday Inn Express, was very protective of me, having a bottle of water ready for whenever I would go jogging and she would insist that I go to the indoor gym when it was too hot or if it was misting outdoors. She told me: "I would like to take you home and put you on a shelf". What do you think she meant?

The Texas weather was favorable: 78 to 80 degrees most days. We visited the Space Center in Houston, where we had a train tour, a movie, a demonstration and a lecture. It was amazing!

Unfortunately, our week of frivolity came to an end as all good things do. On Friday, March 17th, Mark, Kristine and Dylan accompanied us to the airport and we headed for Boston. We had a good flight home.

Carlimo was ready to take us back to Franklin to pick up my Old Silver. We enjoyed a Pizza Hut treat before our return to Mashpee. In early evening, Mark called. That was nice.

On May 3rd, Sydney Claire, Jamie and Tracy's daughter, was born. What a cutie! I visited her every time I would go to Franklin. It was such a pleasure to see the changes that had occurred between my visits; babies grow so fast.

In May 2006, I had a left foot bunionectomy by at the Milford Hospital. After a few uncomfortable days of pain and nausea, I was driving and resuming my regular schedule.

On May 26th, we celebrated Dave's uncle Bill's ninetieth birthday at Pippinelle's Restaurant in Franklin. This was a great reunion for me as I met many new family members.

May 2006 was a rainy month and the Summer flew by as we were busy, hosting visiting friends and relatives. Mark and Kristine came for their first visit together. We spent a day at Six Flags New England, a family outing. Kristine was welcomed with open arms as she became part of the Bourgeois clan. We visited Martha's Vineyard and celebrated the five August birthdays as well as our wedding anniversary.

September brought us to Vermont for an early fall getaway. It was great in Mendon VT where we stayed at Mountain Orchards. During one of our walks, we discovered a very small and old cemetery in which we were told Civil War soldiers were buried.

David enjoyed a chili contest in Woodstock VT. We saw a few movies and found another Christ The King Church. Even with the fairly warm weather, the foliage was starting to be very colorful. And in spite of the rainy return trip home, it was all worth it. I love the Green State.

Thanksgiving has always been at Grandma's house, with most of the family present. Sometimes it was difficult for some family members to attend, as other commitment took priority. I love to have our family together and it is always a good time.

Brianna spent many weekends and school breaks with us. Once our house alarm went off and Brianna, age eight, was petrified and it took some time for her to get over that fear of it happening again. So, the alarm was disconnected .It was more important to have Brianna visit comfortably.

In November 2006, my good friend Lucy Murphy went to her eternal reward. She was sadly missed. On November 24th, we celebrated John's fortieth birthday at a Providence Bruins game, the Boston Bruins hockey farm team.

Christmas 2006 was a big celebration at our home in Mashpee with the entire family. Sydney was the center of attention and such a pleasant baby. To see all the younger grandchildren interacting which each other made it a memorable day for me.

In 1986, Jamie and Lisa Libby, Marcel's step children became part of the Bourgeois family; as I regarded them as my adopted grandchildren. They both received the basic sacraments after their initial instructions provided by St Brendan's Christian Doctrine Program. They were always included in all family activities and celebrations. In 1993, Jamie and Lisa; at age 15 and 12 respectively enjoyed a Summer trip to New Brunswick, Canada with our family.

Lisa, a school teacher along with husband Jack are parenting Nicholas. Jamie, continued his education in technical knowledge and pursued several careers in his young adult life and has become a very involved father to his son Dylan.

CHAPTER 54

2007

In early 2007, seven family members flew to Houston, Texas, to attend Mark and Kristine's wedding. We enjoyed spending time at a picturesque park nearby while practicing our expertise in photography prior to the wedding. Brianna, then nine years old, was overjoyed to be part of these events. This was her first time flying, she had her picture taken with Sam Houston's large statue and she enjoyed swimming at the pool at the LaQuinta Hotel. She was thrilled. Lori-Ann used her many talents as a best person for her brother, everyone's hairstylist and our chauffeur. What a Gal!

The wedding ceremony took place on a gorgeous sunny day at a gazebo outside of Sam Houston Museum, a plantation in Huntsville, Texas. The celebrant was Reverend Richard Poirier, Kristine's sister-in-law's dad. We enjoyed a beautiful reception at this interesting historical venue, with great food, good music and good company, meeting Kristine's family and their friends. Attending the wedding were Mark's manager Ben Orr, and Kristine's supervisor Mary, and her husband Manuel.

Before leaving for home, we visited The Houston Museum of Science, which was fantastic. Although our Texas trip was short, for various reasons, seven individuals returned home with great memories. These were: Phil, Janice and Brianna, Lori-Ann, David Jr., Dave and I. Thanks to Mark and Kristine's very special day. What a FUN trip!

On September 10th, 2007, a right knee arthroscopy was performed at Falmouth Hospital for a meniscus tear suffered during a run on March 11th on the bicycle path in Dennis MA. Persistent pain post arthroscopy required supartz injections for three consecutive weeks, followed by physical therapy, which proved very beneficial.

In October 2007, a special delivery arrived at 129 La LaJa Drive, Angleton, Texas: a precious bundle of joy, Sophia Anne, my eighth grandchild and fifth granddaughter. And we were very anxious to meet her.

In November we had a mini vacation in Stowe, Vermont, where we witnessed the first snow of the season and very cold temperatures. We visited the Von Trapp Family Estate and Museum, which was very impressive, and we had a narrated tour by Maria herself, on video. We met interesting people at The Golden Eagle Resort. One employee by the name of Mark was a llamas farmer, and his wife made hats and mittens from the llamas' hair.

A sad sight during our trip was a deer dying by the roadside after being hit by a vehicle. The good police officers assisted. We searched and found our dear friend Mrs. Reed's gravesite in the small town of Eden. That was special!

Christmas 2007 was celebrated on December 23rd at our home in Mashpee with a few family members missing: Janice and Brianna were in Florida and Mark was at home with his little family, in Angleton TX. The mild temperatures permitted the grandchildren to enjoy a touch football game in the backyard. On New Year's eve, Dave worked at the Heritage Museum and Gardens. Upon his return home after work, we were content to enjoy the celebrations on television. Big Party Goers we are!

CHAPTER 55

2008

New Year's Day 2008 was a quiet day at home.

Later in January, Dave and I attended a one-day seminar entitled Hush your House at CTK with Sister Dympna. It was impressive and beneficial.

Jamie's and Matthew's birthdays were celebrated.

On February 4th, Dave purchased a 2008 Toyota Camry LS. Nice! Brianna was ten years old on the following day; she spent the winter school break with us, and came along to visit John and Laura in New Hampshire.

March brought us to Texas to visit Mark and his family and meet Sophia for the first time. What a thrill to see that precious five-month-old sucking her right hand middle and ring fingers, together. Sophia was smiling a lot; I called her Miss Smiley. It was so much fun to spend time with such a pleasant baby. We were obliged to Dylan, a well-mannered teenager, who let us occupy his bedroom for our stay. Lord Nibbler Bourgeois is a slim black and white, and friendly cat who loved to take naps on a blanket on the floor, sometimes with Sophia.

We visited many interesting places such as The Verna Hogg Plantation and the Houston Museum of Science where we saw the Da Vinci exhibit. Kristine's mom Daviette visited from Austin and entertained us. We enjoyed several restaurants as well as the warm March weather. We visited Mark's workplace and met with many of his coworkers and Mr. Hamm and his wife as well. We had a tour of the facility and were given hats and spent some time with Ben Orr, Mark's supervisor.

Our return flight home was delayed. A gate misdirection in Philadelphia was one more complication but fortunately we were aided by kind angels along the way and we boarded the airplane at the very last minute. Literally, as the door was already shut. The short flight to TF Green Airport in Providence RI went smoothly. Shortly after our arrival at the airport, we were on our seventy-mile trek to our final destination, where we were welcomed by Spunki. We were happy to be home.

In late April, along with the Berardis at the Olive Garden Restaurant in Leominster MA, we celebrated our friend Beverly-An's birthday.

A much awaited visit from Mark, Kristine and ten-month-old Sophia finally arrived in early August and we enjoyed every day of their too-short stay with us. It was a very busy time. We spent some time in Woods Hole, took a lot of photos, and had barbeques. Sophia was the star of the party everywhere she went.

On August 13th, we met with my friend Vicki, a nursing school classmate, and family members and we went to the Boston Museum of Science with Vicki as our guide. She is a good organizer. Tyler was her protégé, after Lori-Ann had to leave early with Matthew for his baseball practice. It was a fun and learning experience for most of us. The day was completed at the Ninety Nine Restaurant in Franklin.

One day, as Kristine was shopping at the Mashpee Commons, I was in charge of the precious little angel, sleeping in her stroller in the shade. I still remember the exact spot where we were and reminisce every time I return to the Commons. While visiting, Mark helped me to improve my computer skills, which was much needed.

August 16th marked our eleventh wedding anniversary and, sadly, a last family get-together prior to the Texas visitors' departure for home the following morning.

Monday, August 18th, was a great day to drive to Kennebunk, Maine, for our vacation. We had a good trip in spite of road work around our familiar area near the Super 8 Motel, our usual lodgings on our yearly trip to Maine. We met with cousin Helen for dinner and visited at her apartment. The next day we took her to Southern Maine Medical Center for medical te sting After some shopping we joined cousins Richard and wife Donna for a pasta dinner.

We had a great time blueberry picking with Helen who, in spite of being legally blind as well as color blind, matched our two quarts yielding. She always has amazed me. Lunch at Mike's Clam Shack in Wells, visiting the Lighthouse Depot, a two-mile walk on the beach and an ice cream treat completed a very pleasant day. The next morning we had a delicious breakfast at Square Toes Restaurant, which is within walking distance. We spent some time at Kennebunkport with Helen and then enjoyed a good game of miniature golf in Wells, where Helen and I both had a hole-in-one, not once but twice. Poor David did not.

Friday morning, we drove about one hour to Acton ME, to a genuine Old-Fashioned County Fair. That was much fun. After our return to Kennebunk, Helen and I went to the River Ridge Rehabilitation Center where Helen works and where I witnessed the dedication of a devoted volunteer, through her musical talent bringing such joy to that facility's clients. We had a great time. We spent the evening in Wells, at the movies viewing The House Bunny, which proved to be fairly adequate, and then a cold treat at Big Daddy's.

The next day, after a few hours spent at Arundel's huge flea market with Helen, I purchased a pretty sailboat wind chime. We headed for home in the afternoon and discovered the high price of automobile fuel in Franklin: $3.49 a gallon.

Early fall promises beautiful days on Cape Cod. We visited with John and Laura in Nashua, New Hampshire, and picked apples at the Lull Farm, a great place to enjoy the harvesting season with loved ones.

On September 30th, we met with Bill and Frances Cotter in Braintree MA and took a River Boat to Boston Harbor. We proceeded to the Boston North End where we walked along the Freedom Trail and visited the Old North Church, a historical landmark, as well as the Paul Revere

House, the Ben Franklin Statue and the Bunker Monument, to name a few. Lunch at Legal Seafood also was a treat.

Great News! Lori-Ann is expecting her third child in early May. She is not feeling very well at times.

On October 2nd, I modeled a Jones of New York outfit at our St. Vincent de Paul Clothes Centre fashion show. All went well in spite of my sore feet: high heel shoes were responsible for that. I purchased the outfit at a huge discount and I wore it at a late fall wedding.

I loved exercising at the Mashpee Gym following physical therapy after my knee surgery. My favorite piece of equipment was the elliptical machine, which I still use at home today.

October 17th was Baby Sophia's first birthday and it was celebrated in Angleton with Grandma Gilbert, uncle Keith, aunt Lisa and cousins Madeleine and Chloe, friends Mary and Manuel, mommy and daddy and big brother Dylan. I was so sorry to miss it.

Meanwhile, on that day, on Cape Cod was the old Franklin Bolts Running Club resurrected Relay Race, in which my niece Nancy participated by running the third leg, 7.2 miles. She did well. It was a great day and a fun event, but shadowed by Dave's missing wallet. I admired his patience in the matter; I would not have been as good. We headed for home, while others went to the motel and dinner in Provincetown. It was a long and slow ride home on very congested route 6A. Nancy brought us home safely. Nice surprise at home: Dave's wallet was on his desk…Thank you, St. Anthony.

I spoke to Mark and Kristine in the evening, Sophia was asleep in her tutu and with frosting in her hair. How sweet! The big bash party was too much for her. She had to rest to celebrate her daddy's thirty-fifth birthday three days later.

On November 4th, Connor celebrated his tenth birthday with family and friends. He is a very quiet, sensitive boy and a great student.

John's birthday always falls near Thanksgiving Day and along with the cool and gloomy days of advanced autumn. Dave and I kept happy and healthy with our busy schedules of work, volunteering and exercising. Our Church, our family and our friends were our priorities.

My work schedule:

Monday - Falmouth Hospital Volunteer

Opposite Monday - Receptionist C-Lab Opposite Tuesday - House Cleaning

Wednesday - House Cleaning

Tuesday - St. Vincent de Paul Thrift Shop

Thursday - Two House Cleanings

Friday - Mashpee Rehabilitation Center

In late November we had our first taste of snow, a dusting, which was repeated on December 6th. An ice storm in Western Massachusetts on December 19th caused power outages, some that lasted about two weeks. On Cape Cod we had approximately three inches of snow. On December 22nd, we had a snowfall of eight inches. It was all gone by Christmas Day. December 31st brought four to five inches of snow followed in the early New Year by icy conditions. On January 10th, we got heavy soaked snow; and on January 13th and 14th, light snow, no accumulations, but cold temperatures followed for the rest of the month.

CHAPTER 56

2009

On January 23rd, Dave's brother Daniel passed away, a few days after a knee replacement surgery at a Boston hospital, at age seventy-six. That was a shocker! There had been no previous sign of a cardiac problem. Dan was a pleasant, engaging man with a great sense of humor, very family-oriented and fun to be with. His two grandsons called him "Bop". I loved Dan. He was always friendly to me.

The calling hours at the Mansfield Funeral Home were well attended in spite of frigid temperatures. The graveside service with military honors was impressive but lacking a religious aspect and somewhat disappointing in David's and my opinion. The funeral day was stormy and cold therefore, I wore hat and mittens, Christmas gifts from Dan. He was buried alongside his parents in Medfield MA. His wife Helen, daughter Helen and son Danny as well as David spoke briefly at the gravesite. After a small reception at the Finkelstein's home in Mansfield, we headed for home.

My car broke down and was left at the Battles Buick Dealer in Bourne MA. Our taxi ride home, 15 miles, was expensive, but the blustery start of this sad day ended with a beautiful sunshine. Sometimes, we see a rainbow when we least expect it.

Frozen pipes in a basement bedroom contributed to a major flood and some expensive repairs during a frigid January 2009.

In early February, we celebrated Brianna's eleventh birthday. She visited us for a few days, which was a very busy time. We went to the movies, played board games, made a bird habitat for a school project. She also accompanied me to Mashpee Rehabilitation Center, where I volunteered and then we went ice skating.

February was a light snow month with continued cold weather. On February 29th, my leap year baby Spunki was celebrated on his seventeenth birthday with lots of treats. He is still looking good and behaving well as always.

Early March brought warm weather, enabling Dave to burn bush in our backyard on a sixty degree temperature day.

I am grateful for my wonderful family who celebrated my birthday at Lori-Ann's house. I am thankful for their love, respect and generosity; it is so important to me to have my family together.

Other March birthdays included my step-granddaughter Lisa on March 7th and my oldest grandchild Angelique on March 12th.

In mid-March, I was summoned for jury duty in Orleans, but did not serve and I was dismissed in early afternoon. The thirty-five-mile ride home felt long as I knew that my husband was sick with a gastrointestinal flu. He recovered after five days of misery and twelve pounds lighter.

Meanwhile, in a Houston hospital, seventeen-month-old Sophia was having tubes inserted in her ears to stop the frequency of ear infections suffered in the past; her daddy had that procedure at about the same age.

March 2009 was difficult for John, unable to cope with his girlfriend's ongoing Illness of breast cancer for the past two years; his own disease surfaced and he was treated at a rehabilitation facility. We helped Paula, with our support and much needed transportation to her treatments.

Easter was a joyous occasion at our home in Mashpee with our family and some friends. Our traditional Easter egg hunt was always a welcomed activity for the grandchildren.

David's older brother Jim suffered from a brain tumor which got progressively worse. After a hospitalization following a fall and a short stay at a rehabilitation facility, he was at home with hospice care under the vigilant eye of his devoted wife Natalie and his daughter Cheryle. David visited him frequently and once one of his old army buddies went along to visit. Unfortunately Jim was not responding well at that time; good effort by Dave and Walter. Two days prior to his seventy-eighth birthday, and ten weeks after his brother Dan's demise, he succumbed to his malignant tumor. Jim was an intelligent man, quiet but also witty. He was a great athlete in his youth and a big brother that Dan and Dave looked up to. On April 13th, 2009, Jim was put to rest in his town of Little Compton, Rhode Island, with a beautiful service. How sad for David to lose his two only siblings that way.

(in such a short span of time).

In mid-April, Brianna, who was then in fifth grade, portrayed Paul Revere in the play Massachusetts on Parade at the John F. Kennedy School in Franklin. She performed well. On April 22nd, little five-day-old Chloe attended the Franklin Spring Parade, the opening day for town sports, with her mom, and myself. The parade was followed by assembly at Fletcher's Field where baseball pre-game activities took place and where cousins Connor and Tyler, in their uniforms, were ready to play ball. Chloe was a very calm and sleepy little angel. What an enjoyable day!

April 2009 was exceptionally warm with days of ninety degrees Fahrenheit. In May, I spent a few days with my cousin Helen in Kennebunk, Maine, lending a helping hand while she underwent ear surgery. She recovered well. I had a flare-up of the PIE syndrome and returned home sick but it felt good to have been able to help my dear cancer-stricken cousin. I always loved to spend time with her.

In June 2009, we celebrated our good friends Fred and Anna Labrousse's fiftieth wedding anniversary in their former hometown of Hubbardston MA. It was a very special day indeed, honoring this wonderful couple, exemplary parents, loving grandparents, who are religious, faithful to God and to one another. You could feel the love in that family.

Father's Day was spent at Jack and Janice's house in South Attleboro MA with good company and great food.

July Fourth celebrations in Franklin are always an exciting time for all. The Zajac boys exhibited their musical talents in competition and Tyler wowed the crowd with "I'll give you love". He took second place, while Matthew and his band got first place. Chloe was my calm little star, cooing and smiling in the middle of these loud musical sounds. Another great day with the grandchildren.

Frequent telephone calls to Texas always put a smile on my face when Sophia says: "I love you, Grandma Doris". How I miss Mark and his family!

We kept in touch with my brother Ronald and his lovely wife Cécile by visiting each other periodically. Their health issues and their family commitments kept them occupied as well.

The St. Vincent de Paul Clothing Center volunteers' appreciation luncheon was celebrated in mid-July at the Flying Bridge Restaurant, which is nestled in one of Falmouth's harbors. This annual event was highlighted by a delicious meal shared with our co workers (fellow volunteers) and a raffle of amazing prizes, which I often won.

Summertime on Cape Cod is always busy with family and friends visiting, which I love. Our children were the most frequent guests; but our friends, the Speronis, the Bourbeaus, the Berardis and Beverly-An, the Kellehers, the Fitzgeralds, uncle Bill and aunt Frieda, my brother Ron and wife Cécile were also frequent visitors. So were friends from nursing school: Vicki, Natalie and Lorrie. All were always welcome to our modest home with the three available bedrooms.

Our frequent get-togethers with our dear friends Ralph and Therese Berardi were memorable, especially when their niece Beverly-An was visiting from Long Island, New York; her friendly and witty disposition made our visits to Leominster a fun time.

With work, volunteering, and social activities, Dave and I had a busy life on Cape Cod.

On Sunday, August 9th, my niece Nancy was at our door at 7:00 am, ready to run the prestigious Falmouth Road Race along with David Jr. With a great view of the finish line, Dave, Tina and I cheered all the runners. Nancy ran the seven-mile course in fifty-three minutes and David ran it in seventy-seven minutes. We were proud of their times and I wished I could have run as well.

After our backyard barbeque was over and the runners had left, Dave and I rushed to Buzzards Bay to attend our former neighbor Liz and her fiancé Jeremy's wedding. It was a glorious day with an elegant affair, near the water. The couple looked radiant and so happy. Liz' daughter Alyssa, a junior bridesmaid, was stunning in her lavender gown. We had the honor of being seated with Pastor Brian Week and his wife Donna and we enjoyed the conversation. It was a wedding to remember.

August 10th to 15th was busy with work, going to the St. Rocco Festival in Franklin with PJ, Brianna and Tyler, and preparing for our trip to Niagara Falls, Canada. We left on August 16th, our twelfth wedding anniversary. We went by way of New York; we had a good trip and crossing the Canadian border was a breeze.

The Travelodge Hotel was pleasant and within walking distance from the Falls. In spite of the hot weather, we did all the activities we chose to do, such as taking a boat ride under the Falls. The shops were also alluring with their novelties.

The Falls under the lights were a phenomenal spectacle. We visited a small historical museum, where I learned some facts unknown to me about Canadian history (especially Ontario). Fort George, which is a National Historic Site in Canada, was involved in the 1812 war between Canada and the United States and we were reminded of that part of history as we drove by Fort George on our way to Niagara-on-the-Lake, a most picturesque small town, bursting with gorgeous flowers everywhere. We had a great Canadian Summer vacation and our return home was also pleasant.

From August 23rd to August 27th, Brianna visited and suffered from an ear infection. That was an unpleasant time…

On September 6th, we headed to Kennebunk ME to visit my cousin Helen who was now undergoing chemotherapy for metastatic cancer. She was always a model of patience for me and I was always so impressed by her acceptance of her illness and by the courage of her fight. She was always ready to undertake a new task. I admired her. Along with Helen, we traveled to Dover, New Hampshire, for a get-together with her brother Richard and her three older sisters, my dear cousins Leona, Dottie and Eva, whom I seldom saw. It was a perfect setting for a late Summer barbeque at my cousin Richard's beautiful home, surrounded by multiple gardens; both vegetable and flower. This spacious and elegant two-family home proves that good relationships between children and their in-laws are real. We returned to Mashpee after a brief stop at Helen's in Kennebunk, a long trip home but we arrived safely.

Our friend Margot, a German lady, came to visit and treated us to homemade bread and a plum cake. Delicious! Her small black Cocker Spaniel Sophie likes Spunki but Spunki was not friendly. There was no problem, however.

In mid-September, we met with our friend Louise Fitzgerald, a realtor, and we looked at condominiums and houses in the Franklin, Bellingham and Medway area as a preview of the real estate market.

My frequent trips to Franklin were primarily to visit with my grandchildren but also for medical appointments. Chloe, the youngest of the five grandchildren living in Franklin, was so much fun to watch as she was growing up in so many ways.

Sydney, age three, was pleasant and generous with the food and so fashionably dressed, with impeccable hair.

My three grandsons played sports, and it was always fun to watch their games.

Autumn on Cape Cod is the best time of the year... BUT what happened to the birds and squirrels that used to occupy our backyard? They are nowhere to be seen at this time. I miss the different species of bird, especially the blue birds.

October 2009 brought some sadness in our lives: our beloved former pastor Father Daniel Gilmartin left this world for a better place on October 8th at age eighty-eight. He had been our shepherd at St. Brendan Parish for twenty-four years and came out of retirement to perform our wedding ceremony in 1997. He was well respected among his colleagues. Viewing hours at the church proved a show of well-deserved affection from the parishioners.

Jack Garden, a neighborhood friend, passed away on October 7th, after a long period of suffering. On October 18th, our good friend Ralph Berardi went to his eternal reward. He was a kind, generous and compassionate gentleman, at times emotional. His motto was: "If you can't say anything good about someone, don't say anything at all". A good rule to follow. There was a huge attendance at the calling hours. My family was present, including six-month-old baby Chloe. The funeral at St. Joseph Church in Medway, officiated by Monsignor Moran, was very impressive. The service was followed by a reception at the new church hall where the Berardi family and friends gathered. My dear friend Therese was lost without her darling Ralph but was courageous and stoic.

In mid-October, John became unemployed from Owens & Minor, a medical and surgical supply warehouse in Franklin, where he had been employed for fourteen and a half years. This was a sad time for John. We welcomed him into our home and helped him to get his life in order. He went through a difficult time and Paula's illness requiring some hospitalizations added stress to their relationship. We helped them as much as we could, which they appreciated.

John, while seeking employment, with Paula's brother's help, made much progress and his church attendance made me happy.

On October 21ˢᵗ, we attended Matthew and Connor's football games and both teams won.

November 2009 was busy from beginning to end. The PIE syndrome flared up with all pneumonia symptoms and all my activities were curtailed for one week, as I felt extremely tired. Dave's uncle Bill, ninety-three, and aunt Frieda, eighty-nine, visited and it was a pleasure to spend time with that wonderful couple.

On the eve of Thanksgiving, our sixteen-year-old granddaughter Jackie spent a special evening with us. She helped me in the kitchen and also enjoyed watching a hockey game with her dad. Our friend Margot was with us on Thanksgiving Day, as well as her two dogs. Jackie made a great impression on us all. Thanksgiving Day with the family brought me much joy, and the tiredness I felt had no comparison to the happiness in my heart that evening. John's forty-third birthday was celebrated. All of my children were present except Mark. We called him, and he informed us of his upcoming business trip to Ontario, Canada, with his manager Ben Orr.

On December 4ᵗʰ, our first snow of the season; only a dusting on Cape Cod.

On December 9ᵗʰ, a shocker: Larry Olson, a famous local runner, had passed away suddenly during a training run. He had been a leader in the running circuit for years. He also coached high school cross country and track. Life was simple for Larry: tending his small sport shop in Millis, where I spent some time on my days off, visiting and learning from his experience. The thin, almost emaciated runner was a guru in that sport. He made many friends, in spite of his fierce competitive nature, he had no enemies. He was well respected by all. His death left a running community in shock, as not only was a great runner gone but also a greater coach. He was a legend with so many accomplishments, such as a 2:19 Boston Marathon. The calling hours at Ross Funeral home in Wrentham proved how popular the man was. He had run 130,000 miles in his career.

December 19th and 20th we had a major snowstorm, about one foot of snow. Our Christmas celebrations were relocated to Lori-Ann's home due to home remodeling being done at our house prior to it going on the Realty Market.

The Capizzi Crew started working on the house siding with Bob, David and John working diligently in the freezing cold. Dave and I kept busy with our regular schedule of work and volunteering.

Phone calls revealed that cousin Helen was feeling poorly. Paula Diggins was hospitalized in Rhode Island with arm pain. But there was some good news: my medical check up with Dr. Woodward was good.

The week of December 20th to December 26th, with the preparation for the floors being refinished as well as preparing for the upcoming Christmas celebration, was a very busy week. Dinner on Christmas eve at a Yarmouth Chinese Restaurant was a disappointment. Christmas Day was a quiet day at home, starting with Church, then gift opening. Our friend Margot was over with her two dogs. John was not feeling well. Spunki loved the Christmas tree, played with ornaments, still very spunky for his age, nearing eighteen years.

December 26th was back to getting the house ready for the Real Estate Market. Early rising, getting the Christmas tree down (how sad), moving more furniture out of specified areas. John was of great help. Then off to Franklin at 1:00 pm for the family Christmas gathering. The Zajac's house was newly renovated and looked beautiful. Baby Chloe looked like a little princess in all her glory and her brothers were so handsome with their new haircuts. We had the traditional ornament swap and the children's gift exchange. It was a great time for all with good food, gifts and family. I was given a digital photo viewer and so was Phil by our children. Lori-Ann got the raffle basket. It was a very fun day as all went as planned.

On December 29ᵗʰ, 30ᵗʰ and 31ˢᵗ, we, along with Spunki, had to move to a small hotel nearby, the Plaza Del Sol, to allow the house renovation to take place. Spunki seemed to like it there and did not want to leave for home on

On New Year's Eve.

These wintry days saw frigid temperatures and there were some inactive days with the outdoor work due to poor weather. The newly refinished hardwood floors looked beautiful, after we had waited in our finished basement for four and a half hours for the floors to dry.

Poor Dave was sick with a cold and sore throat for three days; and a visit to the local clinic was futile as his health insurance was not accepted. He soon recovered on his own.

Lori-Ann called: Little Chloe had her first tooth. Hooray!

CHAPTER 57

2010

Spunki, very weak and thin, stopped eating and drinking in the past two days. He liked cool areas to lie down on, such as near doors and in the garage. Saturday morning he remained the same. I took him to the veterinarian who after a blood test confirmed his fear: renal failure, common in old cats. He was poisoned by the kidney disease. There were two options: to euthanize him today or bring him home to die and suffer another forty-eight hours and have a horrible death. After hearing that explanation, I chose option one. At about 11:15 am on January 9th, Spunki went to Kitty Heaven. Dr. Mark assured me that I had done the right thing and Spunki would thank me for it. I kept apologizing to Spunki. What a hard thing to do. I cried all the way home. After storing Spunki's belongings, I kept saying: "Spunki darling, you were special. We loved you and will miss you always". His ashes, in a tiny mahogany casket-like box with padlock and key, are resting on my desk to this day.

On January 22nd, we attended Dave's sweet nearly ninety-nine-year-old aunt Ruth's funeral. She was very intelligent and pleasant and, although she was deaf, could understand people well and was fairly self-sufficient. I loved her.

The Mashpee Senior Center singers entertained us with patriotic songs. Dave is a member of the group along with a few other gentlemen and eleven ladies. Very enjoyable, indeed.

In the first week of February, I started my new receptionist volunteer position at the C-Lab at the Mashpee Clinic. The work was very easy and I loved it.

We had started looking at condominiums in the Franklin area, with the help of my realtor friend Louise and in anticipation of getting our house on the Realty market we had gotten busy sprucing up the indoors of our home with John's help. Brianna spent a lot of time with us and was a great help with the yard sales and her help was very much appreciated. The house was officially on the market in mid-February.

On February 27th, Dave, John and I enjoyed Jackie's competition in Connecticut, where she was living at the time with the Roach family. Her school performed well and made us proud.

On March 5th, I answered the doorbell and there was Phil with his video camera, and Mark holding Sophia. What a happy surprise! Everyone knew about it except for David and I. Sophia, almost two and a half years old was so sweet, smart and polite. The next forty-eight hours were pure bliss for me. Sophia witnessed her first snowfall and what a joy to see this little Texan making snow angels in our backyard and her delighted daddy videotaping the event.

On Saturday evening, March 6th, I was honored by a surprise seventieth birthday party at the VFW Hall in Holliston, where I was greeted by so many friends, relatives and family members. Most of my brother's family were present, which made me happy, as well as my good friends Therese, Vicki and the Speronis. It was a great celebration of my life with so many loved ones.

On March 11th, five days after our wonderful celebration, my brother had a freak accident when he fell off a steep step in a restaurant /pub in his hometown. He sustained multiple injuries and became progressively worse after being hospitalized. He became comatose for the next thirteen days and was on life support. Unbelievable! He had been the life of the party two weeks earlier. His devastated family kept vigil at his bedside. On March 25th, he expired. He was seventy-five years old on March 19th. In spite of cold and rainy weather, there was a large turnout at the viewing and the funeral, including relatives from New Hampshire and New

Brunswick, Canada. He loved his wife and family dearly. He was a good provider and made people laugh through the years. May he rest in peace.

On March 22nd, John's sixteen-year-old daughter Jackie had gone missing. What a heartbreak! But WHY? Jacqueline is such a beautiful, outgoing young lady, intelligent, with dreams and goals, very energetic, confident and popular among her peers. Cheerleading was one of her passions and obtaining good grades in school was her goal. What could have changed all that? Her mysterious disappearance was very painful for our whole family as we prayed and hoped for her safe return. Oh! Mother Mary, protector of the afflicted and desperate, please cover her with your mantle so no harm comes to her, please. After two long months, Jackie was reunited with our family.

Easter 2010 was celebrated at our home. One-year-old Chloe was charming in her purple dress. Brianna and Tyler enjoyed the outdoor egg hunt on this gorgeous day.

In early April 2010, we received an offer on the house; we made a counter offer and it was rejected. We refused a second and a third offer, but the first bid was changed and we compromised on an agreement. We therefore put a bid on the townhouse in Bellingham and plans were moving to sign the purchase and sale agreement at the end of April. Upon our return from the home inspection at 506 Village Lane in Bellingham, however, we were informed that the deal was off by the buyer; no explanation other than: "too much work". Maybe he was afraid of the large backyard.

Boston Marathon Day was pleasant as Dave's sister-in-law, his niece Helen, my granddaughter Brianna, Dave and I watched the race in Wellesley MA.

The quest to sell our Mashpee property went on and on for several months with garage sales with Brianna's and John's helping hands. The house showings were few and far between, so after the winter break, a new Realty agency took over with Max Carey, a young fresh-out-of-college graduate, very diligent and determined to sell our home. Unfortunately, due to a bad economy, it did not happen; but we remained friends through the years.

September 3rd, 2010 was predicted to be a blustery day (to say the least) on Cape Cod as hurricane Earl made its way towards Nantucket Island and Cape Cod towns, such as Chatham and Wellfleet. We were ready for it, but it spared us on Cape and the Islands. We had rain and wind, but no damage. Thank God!

On September 23rd, 2010, our good friend Alice Melcher, accompanied by her daughter, left Mashpee to take permanent residence in a Laconia NH nursing home. We said our goodbyes in the CTK parking lot after morning mass. Afterwards, the coffee-group ladies were informed of her leaving, which had been a sudden move. Although happy for her, the ladies regretted not having been able to bid her good wishes in person.

On that beautiful afternoon, Dave and I met with Dave's childhood friend Paul Cox and wife Martha at a restaurant in Woods Hole, a very scenic restaurant overlooking the water, with great atmosphere, but the food left something to be desired. But it was nice for Dave and Paul to reminisce on their high school days in Medfield MA.

On this same day, September 23rd, Carl LaBrousse, one of our long-time family friends, succumbed to complications from Lupus at age fifty. So sad!

On October 10th, along with the Darling boys, we climbed Pack Monadnock, a 1200-foot climb, difficult enough, an hour and a half each way. There were no incidents. We had dry and sunny conditions.

Chloe was chatting away and so cute, as all my charming grandchildren were at her age. And still are!

The PIE syndrome started again on October 29th, Tracy's birthday. Following the ordered protocol with Prednisone made me feeling better quickly.

Margot had sprained her ankle. It was improving. She believed that Jesus had knocked at her door at 9:30 pm on Saturday evening.

On November 11th, thirty-four years ago on that day, Phil had his first aneurysm and open heart surgery. He survived by a miracle, and on that day in 2010, he joined Lori-Ann and me in a first visit to our six-day-old great-granddaughter Saydee Marie.

The November birthdays, which included Connor's twelfth and Tyler's eleventh, were celebrated as well as that of new "Papa John" who celebrated his forty-fourth birthday on November 26th.

Thanksgiving Day in Mashpee was very busy and enjoyed with our family. Baby Saydee was hospitalized with viral meningitis for a couple of nights but recovered quickly and continued to thrive. She was a quiet baby. Paula and her three daughters, Caitlin, Rachel and Patty, as well as Jackie, Janice and Brianna added to the joy of a wonderful celebration. The movie Elf was the highlight of the evening.

On December 6th, while visiting at Lori-Ann's, I had chest pain, like a pressure. Coincidentally, I was being seen by my primary physician on the same day. I was scheduled for a stress test later in the week. Eight minutes into the test, my heart rate rose to 193 and my blood pressure to 190/104. Atrial fibrillation was detected and the test halted. I drove home to Mashpee after a short stop at Angelique's in Walpole to drop off some baby needs.

The next day, I started on a blood thinner, which I did not want but agreed to. I spent one night at Marcel's while wearing a Holter monitor for twenty-four hours, and I was treated like a queen by Marcel and Marian. Their big cat Monty attacked me only twice. Marcel and I went to Sacred Heart Church in Hopedale where we were so very welcomed by the pastor. We were invited to bring the offerings to the altar. I was most impressed.

Our family Christmas time celebration was a joyous affair as usual at Eaton Place in Franklin, with the addition of pretty baby Saydee Marie, almost two months old already. Our Christmas celebrations always are a joy. After bringing Angelique, Don and Saydee home, Dave noticed his gift bag was missing. He had mistakenly left it with Angelique's gifts. The bag was recovered a few days later, to Dave's great relief.

CHAPTER 58

Phil's Medical Journey

On June 7th, 2010, at midnight, Phil drove himself to Milford Regional Hospital in severe chest pain. Marcel informed me at 5:00 am that his dad had been airlifted to Brigham and Women's Hospital in Boston with question of an abdominal aneurysm dissection which was ruled out after a few tests were done. He was heavily medicated for these tests. He was therefore groggy and confused, but was discharged home with Jamie. Seeing his dad in this condition, Jamie asked why his dad was so confused and the answer was: "Is he not always like that?" Jamie answered: "No, he is not".

In the hospital parking lot, Phil fell, injuring his leg. He was sent home as planned. The next day, he returned to Milford Hospital with the same pain. Tests showed an infected gallbladder. He was transferred to the Worcester UMass Medical Center, where he was kept NPO (nothing by mouth) and on intravenous antibiotic for about one week, with a plan to do surgery in a few weeks.

Phil's plans to go to New Brunswick were shattered. And this made him anxious and depressed. The foot injury, which occurred at the hospital, was an addition to his pre-existing pain and made life really miserable for him. Father's Day was a very painful one, according to family visitors. Phil's next transfer was to a rehabilitation facility in Milford where the intense physical therapy was very difficult due to numbness from knee to hip and pins and needles in lower right leg. There was not much improvement in ambulation. His blood sugars were out of control due to inadequate nutrition and insulin was given daily (which was new to him).

On June 27th we visited him and he felt so sad and said: "I went to the hospital for gallbladder problems and came out crippled and now I am in a wheelchair".

On July 3rd, at 8:00 pm, I received a call from the rehab center informing me that Phil was being sent to Milford Hospital with chest pain. Marcel met him in the emergency room and at 1:00 am Phil was transferred to UMass, Worcester, again, with question of aneurysm. He was admitted to the Cardiac Intensive Care Unit and monitored. On July 7th, Phil was told: no dissection, a gallbladder problem. Meanwhile his hip, back and leg were still painful.

After Lori-Ann's disappointment with UMass Medical, she insisted that her father be transferred to St. Elizabeth Hospital in Brighton MA, where Phil was known to them. Good idea, Lori-Ann!

From St. Elizabeth Hospital, Phil was sent to a rehabilitation facility in Waltham, then returned to St. Elizabeth Hospital for gallbladder surgery. Finally!

On August 26th, PJ was transferred to another kindred facility in Westborough MA for continued rehabilitation.

On September 1st, we had a much more pleasant visit with Phil. Therapy was going well and the staff was optimistic about a full recovery. Very encouraging.

After four months of traveling from one medical facility to another, Phil made it home. On October 24th, we celebrated his homecoming at his residence at Eaton Place in Franklin, with a small family gathering planned by Janice, assisted by Lori-Ann and Marian. Tracy was ill at the time and missed the party, but Jamie, Connor and Sydney were present, as well as the other grandchildren.

CHAPTER 59

2011

Major renovations were underway at Christ The King Church; all services were held in the parish hall, which was accommodating well.

Our home was being spruced up for the open house and viewing with our dedicated realtors.

Lori-Ann visited with Chloe at the weekend. Chloe is such a pleasant child. She is not a good eater but she is precious. Now two-year-old Chloe says: "What the heck".

Paula was hospitalized at Falmouth Hospital. She is not happy with the medical staff, poor girl. She is having a hard time with that terrible disease now in its fourth year.

Cold and snowy weather continued for most of the month of January with small to moderate snowfalls.

On January 18th, while at mass, I experienced my first near-syncope episode and I was brought home by my friend Barbara, it was very kind of her to do so. Deacon Fantasia blessed me upon exiting the church hall. I recovered quickly from that medical episode and continued with my regular routine of work, volunteering and preparing for a house sale and for a move.

On Friday January 21st, Dave and I attended a special Pro-Life mass in St. Jude Chapel, followed by the chaplet of the Divine Mercy. On our way home we had a dusting of snow, while in the Franklin area, six to seven inches fell.

My best friend Therese celebrated her eightieth birthday and was anticipating her upcoming trip to California with her granddaughter Tracie. She will visit with daughter Donna and her friend Claudia until Spring.

On Saturday, David, with the Senior Singers of the Mashpee Senior Center, performed in a concert to honor soldiers along with other musical groups from surrounding towns. Interesting, to say the least.

On Sunday, January 23rd, at 10:33 am, Jamie Patrick reached Jack Benny's age. A birthday call was placed.

In the afternoon, we met at the home of David's niece in Mansfield MA to celebrate with a belated Christmas family gathering. The Finkelstein's home is always a joy to visit, with great food and company. Our sister-in-law Helen and nephew Danny were present as well. There was much snow in Mansfield with frigid temperatures and the forecast of an upcoming snowstorm.

Our friend Margot made it home safely from visiting her daughter Melissa in Las Vegas, Nevada.

On January 31st, we welcomed our new realtors, Shannon and Maxwell. They paid us their first visit on this very cold afternoon. They are both young and energetic. We were impressed. Good vibes.

On February 4th, fifty years ago today, I left the novitiate and was greeted by mountains of snow in Grande-Digue, along with bitter cold. I made a fairly good adjustment. I lived at my sister's house and worked at the Poirier Corner Convenience Store for a while. Our parish pastor's funeral had just taken place the week prior to my arrival to my old parish. On February 12th, my brother Ronald and his wife Cécile were married, fifty years ago in Waltham MA. I was unable to attend. Those two missed major events saddened me as I was starting my new secular lifestyle.

John and Paula visited frequently from Wareham. Paula continued her cancer treatments and Dave helped with transportation while John and I worked. She was very pleased to be able to attend a Feel Good and Look Good class in Hyannis. Dave is a very generous man, always helping others.

Valentine's Day! and temperatures were in the low forties. David, even though sick with a fever, chills and achy feeling, had gone out to purchase a valentine card for his wife. That deserved double credit, according to Max, our new young realtor.

On February 16th, nine years ago on that day, after twenty-eight years of employment, I had retired from Milford Hospital. Lori-Ann gave her resignation at Cheri Cheryle that week after nearly eighteen years.

Meanwhile, we continued our search for a new abode and Shannon and Max were doing their best to sell our house. My preferred condominium was the one we saw located in Bellingham, on Village Lane, and offered by my friend Louise.

Along with hunting for a house, we were also looking to adopt a cat. We visited a cat shelter in Centerville a few times and both of us were scratched by Darcy at different times.

On those cold evenings, playing cards and board games were very welcomed activities. We played Boggles, Aggravation and Phase Ten. Movie watching was also a fun distraction. We became avid American Idol fans in those days.

We received good news on Paula's PET scan result: no liver involvement or new spots on bones. She was a very happy girl.

On March 4th, my birthday was celebrated quietly with Janice and Brianna, with dinner at Bobby Burns Restaurant at Mashpee Commons, followed by a delicious cake at home and several phone calls from family and friends and multiple birthday cards. It is a well-known fact that I love mail! I am blessed with many friends. Janice's little Shih Tzu, Reeses, was well behaved on her first visit to our home. Lori-Ann was in the Bahamas at the time.

Paula was continuing her chemotherapy journey with multiple problems and frequent short-term hospitalizations at the Tobey Hospital in Wareham and at the Falmouth Hospital. David and I helped her as much as we could and she was very appreciative. She would often express her feelings in written notes. We celebrated her forty-eighth birthday quietly at our home in early March. A cold and snowy month continued, feeling more like late November.

March 24th to March 31st A Boston Medical Center visit with David on a blustery day. In remembrance of the first anniversary of my brother Ronald's demise, we celebrated with a mass in North Dighton MA. The mass was followed by a get-together at the Léger residence to honor my niece Nancy on her forty-fourth birthday. We had a nice time.

On March 31st, Good Humor Ice Cream (formerly Sealtest) closed its doors and moved to Tennessee. This left Marcel unemployed after twenty-seven years with the company.

Early April brought a few annual events, such as our group of nursing school alumni getting together to celebrate a few birthdays, particularly that of our sweet friend Helen Brule.

The Franklin Davis Thayer School talent show, which is co-chaired by Lori-Ann, is always a most welcomed and enjoyable evening. The talent show is a family affair: Lori-Ann as co-chairlady, Tyler a fifth-grader MC along with three other students, Tyler displaying his musical talents with a drum solo and a song, his dad in charge of sound and lighting. Brianna and friends, Phil and Janice joined Dave and me as well as Tyler's paternal grandmother Nana and Papa Warren.

Toby, our new cat, was out on a leash today. He was very frightened. We are not planning to continue this exercise.

On April 15th, after spending eleven days at Morton Hospital in Taunton, my sister-in-law Cécile was discharged to Longmeadow Rehabilitation Facility.

Today was a fun day at the Mashpee Rehabilitation Center where I volunteer, as four hundred and thirty-three words broke our previous record for The Word Game that we play with the patients in the clients' activities room, and where I assist every Friday morning, and loving. it.

On April 16th, seventy years ago, my mother went to her Maker. What a pity to leave a husband and three young children. May she rest in peace in the Heavenly Kingdom.

April 18th This year we enjoyed viewing the Boston Marathon on television. It was a great feat with several broken records, a great day for the USA. On the following day the Red Sox and the Bruins were also victorious.

April 20th marked Chloe's second birthday celebration. She remains charming, inquisitive, so lovable a child.

On April 21st, Marian's dad Robert Hart, at nearly ninety-three, went to his eternal reward after many years of suffering with Guillain-Barre. Mrs. Hart is coping fairly well and is residing at the Holliston Nursing Home.

David and I attended the Holy Thursday evening service. On Good Friday afternoon, the Christ The King youth ministry performed The Stations of the Cross with modern music and appropriate song messages. Well done! We also attended the evening service.

Holy Saturday was the day for the Easter food preparation, which this year included the forty-seventh baking of my Bunny Cake. At the Easter vigil celebration, I became faint and required some assistance from usherette June, who was very comforting.

April 24th was Easter morning, a beautiful day for an outdoor egg hunt, which is always fun for the young grandchildren. Among our invited guests were parishioners Barbara and David Berglund, our friend Margot and the Bourgeois-Darling clan. It is always fun to get together. Dave and I enjoyed having the family in our home in Mashpee. The afternoon temperature reached the low 70s allowing for dessert to be consumed on the patio.

\What a day! Great company and food plentiful! We missed John and Paula who were working and we repeated the Easter meal at a later date.

April 27th was Mr. Hart's funeral, followed by a reception at The 45 Restaurant in Medway. Later we visited David's elderly uncle and aunt in Franklin. As the good weather continued, David took advantage and worked diligently at embellishing our yard and he seemed to enjoy it. The spring blossoms were in their full glory. A beautiful time of the year! Dave seemed to enjoy his new battery-operated lawn mower.

On April 29th, we signed a new contract with a new agency, the Real Estates Associates, a transfer from Century 21. All went well. Frequent open house sessions were scheduled but so far, no offers.

On April 30th, Paula had to be admitted to the Falmouth Hospital as she was febrile, nauseated with achy feeling, and had cirrhosis of the liver. Sadly, Paula is losing her battle with the Big C. I contacted her brother Jeff.

On May 1st, Osama Bin Laden was assassinated by the Navy Seals. Victory for America!

On May 7th, we went to Jamie's house to celebrate granddaughter Sydney's fifth birthday, my friends Therese and Beverly-An also attended. We had a great time with family and friends.

May 8th was Mother's Day, a cool and drizzly day. We attended the 8:30 am mass. In the afternoon, I visited Paula in the hospital. I received telephone calls from my children as well as from Jeff Bellin, Paula's brother. Paula is confused at times and requires pain medication for her suffering. It was a sad sight to witness.

Mark called. He was disappointed with the outcome of his search for a marketing position with Eaton in Wisconsin. He continued his search for suitable employment. Prayers were needed.

Paula was a patient at Bourne Manor, near the Cape Cod Canal, and her time there proved to be such a miserable time for her. She was so unhappy there. Meanwhile her condition worsened and after a few admissions to Falmouth Hospital, she was admitted to McCarthy House, a hospice facility in Sandwich MA. She was still responsive but confused. It was very sad for John and her three daughters, who also visited with their father.

It was a surprise for us to meet Paula's biological mother, Carolyn Caplan, from Colorado, a very pleasant lady. There was a striking resemblance between the two women. Unfortunately, Paula never knew her, having been adopted soon after birth. Her also adopted brother Jeff, became her health care advocate. A reconciliation telephone conversation had taken place between Paula, her adoptive mother Sandra and Jeff earlier, while Paula was still alert and still responsive. That was great news for me!

Saturday May 28th, 2011, while I was at MG Salon and Spa in Medway MA. for a hair appointment with Lori-Ann, I received the sad phone call from John. Paula had expired at 12:45 pm. John was devastated. The events for that very busy late spring day took place as planned, which included a winning baseball game for Matthew's team, dinner at Rick's Restaurant, followed by Sydney's dance recital. We arrived home late in the evening. John was being assisted by Jeff and his friend Gigi.

My Canadian cousin Germaine, who had been so kind to me through the years, providing me with many family informative papers and photographs, returned to her Maker as well. That was a memorable weekend.

Memorial Day was David Jr.'s girlfriend Tina's celebration on receiving a well-earned doctorate degree in Forensic Sciences. David attended. John, who was in much need of moral support, and I stayed home.

On Thursday June 2nd, 2011, Ascension Thursday, was Paula's graveside funeral service with Jewish traditional rites. Dirt was shoveled onto the casket in the grave. The service was well attended by family and friends. A very sad day for her three young daughters: Caitlin, Rachel and Patricia;

for John and for his daughters Angelique and Jacqueline as well. The Rabbi read the eulogy that had been prepared by Jeff and John. Paula's adoptive mother was unable to attend due to poor health. May God rest Paula Diggins' soul. She will be missed.

In early June, Dave and David Jr. went on a pleasurable trip to Cooperstown, New York, for a couple of days. They both very much enjoyed their relaxing stay and returned home on a warm 80+ degree day.

On Thursday June 9th, we took Toby to the veterinarian for a rabies shot. He is a large healthy cat of 15 lbs 14 oz. He behaved well and had his nails trimmed. Lucky kitty.

June 10th was another WORD RECORD DAY. The winning phrase: Accused of impersonating a Falmouth Officer (from the Cape Cod Times, a local newspaper). Four hundred and eighty-three words.

On June 13th, the Thrift Shop's annual luncheon was held at The Flying Bridge Restaurant. It is always a fun time.

June 15th The Bruins won the STANLEY CUP! after thirty-nine years, in a very impressive last game with a shutout 4-0 against the Vancouver Canucks. A riot ensued in the streets of Vancouver. What a shame!

June 18th We went to the Melody Tent Hyannis for Siobhan Magnus' concert with the Ultrasonic Rock Orchestra. We were disappointed and we left for home early. The following day, Father's Day, was another disappointment at the PawSox game, where ten family members attended and the Sox lost 2-0.

House showings continued without any offers. I was unable to attend my friend Cindy's retirement party in Milford due to health issues but I met with her in Franklin at a later date. Cindy and I became good friends after working together at Milford Hospital for several years.

June 22nd The FBI apprehended and arrested James Whitey Bulger, a well-known Boston area mobster along and his girlfriend Catherine Greig, in California, after sixteen years on the run. Great job, FBI!

Jamie returned to his plumbing employment after nearly two years of being laid off. Wonderful!

On July 1st, a near-syncope occurred during mass and paramedics were called. I refused to go to the hospital, recovered, and went home. I was ordered by my primary physician, to be seen at Falmouth Hospital emergency room, which I did. A chest x-ray, a head scan and intravenous fluid were administered. I was sent home with a Holter monitor for twenty-four hours. I felt better the next day and the following days as well.

On July 4th, we watched the Boston Pops on television and listened to fireworks from the nearby town. Otherwise the day was uneventful.

Great news from Mark J. in Angleton TX. He was very excited about a pending marketing position in Nacogdoches TX, which is the oldest town in Texas.

The Barnstable County Fair takes place on the third week of July, yearly, and attracts fair goers from surrounding towns. The fair was always enjoyed by my grandchildren. Little Chloe, then two and a half years old, her mommy Lori-Ann and I attended The Wiggles Show at the Melody Tent in Hyannis. What fun for Chloe.

Dave's birthday on August 12th was celebrated at Bobby Byrne's Restaurant in Mashpee, followed by our fourteenth wedding anniversary in Kennebunk, while vacationing in my favorite part of Maine.

Old friends Anna LaBrousse and Bella Cardoos visited from Virginia and from Bridgewater MA. We had a very enjoyable day.

On August 27th and 28th, Hurricane Irene came to visit New England. Cape Cod was mostly affected by high winds, with gusts of seventy miles per hour in Mashpee. Some flooding occurred after heavy downpours and there were power outages off the Cape. Vermont was a total disaster.

On Labor Day, miniature golf with Dave in West Yarmouth turned out interesting as he beat me by four points in the first half and I did the same in the second half of the game. We both had holes-in-one. It was a fun day!

Saturday September 10th was special for me at Candlepin Bowling, with Dave and John. I scored 109 in the first string and left them trailing. They certainly improved in the second string, and I declined.

September 12th, a warm fall day, was spent with John and Laura who were visiting from Nashua NH. We visited the Glass Museum in Sandwich MA and watched a glass blowing demonstration, which was mind boggling. We had lunch at Seafood Sam. It was a beautiful day.

A mild case of the PIE syndrome was kept under control with my bystander Prednisone. I experienced a near-syncope episode at church again.

Mark started his new marketing manager position with Elliott Electric Supplies in Nacogdoches and he was feeling good about it. Great news!

We enjoyed a fun time with Lori-Ann, Chloe and John at Craigville Beach, at Pizza Primo, and at the Polar Cave, Cape Cod's voted # 1 Ice Cream Parlor.

October brought Dave and me to Lake George, New York, for a well-deserved vacation to enjoy fall weather in this area, away from the hustle and bustle of New York City. We found it to be a relaxing as well as a learning experience. The cruise on the Horicon ship was full of interesting facts. We visited the Blessed Sacrament Church and across from the park were monuments of the French missionaries Saint Isaac Jogues, Saint Jean de Brébeuf and their companions, who were martyred for their faith by the Mohawk Indians. They are known as the North American Martyrs. They are co-patrons of the United-States and Canada. The massacres occurred between 1642 and 1649 in Canada and in the

US, respectively. A shrine in their honor is located in Auriesville, in the vicinity of Lake George, New York, and one is also situated near Midland, Ontario, Canada. I felt privileged to have witnessed such a site. Therefore our short trip to Lake George was very fruitful.

Upon our return home, my Buick Century greeted me with a large problem with the ignition. This left me without a vehicle for over a week, waiting for parts. It was also very costly. Thankfully, David was my patient chauffeur.

On October 17th, my granddaughter Sophia celebrated her fourth birthday in California, while visiting with her mom.

October 23rd We enjoyed another day trip with the 50+ Club to Newport, Rhode Island, where we saw the comedy show Social Security; it was hilarious A delicious lunch and a cabaret show followed.

From October 27th to October 29th, there was a snowstorm with power outages off Cape. High winds and rain on Cape.

November 4th marked my great granddaughter Saydee's first birthday. We had lots of fun. Janice played the part of Saydee's favorite Disney character, Mickey Mouse. We had lots of laughs.

November 10th Thirty-five years ago on that day, Phil had his first heart problem. On that day in 2011, another Phil succumbed to a heart attack, unexpectedly. He was a prominent member of our community and an active parishioner of Christ The King Church.

On November 20th, my grandson Tyler turned twelve years old. How time flies! Thanksgiving Day was spent in South Attleboro MA at Jack and Janice's home with a large turnout and abundant food. Good times!

November 26th was John's birthday. He celebrated with his daughters in Walpole.

Our house went on the market again with Keller Williams Realty and the showings increased with Donna Davis-Hickey and Stephen; very aggressive realtors.

December 3rd A very special day indeed: John had a counseling session with Monsignor Hoye, which made me happy. John had been very sad since Paula's passing.

There were two house showings on that day, but no offer.

Mild temperatures for the season. Lori-Ann was devastated on the outcome of the court decision regarding the Hair Salon case. Oh! God, may something good come out of this terrible experience for Lori-Ann.

December 18th We enjoyed watching Sydney, age five, as she performed in The Nutcracker with her school of dance.

Christmas Day A quiet day at home. After church service with John, we had a few guests for dinner: Margot and Marion Pomfret, a CTK parishioner. A pleasant afternoon was spent with movies, and pleasant conversation with good company. We received family telephone calls on this special day.

Our usual Christmastime family celebration took place at Eaton Place Hall in Franklin, and as always, it was a fun-filled day with family all in attendance except Mark, who was at home with his family, in Nacogdoches TX.

CHAPTER 60

Face the Truth, Mom

A young mother's story written in 1970 but which still applies today.

FACE THE TRUTH, MOM

---◆:◆:◆---

This article has not been written by a college graduate, but by a thirty-year-old housewife who would like to express her opinions on one of the leading topic of conversation among women of childbearing age: Birth Control.

It is talked about by many others as well, including clergymen, physicians, politicians, all professionals and the rich and the poor. In these modern times it appears that man is trying to become superior to his Master and has obviously forgotten his goal in life, which is to Know, Love and Serve his Creator, to whom he shall return to receive his reward for his good deeds, so says the Scriptures.

Although there are still men of good will on earth, Thank God!, it seems that the Evil Spirit is busy spreading his disastrous message of disguised truth in our confused world with an unbelievable speed. Therefore, apparently we are fighting a losing battle; but with the grace of God, we shall overcome.

Since the beginning of time there has been problems in our world, but there has always been a solution; so hopefully a solution will be in the future. Will God our Father let His children rule Him and show Him how to run His earth much longer? Will He strike and show His anger as He did in the Old Testament? Has man earned the right to call His Creator's laws unfair?

Man has found many answers, but concerning life and death God is still the undefeatable One, and let us not forget it. We do not have the right to interfere with God's creation of a new life or to determine when to end that life. Neither do we have the right to invade people's private lives to regulate the number of lives, with God's given power, they can create. Man changes God's laws to suit his needs, understandably, but God is still in charge and that will never change.

Now, if you let your imagination wander, you may inject your own comments to this conversation.

Letter from a mother to her unborn son

———◆•◆•◆———

Dear son:

We hope you are happy in your non existing world. Your father and I are sorry to tell you that we are unable to grant you the gift of life, that you requested. It was our deep and true love for you that brought such a decision regarding your destiny.

Dear son, you know that we would not want to see you unhappy, hungry or suffering, so we have to refuse your right to be born for these logical reasons, I pray you will understand.

Morality: The young generation today, has more than its share of juvenile delinquency, drug addiction, protests and demonstrations, be it against wars, laws or the establishment. Things are so much different now than when your father and I were young; the standard of moral values has changed tremendously. Son, we are living in a confused world and changing times have brought us to revolution in the church, and in the government affairs and other medias. Society is revolting against next to everything; is that the kind of life you would like to live?

You see, son, by refusing you the right to be born, we are protecting you from such problems. I also want to point out to you another view of today's life picture. Finance: If you would be born in 1970, your birth fee would be about $1,500.00 and until you have reached your eighteenth birthday, you would have cost us ten times more. The cost of living today is very high and rising, as well as the cost of education. To fit in the groove of today's generation, you need to be from a well-off family; but unfortunately your father's income does not meet these standards.

I admit, we enjoy a few frivolities such as: having an extra television set in our bedroom, two cars in the garage, a fur coat in my closet and a weekly night out (including dinner and dancing or a movie). You would not want us to deprive ourselves of the simple pleasures of life, now would you, son? After all we do not harm anyone and we are living a good life, even though we miss church on Sundays now and then.

So, dear son, we are very sorry, we cannot afford another mouth to feed, as we are financially handicapped and I cannot face the responsibility for I have already exhausted my energy and patience with your brother and sister. Besides, the trend is two children per family.

Sorry, son.

Your would-have-been mother

Letter from unborn son to his mother

---•◆•---

Dear mom:

I do not know why I call you by that precious name as you are not my mother and never will be, by your own choice.You preferred not to be so to spare me all the miseries of an ill fated destiny (as you explained).

Well, dear parents: Be aware that being rejected by your own parents is a worse fate than any other to me. I plead to you to give me a chance to be born and show you what I can do with my life.

I understand that parents have great responsibilities but some parents ignore them and prefer their comfort to the welfare of their offspring. For example, I see you and dad drink martinis every night until you are blinded and do not wonder or care how or where my teenage brother and sister are spending their evening.

To you, mom, your bridge club is more important than dealing with my sister's problems. Dad will take an evening out with the boys instead of having a serious conversation with his son, anytime.

You mentioned the sad shape the world is in. Who is to blame, if not the parents who are too lazy, selfish or unwilling to sacrifice their own comfort zone to work harder in bringing up their children to become good Christians and decent citizens.

Sometimes parents are too immature to live up to their parenting expectations; therefore the children suffer from their upbringing. I believe that if parents would take better care of the children they already have, there would not be any reason to make use of birth control in fear of additional children. Why should we, legitimate sons and daughters, be penalized while our illegitimate counterparts are adopted into good families and we are still waiting to be born into your world. If parents brought up their teenagers in the fear of God and respect for the sixth commandment, some of us legitimate unborn children would be where we belong.

By limiting your family to two offsprings, you might be saving monetary assets but it will not buy your eternal life. By playing with fire (birth control) you might get burned, maybe even eternally.

With due respect, mom, I'd rather stay in my non existing world than to be part of your corrupt one.

May God forgive you, mom.

Your never-to-be-born son

======== CHAPTER 61 ========

Challenges

1972 -- 1996 Our beloved pastor Father Daniel Gilmartin shepherded his flock at St. Brendan Parish in North Bellingham MA for twenty-four years. He remained a friend until his demise in 2009.

In the summer of 1996, Father David J. Mullen became our new young and energetic pastor, with a high regard for the pro-life movement and for the Catholic Church magisterium and a promoter of the sacrament of Reconciliation.

In 2002 there was a scandal in our Church involving priests and the Boston Archdiocese was in a crisis.

Father Mullen took it upon himself to address the problem with his pastoral superior, Bernard Cardinal Law. With his permission, here is a copy of his letter to His Eminence Cardinal Bernard Law:

REV. DAVID J. MULLEN

Saint Brendan Parish

384 Hartford Avenue

Bellingham, Massachusetts 02019

June 5, 2002

His Eminence Bernard Cardinal Law

2121 Commonwealth Avenue

Brighton, Massachusetts, 02135

Your Eminence:

I write to you on the twentieth anniversary of my ordination. I call upon the grace that the Lord gave to me twenty years ago in order to express what I must. Men are sometimes called to do hard things; this letter is one of them. It makes no use to prepare to be a man, a Christian man - and a priest no less; but not to have the courage to act or speak like one when the circumstances require it. Our present circumstances do certainly require it. This is an attempt to speak like a real Christian man, a real priest - with truth and charity. Over the years I have been a great supporter of yours. This is the same priest who during the "Last Temptation of Christ" controversy stood in front of the Globe building on Morrissey Boulevard with Dr. Joseph Stanton and about a dozen others defending your right to caution the Faithful regarding the movie.

You might recall that a day or two before, the editorial cartoonist Szep, had ridiculed you in the Globe. This is also the same priest who supported you with an editorial article printed in the Boston Herald when you asked pro-lifers to stay away from the abortion clinics after the clinic shootings. Many pro-life people were critical of you then but I asked them to trust in your prudence.

But now I must write to you not to praise, and certainly not to condemn but to admonish.

I have also enclosed within this envelope my contribution to the 2002 Cardinal's appeal. The donation is doubled in comparison to last year. In order to make up for the many who will not give this year as a way of protesting against you and the central part you have in the scandal that has engulfed the Archdiocese of Boston. It is indeed hard to fathom the depth of the sin and evil that has been both tolerated and caused by the curia of the Archdiocese of Boston. It is untruthful to contend that what has brought about our present situation was the misunderstanding of child abusers or bad record keeping. Simply said what brought it about were many objective mortal sins. It brings the Church into disrepute for us to preach to the people of God about sin and the need for reparation and penance, when at the same time regarding the subject of abuse of children by priests and the protection of the latter by the Archdiocese; we talk of "mistakes" instead of sin. But this about sin, not just of the priest perpetrators but also of the administration.

There was the sin of failing to be effectively concerned with the moral and spiritual health of the children who were victimized. As a result, hundreds of children were assaulted continually and sins against the sixth commandment of the Decalogue were committed against them. It is quite clear from the official correspondence in the Geoghan and Shanley files concern for the children did not figure largely in the various considerations that were made; indeed they were hardly ever referred to. This is despite the fact that Our Lord tells us in Sacred Scripture that it would be better to be thrown into the sea with a millstone around the neck than to bring one of the little ones to sin (Mtxv111.6).

There was the sin of scandal that causes the entire preaching of the Church to be compromised. The catechism of the Catholic Church tells us that scandal "takes on a particular gravity by reason of the authority of those who cause it". (#2284). This scandal is truly serious because it involves the Archdiocese of Boston bearing false witness. The false witness was exemplified in the sending of the offending priests to new parishes or pastoral responsibilities for those thus ministered to by them would assume that the priest sent to them would give good spiritual care. But the Archdiocese knew that they would not. Certainly this was true in the case of Shanley who was notorious in his rejection of the moral doctrine of the Catholic Church regarding sexuality. The Archdiocese knew that Geoghan, Shanley, Birmingham, Mahan and others had repeatedly abused many children and thus had no rational reason to think that they would not do so again. The Archdiocese had no need of "expert opinion" regarding such men, for it possessed documented evidence of their evil habits. Despite this they were sent to new pastoral assignments. The people of God had the right to expect and assumed that the priests sent to them would be good men.

There was the sin of leaving bad priests in the ministry of the Boston presbyterate. This is an offense against the priests. A man gives up many things to be a priest, but this should not include his good name and reputation as a Christian. You had no right to allow child molesters to be active among us. Not only does this seriously compromise our ability to spread the Gospel, but it is an offense against our dignity. It was your job to keep us free of such people. You obviously refused to do so. There was the sin of not protecting the abusive priests. Catholic morality tells us that we should be put in an unnecessary occasion of sin. Yet these priests were put in a situation that had already proven to be their moral downfall. Where was the priestly fraternity in that? In many cases their brother priests in the same assignments were not warned of the priest's proclivities so they could guide them away from difficulties.

If it is true that you told someone who had been abused that you "bound him by the power of the confessional" not to speak to anyone about the abuse, then this is in itself a serious abuse of the Sacrament of Penance and thus a sacrilegious sin. No priest, bishop or cardinal has any authority to bind anyone in such a way. We, not the lay faithful, are bound by the sacrament, specifically by the seal of confession.

We are told in Sacred Scripture that we are not to judge lest we be judged. So I do not know and will not judge the responsibility before the eyes of God that you or others have for these sins. But there is no doubt that objectively these and more sins were committed. This should be admitted to the people of God.

Because of this scandal the local church is prostrate before the pagans. You have lost your ability to improve the public mind on matters of morality. Indeed all priests have been compromised as moral authorities. In these circumstances the opponents of Christian morality will try to further undermine marriage and family life. They are likely to have success, especially since dissenters in the clerical ranks who favor such outrageous as gay marriage have, be emboldened to join them. At the same time, anger and confusion among the laity increase as they look away from their shepherd and refuse to hear his voice.

Monsignor Frederick Ryan of St. Joseph Parish in Kingston was thinking of the good of his parish when he sent his resignation to you. On your part the present situation requires an act of self-sacrifice that will also be penitential and reparative of some of the evil that has been done. In addition, the Holy Father must be informed of the substance of all the documents that have been released by court order so that he will not mistakenly think that the scandal came from following the advice of experts or because of bad "record keeping".

I pray to God that you will have the courage and love of the Gospel that is necessary in order to do what you must.

Obediently,

Rev. David J. Mullen

cc: Most Rev. Walter J. Edyvean

Most Rev. Francis X. Irwin

Most Rev. John P. Boles

Most Rev. Emilio S. Allue

Most Rev. Richard J. Malone

Most Rev. Richard G. Lennon

CHAPTER 62

More Tidbits

Strange but true: The truly remarkable similarities between Abraham Lincoln and John F. Kennedy:

They were elected one hundred years apart; both were assassinated with their wife present, on a Friday; and both were succeeded by a vice president named Johnson.

Most people spend the first half of their life deciding what to do with their life and spend the second half, regretting they never did.

J. Betterman

My Promise to my Children

For as long as I live, I will always be your parent first and your friend second.

I will stalk you, flip out on you, lecture you, drive you insane, be your worst nightmare and hunt you down like a bloodhound when I have to, because I love you.

When you understand that, I will know you have become a responsible adult.

You will never find anyone else in your life who loves, prays, cares, worries about you more than I do.

If you don't mutter under your breath "I hate you" at least once in your life, I am not doing my job properly

Author unknown

Great minds discuss ideas.

Average minds discuss events.

Small minds discuss people.

Author unknown

What is an OKAPI? A part giraffe and part zebra.

Houston Zoo

One hundred years from now

It will not matter what kind of car I drove,

What kind of house I lived in,

Or how much money I had in my bank account,

Nor what my clothes looked like.

But the world may be a little better

Because I was important in the life of a child.

Margaret Fishback Powers

A SMILE

It goes a very long way toward making life worthwhile.

It costs the least, yet does the most.

A smile which comes straight from the heart

Which loves its fellow man,

And drives away the cold and gloom

And brings the sun again.

It's full of warmth and kindness too;

With no real effort spent.

It's worth a million dollars; yet it doesn't cost a cent.

Author unknown

Certain people are a Joy to know

People who know how to brighten a day with heart warming smiles and with kind words to say.

People who know how to gently impart the comfort it takes to

cheer someone's heart.

People who know how to always come through when there's

anything they can possibly do.

People who know how to give and

who know how to care and

who know how to let all their warm

feelings show.

Are people that others feel lucky to know.

Amanda Bradley

A PARENT'S PRAYER

———————◆•◉•◆———————

I free you from my anxiety, from my personal idea

of what constitutes happiness for you.

I trust the spirit of God in you to illuminate you,

to guide you,

to show you the way that is right for you,

that is for your highest good,

the way that means happiness and success for you.

I place you lovingly in the hands of the Father.

I stand by in faith;

I refrain from imposing my will on you.

You are God's child, you are here to fulfill your own purpose.

As close as I am to you, as much as I love you,

I cannot live your life for you.

Your destiny, your fulfillment is between you and God.

I know that we are one in God and that as I trust God in my life

and trust Him in your life, all is well.

Author unknown

Quotes to live by:

It does not get harder, you get stronger! How true!

When you get into a comfort zone, it is beautiful but nothing grows there.

For ALL girls to hear:

Mirror, mirror on the wall

It doesn't matter if I'm short or tall

Or if I have skinny legs or my hips are wide...

It only matters what I am inside.

Blue eyes, brown eyes, black or green

What makes beautiful cannot be seen.

When you look at me, don't judge me by my parts

The most beautiful thing about me, is in my heart.

Ms Moem, English poet

RECIPE FOR MARRIAGE

One carefully selected man

One carefully selected woman

Pre-heat the home to the nth degree.

To the man, add abilities to be a good provider and give affection

To the woman, add abilities to be a good homemaker and

Stir in loyalty, tenderness and creativity.

Boil until all traces of nagging evaporate.

Carefully blend two together.

Grease with maturity.

Flour with common sense.

Add heaping amounts of respect and honesty

Consistently, add kindness and understanding.

Drain all impurities, but retain individuality.

Whip in sense of honor.

Grind in responsibility.

Stir in ability to sacrifice.

Soften with trust.

Cut out all traces of selfishness.

Add richness.

Blend in plans and dreams and work them out together.

Season with children…

Author B. Daniel

When you can't put your prayers into words, God hears your heart.

TRUST IN HIM

———◆•◆•◆———

God has our entire lives in the Palm of His Loving Hand. We can rest secure about our past, present and future; for he loves us.

Mother Angelica

April 20, 1923 - March 27, 2016

Some wise person came up with this one:

1. Faith is the ability to not panic.

2. If you worry, you did not pray. If you pray, don't worry.

3. As a child of God, prayer is like calling home every day.

4. Blessed are the flexible for they shall not be bent out of shape.

5. When we get tangled up in our problems, be still!

God wants us to be still so He can untangle the knot.

6. Do the math; count your blessings.

7. God wants spiritual fruits, not religious nuts.

8. Dear God: I have a problem: It's me.

9. Silence is often misinterpreted, but never misquoted.

10. Laugh every day, it's like inner jogging.

11. The most important things in your home are the people.

12. Growing is inevitable, growing up is optional.

13. There is no key to Happiness, the door is always open.

14. A grudge is a heavy thing to carry.

15. He who dies with the most toys is still dead.

16. We do not remember days, but moments.

Life moves too fast, so enjoy your precious moments.

17. Nothing is real to you until you experience it, otherwise it's hearsay.

18. It's all right to sit on your pity pot every now and again.

Just be sure you flush when you are done.

19. Surviving and living your life successfully requires courage.

The goals and dreams you are seeking require courage and

risk taking. Learn from the turtle: it only make progress when

it sticks out the neck.

20. Be more concerned with your character than your reputation.

Your character is what you really are, while your reputation is

merely what others think you are.

Author unknown

WHAT CANCER CANNOT DO

It is important to remember what cancer Cannot Do.

It cannot cripple love

It cannot shatter hope

It cannot corrode faith

It cannot destroy peace

It cannot kill friendship

It cannot suppress memories

It cannot silence courage

It cannot invade the soul

It cannot steal eternal life

It cannot conquer the spirit

Author Unknown

Someone once said:

If there is a light in the soul

There will be beauty in the person.

If there is beauty in the person

There will be harmony in the house.

If there is harmony in the house

There will be order in the Nation.

If there is order in the Nation

There will be Peace in the world.

Author unknown

Four things you can't get back:

The word after it's said

The stone after it's thrown

The occasion after it's missed

The time after it's gone.

Evolver Social Movement

From William Golding's desk:

I think women are foolish to pretend they are equal to men.

They are far more superior and always have been.

Whatever you give a woman, she will give greater.

If you give her a sperm, she will give you a baby.

If you give her a house, she will give you a home.

If you give her groceries, she will give you a meal.

If you give her a smile, she will give you her heart.

She multiplies and enlarges what is given to her.

SO, if you give her any crap,

Be ready to receive a ton of it in return.

William Golding, Novelist, Playwright and Poet

1911-1993

In life, we cannot change the time; but we MUST make the best of each year.

Anonymous

REWARDS OF GIVING

———◆•◈•◆———

May your home be blessed with the courage

of compassionate hearts,

seeing the greatness in every soul.

May the garden of your heart blossom

with even the smallest of kind acts,

giving your life the gift of divine PURPOSE.

Anonymous

TIME IS PRECIOUS; DO NOT WASTE IT.

Anonymous

BEING A FRIEND

———————◆•◆•◆———————

Love

I love you,

Not only for what you are,

But for what I am

When I am with you.

I love you,

Not only for what

You have made of yourself,

But for what

You are making of me.

I love you

For the part of me

That you bring out;

Doris Bourgeois-Darling

I love you

For putting your hand

Into my heaped-up heart

And passing over

All the foolish, weak things

That you can't help

Dimly seeing there,

And for drawing out

Into the light

All the beautiful belongings

That no one else had looked

Quite far enough to find.

I love you because you

Are helping me to make

Of the lumber of my life

Not a tavern

But a temple;

Out of the works

Of my every day

Not a reproach

But a song.

I love you

Because you have done

More than any creed

Could have done

To make me good,

And more than any fate

To make me happy.

You have done it

Without a touch,

Without a word,

Without a sign.

You have done it

By being yourself.

Author: Elizabeth Barrett Browning

NEW ENGLANDERS

Forget Rednecks. Here is what Jeff Foxworthy has to say about New Englanders:

"If someone in a Home Depot store offers you assistance, and they do not work there, you are in New England".

"If you've worn shorts and a parka at the same time, you live in New England".

"If you had a lengthy telephone conversation with someone who dialed the wrong number, you live in New England".

"If vacation means going anywhere south of New York City for the weekend, you live in New England".

"If you measure distance in hours, you live in New England".

"If you know several people who have hit a deer more than once, you live in New England".

"If you have switched from heat to A/C in the same day and back again, you live in New England".

"If you can drive 75 mph through two feet of snow during a raging blizzard without flinching, you live in New England".

"If you install security lights on your house and garage, but leave both unlocked you live in New England".

"If you carry jumpers in your car and your wife knows how to use them, you live in New England".

"If the speed limit on the highway is 55 mph, you're going 80 and everyone is passing you, you live in New England".

"If driving is better in the winter because the potholes are filled with snow, you live in New England".

"If you know all four seasons: Almost winter, winter, still winter and road construction, you live in New England".

"If you have more miles on your snow blower than your car, you live in New England".

"If you find 10 degrees "a little chilly," you live in New England".

"If there's a Dunkin's Donuts on every corner, you live in New England".

"If you actually understand these jokes and send them to all your New England friends and others, you live or have lived in New England".

GOOD THOUGHTS FOR THE DAY

I've learned... that the best classroom in the world is at the feet of an elderly person.

I've learned... that when you're in love, it shows.

I've learned... that just one person saying to me: "You've made my day!" makes my day.

I've learned... that having a child fall asleep in your arms is one of the most peaceful feelings in the world.

I've learned... that being kind is more important than being right.

I've learned... that you should never say no to a gift from a child.

I've learned... that I can always pray for someone when I don't have the strength to help in some other way.

I've learned… that no matter how serious your life requires you to be, everyone needs a friend to act goofy with.

I've learned… that sometimes all a person needs is a hand to hold and a heart to understand.

I've learned… that simple walks with my father around the block on summer nights when I was a child did wonders for me as an adult.

I've learned… that life is like a roll of toilet paper; the closer it gets to the end, the faster it goes.

I've learned… that we should be glad God doesn't give us everything we ask for.

I've learned… that money doesn't buy class.

I've learned… that it's those small daily happenings that make life so spectacular.

I've learned… that under everyone's hard shell is someone who wants to be appreciated and loved.

I've learned… that to ignore the facts does not change the facts.

I've learned… that when you plan to get even with someone, you are only letting that person continue to hurt you.

I've learned… that love, not time, heals all wounds.

I've learned… that the easiest way for me to grow as a person is to surround myself with people smarter than I am.

I've learned… that everyone you meet deserves to be greeted with a smile.

I've learned… that no one is perfect until you fall in love with them.

I've learned.... that life is tough, but I'm tougher.

I've learned... that opportunities are never lost; someone will take the ones you miss.

I've learned... that when you harbor bitterness, happiness will go dock elsewhere.

I've learned... that I wish I could have told my mom that I love her one more time before she passed away.

I've learned... that one should keep his words both soft and tender, because tomorrow he may have to eat them.

I've learned... that a smile is an inexpensive way to improve your looks.

I've learned... that when your newly born grandchild holds your little finger in his little fist, that you're hooked for life.

I've learned... that everyone wants to live on top of the mountain, but all the happiness and growth occur while you're climbing it.

I've learned... that the less time I have to work with, the more things I get done.

HAPPY FRIENDSHIP WEEK TO ALL !

Andy Rooney

QUOTES TO LIVE BY

The dream is the motivation,

If the dream is big enough the facts don't count...

Never lose sight of your dream.

Don't let anybody steal your dream.

There is no luck involved in success,

It is the result of hard work.

The person who says: "I can't do it"

Is defeated before he begins.

Success is a decision.

Be a winner not a whiner.

Either control your attitude

Or it controls you.

If you don't stand for something,

You will fall for anything.

Enthusiasm is contagious.

Aspiration requires perspiration.

Nothing good never comes easy.

Never make a promise you can't keep.

You are the master of your own destiny.

Listening is as much an art as speaking.

A goal is a dream with a plan.

Keep your criticism to yourself…

People have enough of their own.

A lot of people fail because

They believe they aren't good enough to succeed.

Author unknown

May you have…

———————◆•◈•◆———————

Enough Happiness to keep you sweet

Enough Trials to keep you strong

Enough Sorrow to keep you human

Enough Hope to keep you happy

Enough Failure to keep you humble

Enough Success to keep you eager

Enough Friends to give comfort

Enough Wealth to meet your needs

Enough Enthusiasm to look forward

Enough Faith to banish depression

Enough Determination to make each

Day better than yesterday…

Doris Bourgeois-Darling

Irish poem Author unknown

THE STORY OF FOUR PEOPLE

———————◆•◉•◆———————

There is a story of four people named:

EVERYBODY, SOMEBODY, ANYBODY and NOBODY.

There was an important job to be done and

Everybody was asked to do it.

Anybody could have done it,

But Nobody did it.

Somebody got angry about that because

It was Everybody's job.

Everybody thought that

Anybody could do it,

But Nobody realized that

Everybody wouldn't do it, consequently, it wound up that

Nobody told Anybody, so Everybody blamed Somebody.

Author unknown

TODAY > TOMORROW > YESTERDAY

Let us live but one day at a time: TODAY.

HEAVEN'S GROCERY STORE

I was walking down life's highway, a long time ago; one day I saw a sign that read: "Heaven's Grocery Store".

As I got a little closer, the door came open wide, and when I came to myself I was standing inside.

I saw a host of angels, they were standing everywhere. One handed me a basket and said: "My child, shop with care".

Everything a Christian needed was in that Grocery Store. And all you could not carry, you could come back the next day for more.

First, I got some Patience. Love was in the same row. Further down was Understanding, you need that everywhere you go.

I got a box of Wisdom, a bag or two of Faith. I just couldn't miss the Holy Ghost, he was all over the place.

I stopped to get some Strength and Courage to help me run this race.

By then my basket was getting full, but I remembered I needed some Grace.

I didn't forget Salvation; for Salvation, that was free, so I tried to get enough of that to save you and me.

Then, I started to the counter to pay my grocery bill, for I thought I had everything to do my Master's Will.

As I went up the aisle, I saw Prayer and I had to put that in for I knew when I stepped outside, I would run right into sin.

Peace and Joy were hanging near, so I helped myself.

Then I started toward the counter and said to the Angel: Now how much do I owe? He just smiled and said: "Take them everywhere you go."

Again, I smiled and said, "How much do I owe?"

He smiled again and said: "My child, Jesus paid your bill a long time ago."

Author unknown

CHAPTER 63

CJCA

Christian Foundation For Children and Aged

For many years, David and I sponsored young boys from Mexico through the above or through our Parish. The boys were between eight and fifteen years of age. The pledge was twenty dollars monthly to help their family while they attended school. Their sponsorship would end when out of school.

We sponsored Mario, Jose and Jesus.

Here is a letter sent to us in 2009 by Jose Angel:

Dear David and Doris:

I hope you are doing well. We are pretty fine too.

My birthday was on April 19th; my brother's birthday was on April 11th.

We had a family gathering and it was great. I'm 15 years old now and my brother is 12.

I'm finishing middle school. My favorite subjects are: Math and Physical Education. I like running and do exercise. After finishing middle school, I am going to study Mechanics, because I really love cars.

Let me tell you that we visit our grandparents on summer vacation, we

all go to a river and have a nice picnic.

I'm going to study harder next year. I just want to learn more about

mechanics. It would be great if I run my own business (a workshop).

There was a virus called Influenza, some days ago. We were washing our hands lots of time and were wearing mouth covers. My family and friends didn't catch that virus.

Well, Bye for now,

Your Godson,

Jose Angel Alvarez

Translated by Noe Guerra

CHAPTER 64

Volunteers

This poem was given to me by our three leaders at the St. Vincent de Paul Thrift Shop: Mary, Pat, and Maury who described our work as truly a "Mission of Love and Friendship".

VOLUNTEERS

Many will be shocked to find, when the day of judgement nears,

That there's a special place in Heaven, set aside for volunteers.

Furnished with big recliners, satin couches and footstools,

Where there are no committee chairs,

No yard sales or rest area coffee to serve.

No traffic problems, Sunday mornings.

No classes to prepare or activities to do.

Telephone lists will be outlawed.

But a finger snap will bring cool drinks.

And gourmet dinners and treats fit for a king.

You ask, who will serve these privileged few

And work for all they're worth.

Why, all those who reaped the benefits,

And not once volunteered on Earth.

Author unknown

HAPPY NATIONAL VOLUNTEER WEEK

TO OUR GOOD FRIEND, DORIS!!!

All the residents and staff want to thank you for all that you do and for coming here every Friday with all the fun and support.

You are a gem and we would like to present this little gift in honor of National Volunteer Week!

Best wishes from all your friends at Mashpee Care!

"CELEBRATING PEOPLE IN ACTION"

I started volunteering at the Milford Regional Medical Center in November 2014 and I volunteer to the present day, hopefully bringing smiles to patients and staff as I deliver books and magazines for their use and pleasure.

Helping with the food pantry "Fish and Loaves" luncheons at our neighbor's parish St. Blaise in our town, as well as helping my friend Palma from St. Brendan Parish with the "Baby Shower" for needy mothers in the archdiocese of Boston.

Volunteering is a very satisfying activity and I firmly believe that we get more satisfaction from volunteering than the recipient does.

CHAPTER 65

The Millenium Review

June 2000 David retired from his 30-year employment with the Town of Wellesley.

July 2001 The purchase of our home in Mashpee MA.

September 11th, 2001 Disastrous terrorist attack on our country.

February 3rd, 2002 The NE Patriots won the Super Bowl with Adam Vinatieri's help (my hero!).

March 2002 My retirement from Milford Regional Hospital after twenty-eight years.

May 2002 Lease of Franklin condo to Jeff Recker.

May 22nd, 2002 Move to Mashpee.

May 15th, 2003 Closing on 2007 Franklin Crossing condominium.

May 27th, 2003 Purchase of a new silver Buick Century. Very exciting!

June 5th, 2004 Jack and Lisa's wedding. Beautiful!

July 4th, 2004 Celebrations in Franklin.

October 4th, 2004 Pennsylvania trip with the 50+ Club. Amazing!

April 2nd, 2005 Another fantastic trip to Washington DC with the 50+ Club.

May 19th, 2005 Father's Day PawSox game in Pawtucket RI was a blast.

May 21st, 2005 Farewell party for Mark J. moving to Houston TX.

July 1st to 4th, 2005 Mark's trip to Texas (I was thrilled to hear from him every evening).

July 8th, 2005 Flight to Grand Rapids, Michigan, with David Jr. and Tina to Dave's nephew's wedding.

November 27th, 2005 Lisa Libby Birren's baby shower at Ma Glockner's Restaurant, Bellingham.

January 11th, 2006 Auto accident near home in Mashpee.

March 10th, 2006 Flight to Texas to visit Mark and Kristine.

March 22nd, 2006 A great trip to Newport RI with the 50+ Club.

May 13th, 2006 Brianna's First Communion at St. Brendan Church in Bellingham.

May 15th, 2006 Foot surgery by Dr. Lepley at Milford Hospital.

May 28th, 2006 Dave's uncle Bill's ninetieth birthday party at Pippinelle's Restaurant in Franklin.

June 25th, 2006 Sydney's Baptism at St. Brendan Church in Bellingham.

July 8th, 2006 Mark and Kristine's visit.

August 17th, 2006 A trip to Martha's Vineyard.

August 26th, 2006 Dave's fiftieth class reunion at Glen Ellen Club in Millis.

September 28th, 2006 A trip to Vermont was most enjoyable.

November 8th, 2006 Lucy Murphy expired at age eighty-six.

November 2006 Providence Bruins game in honor of John's fortieth birthday.

April 28th, 2007 Mark and Kristine's wedding in Huntsville TX. Lovely!

May 27th, 2007 Cousin Jeannette Sousa lost her long fight to cancer.

May 29th, 2007 Mrs. Reed also went to her Maker at age ninety-two.

August 15th, 2007 Trip to Maine and Nashua NH.

September 10th, 2007 Right knee arthroscopy done by Dr. Paul Dimond, after a running injury.

October 17th, 2007 Sophia Anne Bourgeois was born, a healthy baby.

November 5th, 2007 Trip to Vermont, cold and snowy.

February 4th, 2008 Dave purchased his brand new Toyota Camry, which he still drives today.

March 25th, 2008 To Texas to visit five-month-old Sophia.

August 9th, 2008 Mark, Kris and Sophia came for a most welcomed visit which we all enjoyed.

April 20th, 2009 Chloe Jane was born. Her two brothers were thrilled to have a baby sister.

January 9th, 2010 Spunki expired at Dr. Mark's office, from kidney failure. He was almost eighteen years old.

February 27th, 2010 To Connecticut to watch Jackie's cheerleading meet. Impressive!

March 11th, 2010 My brother's freak accident, a bad fall.

March 25th, 2010 Ronald went to his Maker, after a week and a half in a coma.

July 13th, 2010 My cousin Helen Delorey expired at a Hospice facility in Scarborough ME.

CHAPTER 66

Happenings, Here and around the World

April Fool's Day 1997. Blizzard conditions hit our area. Living at the Franklin Crossing condominium at the time, we got buried with thirty-two inches of snow in twenty-four hours. Worcester suffered the highest snowfall amount since 1905.

On September 5th, 1997, Mother Teresa of Calcutta, beloved missionary of the poor in India, died at age eighty-seven. She founded the religious order of the Sisters of Notre Dame and was the recipient of the Nobel Peace Prize in 1979 for her prestigious work with the poor.

September 11th, 2001 at 8:45 am, American Airlines Flight 11, en route to Los Angeles from Boston crashed into the North Tower of the New York World Trade Center.

At 9:03 am, United Airlines Flight 175 also en route to Los Angeles from Boston crashed into the South Tower of the World Trade Center and by 10:29 both towers had collapsed.

At 9:43 am, American Airlines Flight 77 from Washington to Los Angeles crashed into the Pentagon.

At 9:48 am, the Capitol and the West Wing of the White House were evacuated. President George W. Bush calls the crashes "an apparent terrorist attack on our country".

At 10:37 am, confirmation that United Airlines Flight 93 en route to San Francisco from New Jersey had crashed in Pennsylvania; none of forty-five people aboard survived.

In early afternoon President Bush was flown to an undisclosed location. The Boston Herald provided this information.

The mastermind of the 9/11/01 terrorist attacks, Osama Bin Laden was killed by a US raid in early May 2011, a Great Feat for America, a decade later.

April 2005, our beloved Pope John Paul II went to his eternal reward after serving as our shepherd for twenty-seven years. He had visited Boston in 1979 and was very popular with the young generation, high school and college students. He was famous for his many trips around the world and especially for the "World Youth Day". He was canonized on April 27th, 2014, along with his predecessor Pope John XXIII. It would be wise to invoke those two saints to intercede in our behalf.

April 29th, 2011 The Royal Wedding. Former college sweethearts British Prince William and Kate Middleton, a commoner, now known as the Duke and Duchess of Cambridge, exchanged their wedding vows in front of 2,000 guests at Westminster Abbey in London and billions of TV viewers worldwide. The elegant ceremony took place at the same altar where Prince William's parents were married thirty years ago. The Duke and Duchess of Cambridge are now the proud parents of Prince George and Princess Charlotte and a third child is expected.

CHAPTER 67

2012

This was the year of many changes. On January a Reveal monitor was inserted under the skin in my upper chest to determine if near-syncope is related to heart. The procedure was done at Milford Hospital by Dr. Scott Brownstein assisted by Joseph O'Brien, a technician with Medtronic Device. Dr. Sabeen Chaudry became my cardiologist, whom I still see today.

On January 30th, David had MOHS micrographic surgery to treat skin cancer. This procedure was done successfully at a medical center in Watertown MA.

On March 17th, 2012, my granddaughter Jacqueline gave birth to Bradley Francis at 4:53 am in a Connecticut hospital. Her dad John and I visited in the afternoon. Jackie was uncomfortable but happy.

On April 12th, a permanent pacemaker was implanted by Dr. Scott Brownstein and procedure was tolerated well.

Upon my return from Milford Hospital, arrangements were made for two house showings on the following day. One was an offer that was accepted and the buyer wanted to move in, with her six cats, in a short time.

I could not lift over ten pounds for a month; therefore my children were of great help for a few weeks. Brianna was our garage sale coordinator and her services were much appreciated.

A Millis MA Stoneybrook apartment became our new dwelling from mid-April to mid-July. NOT our or Toby's favorite place.

Finally, it came to an end as we closed on the house on May 17th. The previous day, I had spent eleven hours of preparation and had made a wrong turn on the way to Millis on our way home, arriving home at 11:30 pm. That had made for a very long and exhausting day. We were in Centerville the following morning. All went well, including the walk through. The closing on our home at 9 High Sachem Road, Mashpee, was with mixed feelings, after ten years at that address. Our consolation was that we would be closer to our family.

On July 18th, we moved to our new abode: Townhouse 302 Village Lane, in Bellingham MA. We were happy to be THERE. We met our friendly neighbors at our new 55+ community. I thought to myself: "I think I'm going to like it here", like Annie said at Daddy Warbucks' house. Our Lane is a happy one at Village Lane, Bellingham. We finally settled in, with our friend Louise's help; she is a very neat painter. On August 5th, a freak accident in our garage required eleven sutures on Dave's right eyebrow.

August 16th, our fifteenth wedding anniversary was spent in Kennebunk, Maine.

On December 14th, Sandy Hook Elementary School in Newtown, Connecticut, became a horror scene. A deranged young man shot twenty young students and six adults. Our whole country was deeply affected by this senseless carnage.

CHAPTER 68

Lori~Ann's Medical Journey

On Labor Day 2012 Phil, Lori-Ann, Chloe and I went apple picking at The Big Apple in a nearby town. Lori-Ann was our driver. She complained of neck pain and frequent headaches.

The following week, after experiencing blurred vision, she was advised to see her primary care physician, Dr. M. Woodward, a visit that she delayed due to a change in her health care insurance.

She drove herself to the Milford Hospital Emergency Room at 10:00 pm on September 13th and she was admitted.

The following day, after a CAT scan and an MRI, two lesions were detected in her head: one frontal and the other at the base of her skull. That may explain the neck pain.

After being seen by Dr. Woodward, Lori-Ann was admitted to Boston Medical Center, where she underwent several tests, such as blood work, bone scan, MRI, PET scan and x-rays. On September 21st, she heard the bad news: a diagnosis of Multiple Myeloma.

Multiple Myeloma is a rare type of blood cancer which affects the plasma cells in the blood of bone marrow, which weans away portion of the bone. The plasma cells, a type of white blood cells, are part of body's immune system and when healthy, help to fight infection and disease by producing antibodies. The cause of Multiple Myeloma is unknown and it is incurable BUT it is treatable!

On September 24th, a plan of action was presented to my daughter. On September 25th, she was discharged to home. She started radiation therapy a few days later, from Monday to Friday for ten days, and lab tests daily. The side effects from steroids that she experienced included worsening vision problems, headaches, anxiety, weakness, tiredness, and insomnia.

Dana-Farber / Brigham and Women's Cancer Center opened its doors across the street from Milford Medical Center in 2008 and has been a godsend to our community. Lori-Ann was privileged to be treated at that amazingly well staffed medical facility, under Dr. McNulty's care, and at a nearby facility, this great oncology center approximately ten miles from her home. One of her caring nurses at Dana-Farber was her childhood friend Mary-Beth Rapko Proulx.

Multiple Myeloma has few risk factors; however, some risk factors have been identified, including: being fifty years old, or, usually being in mid-sixties; being male; being African-American; being overweight or obese; having been exposed to radiation; being employed in the petroleum industry. Lori-Ann, at age thirty-six, obviously did not fit those criterias.

Among the possible symptoms of the illness Multiple Myeloma are: Calcium/Renal/Anemia/Bone (CRAB). Kidney failure can be caused by elevated levels of the M protein. Anemia-related fatigue occurs when having too few red blood cells or when the red blood cells are being replaced by Myeloma cells in the bone marrow.

Additional possible signs: weakness or numbness, especially in the legs; unintended weight loss; bone injury, pain or fracture, especially in back, pelvis, ribs and skull. The best tool for diagnosis is a bone marrow biopsy, which can be very painful; not Lori-Ann's favorite.

On October 23rd, chemotherapy started with two weeks of treatment and one week off. It was well tolerated, with no side effects. Lori-Ann's vision improved and she had fewer headaches. She even worked part-time for some time; then she was off for months.

There were good and bad days ahead. She was seen by Dr. Kumar, a neurologist, after experiencing tingling of her left eye, face and limbs, ringing in the ears, and a sloshing feeling in her head, followed by headaches, weakness and tiredness.

By early November, Lori-Ann stated feeling better and she had no more headaches. The chemotherapy continued until mid-April and the preoperative protocol was started for the Self Stem Cell Transplant. Lori-Ann was admitted to Brigham & Women's Hospital in Boston on May 12th, Mother's Day. Millions of cells were harvested and blessed. Matt witnessed the blessing. The successful transplant took place on May 15th and Lori-Ann returned home two weeks later on Memorial Day. She was to recuperate at home with her devoted family, her husband Matt, their sons Matthew and Tyler, and her mother-in-law Carol. Even little Chloe was a great help. Her wonderful neighbors, friends and coworkers provided meals and housekeeping, which she very much appreciated. I joined the effort as much as I could as well.

Praise to all her coworkers at MG Salon and Spa in Medway MA for all their generous support in so many ways. What impressed me the most was that those coworkers picked up many of Lori-Ann's clients and gave her the money. How amazing is that?

With a lot of prayers, support and medical intervention, Lori-Ann made a complete recovery and, in my opinion, became physically stronger and mentally more highly spirited.

Here is a message from Lori-Ann prior to her self stem cell transplant:

March 13th, 2013

Howdy:

Just wanted to give you an update: Starting my second round (4 weeks) with the new treatment. I'm happy that with this new treatment I have a lot more energy, no nausea and a lot less burning and tingling in my feet. It still looks like the stem cell transplant prep work will be starting at the end of April. It takes a couple of weeks before the actual transplant; like heavy chemo, shots, x-rays, stem cell collecting and my least favorite:

bone biopsy. I believe the transplant itself is really easy:) I will be in the hospital for about 3 weeks. Then, just rest and keep away from germs when I come home. Maybe my germ freak friends could give me pointers; you know who you are:)

And by the time I get home, the snow should be all melted!

I hope everyone is doing well.

Love,

Lori-Ann

Worry looks around

Sorry looks back

Faith looks up

So Have Faith

Anonymous

On May 1st, 2016: Multiple Myeloma Research Foundation Road Race

Participant Lori-Ann Zajac

Distance 5K (3.1mi.)

Time 25:44 Pace 8:17

Place 140 overall

Division 30-39 Place 17

CHAPTER 69

2013

On February 8th started the blizzard of 2013. It lasted until the following day and dumped two feet of snow in our area, but there were no power outages.

I was afflicted with the PIE syndrome at that time. Our cat Toby seemed amazed at all the outdoors covered in white and he was unable to enjoy his morning stroll. Fortunately the rest of the month was not very stormy.

We enjoyed Connor's impressive performance at a swim meet in Framingham with first, second and fifth place, respectively. Connor is very dedicated to his sport but he is also is a great student. He makes us proud.

On February 28th, 2013, Pope Benedict XVI's resignation came as a shock to the world. The eighty-five-year old German Pope, after eight years of Papacy, stepped down as the 265th leader of the world's 1.2 billion Catholics. He will keep the name Benedict XVI and will be referred to as Pope Emeritus and will continue to wear the white cassock. The Fisherman's ring, which is used to officially seal documents to ensure authenticity, was destroyed. This is to make sure no one will forge a document in the pope's name after he retires or dies. He will not wear the signature ruby red shoes in retirement, but the Pontifical Swiss Guard will continue to guard Benedict in his retirement. Pope Emeritus Benedict XVI has pledged to place himself entirely under the authority of the new pope, even though the decision to live at the Vatican in his retirement, to be called "Emeritus Pope" and your "Holiness", and to wear the white cassock were his choices.

On March 13th, Cardinal Bergoglio of Argentina became the 266th Pope of the Catholic Church, the first from Latin America, and the first Jesuit to become pope. He humbly took the name Francis in honor of St. Francis of Assisi, venerated for his spirit of reform and for his care for the poor. The 76-year-old Pontiff was labeled "a gift to Latin America", where the people of Buenos Aires were elated. His views on abortion, same-sex marriage, transgendering, and adoption of children by same-sex couples are very strong, which has brought him some controversy in Argentina. While addressing the throng of faithful, in his humility, Pope Francis asked for prayers to his intentions. In September 2015, Pope Francis came to America and was most welcomed in Washington DC, in Pennsylvania and in New York. Pope Francis is well liked by most, including non Catholics.

April 15th The Boston Marathon Terror Attack: Dave and I were volunteering with Dana-Farber in Newton near the 17th mile mark of the 117th running of the famous Boston Marathon. Our shift was from 11:00 am to 3:00 pm. At the close of our shift, emergency vehicles with sirens blaring went speeding by our post. Runners were still going by. We learned of the explosion via the car radio on our way home: at 2:50 pm an explosion had gone off near the finish line. This explosion was followed by another one ten seconds later and a hundred yards further. The ground trembled. The finish line area became like a battle zone. There was a selfless rush of people to help others. Three spectators were killed and at least 264 were wounded. Another life was lost in relation of this vicious attack when MIT police officer Sean Collier, 26, was also killed, a few days later by one of the attackers. President Obama vowed that those responsible for this horrible event will feel the full weight of justice. He also praised the heroism of responders in Boston. On that INFAMOUS day, the new motto "Boston Strong" was created.

On the evening of April 19th, in Watertown MA, the Boston Marathon attackers were captured: two brothers of Chechen origin. One was killed by the police during the capture. This brought an end to the nightmare. President Obama applauded Boston for not allowing the terrorists to prevail: "They failed because the people of Boston refused to be intimidated."

On Saturday April 27th, Toby left on a two-day adventure which left me in distress. I initiated an extensive search for my beloved pet with posters on telephone poles, which did not bring him home. He returned home at 4:30 am on Monday, looking healthy. His whereabouts? He never divulged his secret yet. He also did not resist his welcome home hug.

August burst out with activities: Marcel's fiftieth and Dave's seventy-fifth birthdays were celebrated. We also attended Dave's class reunion, with very friendly people. I joined the Circle Of Care, a home-care agency and I enjoyed caring for the elderly, especially a nice gentleman, Phil Baril; and a very special lady, Millie Lombard, who in a short six months left an imprint on my soul. She was very intelligent, spiritual and very witty.

Janice's forty-ninth birthday was celebrated at our home with a surprise visit from our friend Beverly-An and Janice's friend Christine from Texas. The birthday cake was homemade by Phil and Brianna. We had a great time.

Dave and I participated in one of the Damplo / Berardi family traditions by attending the celebrations for the feast day of St. Agrippina, an Italian princess and the patron saint of a small town in Sicily.

On August 13th, Dave and I drove to Mystic and Stonington, Connecticut, where we enjoyed a few wonderful days.

September and October, we headed north. Kennebunk ME was gorgeous at that time of year. The Boston Red Sox won the World Series defeating the St. Louis Cardinals 6-1 in game 6. This was the Red Sox' eighth championship since 1903. We are very proud fans and the Boston festivities proved it.

CHAPTER 70

2014

On Sunday, January 12ᵗʰ, eight-year-old Lexi and seven-year-old Sean Munroe suffocated in a chest at their home in Franklin MA. A devastating tragedy for not only the family but for the whole town.

On Monday, April 21ˢᵗ, Team Hoyt: Dick and Rick, a father and son racing team, completed their thirty-second and last Boston Marathon. Rick, 52, has cerebral palsy and is a spastic quadriplegic. They form a very impressive duo and the 73-year-old Dick has always been an inspiration to all.

Lori-Ann and her family left for a twelve-day trek to England to visit their friends. On May 12ᵗʰ, Amelia (Millie) Lombard expired. Dave and I were Texas bound at the time. More to follow on that great adventure.

On June 6ᵗʰ, we celebrated my oldest grandson Matthew's high school graduation in Franklin.

On June 30ᵗʰ, we were off to New Hampshire's Mount Washington with Dave Jr. and Tina to ride The Rail. Interesting.

We enjoyed the July Fourth celebrations at the Franklin Commons, as we always do, with the Zajac boys.

On July 13ᵗʰ, Mark Jason was hospitalized with cardiac problems. Stents were successfully inserted for blocked arteries. Mark was doing well and returned to work four days later. A change in lifestyle has been very beneficial to him.

On July 23rd, Connor participated in a swim meet in New Brunswick, Canada. He performed well as usual.

On August 6th, the demolition of the fieldhouse at the old Franklin High School began. The rest of the building was gone.

On August 10th, we attended Janice's fiftieth birthday party at Eaton Place in Franklin.

On August 17th, we had a family get-together at Village Lane to bid Phil a safe solo trip to New Brunswick.

In mid-September, we left on another trip to Kennebunk ME. We had enjoyable fall weather.

On September 29th, John started his new employment at McKesson in Walpole MA.

On October 30th, the longest-serving Boston Mayor, Thomas Menino, lost his battle to cancer at age seventy-one. He was remembered for his dedication to public service for over twenty years. "I just did my job. Nothing special". He was the city's first Italian American mayor and he said he loved every minute of it. He left an imprint on the HUB.

The Ebola virus was in full swing with four cases reported inside the United States.

November marked the beginning of my new assignment: Milford Regional Medical Center VOLUNTEER.

December 7th was the occasion for Sydney's fun-to-watch swim meet at Keefe Technical School in Framingham. It had been a cold month but no snow as yet.

CHAPTER 71

A very Special Trip to Texas

On May 12th, 2014, at 5:30 am Dave and I started out on our trip to Texas to visit Mark and his family. We followed the route mapped out by AAA. It was a very slow morning through Connecticut and New York, with multiple slow-downs and gridlock due to an accident on route 287 West. Finally we entered New Jersey at 11:00 am. Vehicle fuel was $3.55/gal.

In the afternoon, after an hour and a half at the driver's seat, we had moved 2.3 miles. A seven-car pileup on I-78, about six miles ahead left three people dead when a tractor trailer hit a vehicle and caused a domino effect. After being advised by a young truck driver to divert to a side road, and after circling around for a while, we were saved by our GPS. I could sense Mark's disappointment when he called us that evening. We were safe! God rest the souls of the three who did not survive that tragic accident. That was a disheartening day.

Day 2 We had a good early start and were proceeding on Route 81W with speed limit 70 mi/hr. There were more trucks on the road than I had ever seen in my entire life. I prayed for their safety. We arrived at Kingsport TN at 4:00 pm and the Comfort Inn looked very inviting after reaching 757.7 miles. We met a very talented and interesting young man at Pizza Hut. Car fuel was $3.75/gal. This was a good traveling day. Mark was pleased with our progress that day.

Day 3 I drove through the center of Birmingham, Alabama, at noontime in pouring rain. Traffic was busy and it was nerve-wracking but I managed well. The time zone changed somewhere in Alabama. Today, at Tombusca Mississippi's Visitors' Center, where the staff was very friendly and helpful, I tried to call my friend Geri Lapio, a Mississippi native, and mistakenly called my neighbor Edna in Bellingham. Edna was sick on that day. Mile 1363 and 150 miles from Louisiana. A cool evening, temperatures being in the 40s.

Day 4 Thursday, May 15th, we left Tallulah, Louisiana, at 6:30 am after a hearty breakfast at the Waffle House. There we encountered a sheriff, who strangely parked very close to our vehicle. We arrived at Nacogdoches, Texas, at noon and Mark met us in front of the library and guided us to his neck of the woods. His employer, Elliott Electric Supply Company, and the Best Western Motel where we stayed are in the vicinity of Mark and Kristine's apartment on Old Tyler Road. This location is very convenient for the Bourgeois family, as both Mark and Kristine work at Elliott Electric.

After we had registered at the Best Western Motel, Kristine picked us up and we went to the Christ Episcopal School and surprised Sophia. We all were very excited and we took her home, where we spent time with her. She introduced us to her friend "the big old tree" where she spends much time playing near this huge tree in her backyard. Sophia is very energetic, with a vivid imagination. The entertainment tonight: Frozen theme songs and dance. Good choreography by Sophia.

Friday, May 16th Mark was off from work and took us to visit his workplace. He was very proud of his lovely new office, its decor reflecting Mark's taste, the bacon trivia especially, and his own abstract graphic art. We met many of the hundred staff members, all very welcoming and pleasant. Kristine worked until noon, then we had lunch at The General Store Restaurant. Sophia spent the night with us at the motel, where we watched the movie Frozen on her Touch Pad. Mark, Kris and her son Dylan, 19, went to see the movie Godzilla.

On Saturday morning, May 17th, after our continental breakfast, Sophia and I had a thirty-minute walk on a quiet road on this beautiful morning. Later, we met with Mark and Kristine and went to the Visitors Center for a walking tour of the oldest town in Texas: Nacogdoches. The hour-and-a-half walk was long for little six-year-old Sophia. She was happy to ride on her daddy's shoulders. We still enjoy wearing our special 9 Flags tee-shirts as a reminder of that special day. Lunch at Butcher Boy was great. That is where I sampled fried green tomatoes. Sophia spent another night with us at the motel; a quiet evening with bath and reading time.

Sunday, May 18th We went to mass at Sacred Heart Church, a nice church with many similarities with St. Brendan Church. After spending some time with Sophia at the church's children playground, we went to Lufkin, about thirty miles away, to visit a zoo. It had multiple species of animals, birds and reptiles and some ostriches showing their beautiful plumage. We also enjoyed a train ride during which Sophia lost her favorite hat, which was later retrieved by Grandma.

Monday, May 19th Mark and Sophia, Dave and I went to a park and then we proceeded to Millard's Crossing, a small village assembled from old homes moved from downtown Nacogdoches. Mrs. Millard, a very influential socialite from that town, raised funds and provided funds to move many historic homes from sections of town in fear that those homes would be destroyed or used as business buildings. Instead, these relocated old homes became small museums and tourist attractions. We had an interesting tour of these preserved treasures, which included a church and a school. Sophia was very excited and we were all having fun. We all enjoyed a Chinese food dinner, followed by dessert at the Marble Slab Creamery. In the evening, Sophia and I planted some purple petunias in their front yard.

On Tuesday, May 20th, Kristine picked us up at the motel in her nice Nissan Versa and we spent more time at Elliott Electric, meeting with Mark and other coworkers, all pleasant individuals including their CEO William Elliott. We watched Sophia's gymnastics class then enjoyed a delicious pasta dinner by Dylan. Kudos to the chef!

Wednesday, May 21st We went to Sophia's school at 8:00 am for the 8:15 chapel time, presided by the principal, Mrs. Russell. Christ Episcopal Church School is very well organized and conducive to well-mannered and disciplined children. My granddaughter thrives there and loves attending the school, which makes me very happy. It was a pleasure to meet Mrs. Unger, Sophia's teacher, and her best friend Preston and his parents, Jeremy and Heather. The evening brought photo sessions and sad goodbyes as we were preparing to return home the next morning.

Thursday, May 22nd On the road again, along Route 20E heading towards Louisiana on a crispy 470 F early morning. I drove the first 120 miles then felt tired, sensing the PIE syndrome coming on. David felt good and drove most of the day. I started on my prescribed medication for my thirty-year-old medical problem, with some relief. I prayed a lot and we listened to music as well. We had breakfast at the Waffle House in Tallulah LA and, again, the same parking space, the same table, the same waitress; but no sheriff this time.

In Mississippi, between Monroe and Vicksburg, a mishap happened. We hit a large truck tire lying on the road, which could not be avoided. Upon examination, the front bumper of our car was damaged and fluid was dripping midway under the vehicle. We stopped at the Visitors' Center where we were instructed to proceed towards Vicksburg, to the Cannon Toyota Dealership. They took good care of us, at no cost. Evidence of Southern Hospitality. The diagnosis: a damaged engine cover, which could be repaired at a later time; and the dripping was from the air conditioner, which is normal. Praise the Lord! The numerous prayers recited throughout the trip kept us safe; no doubt.

Friday, May 23rd A smooth riding day, uneventful in spite of the start of the Memorial Day weekend. I was feeling better, so I drove a longer distance that day, but felt very tired afterwards. We had an early night at the Days' Inn Motel in Virginia. After a restful night, we left early on our last leg of our journey home. Dave did most of the driving. My PIE syndrome was getting worse.

Saturday, May 24th We were heading towards Harrisburg, Pennsylvania, when we lost our way but our faithful GPS took us back on track, avoiding the Catskills Mountains. Going through Connecticut, the fuel was the highest seen on the entire trip at $4.02. We arrived home at 5:35 pm, tired but so happy to be home and to reunite with our big cat Toby. We had trekked approximately 3,450 miles (round trip) and were proud of ourselves for our accomplishment.

We called my granddaughter Jackie on her twenty-first birthday. Although it was a slow progress, I fully recovered from the PIE syndrome episode.

CHAPTER 72

2015

January 1st Our annual Christmas celebrations in Franklin and a great time with the family as usual.

January 18th The New England Patriots' Big Win! their Super Bowl qualifier.

January 26th Waking up from a sleepy winter, we were surprised by a blizzard with high wind gusts, low temperatures and an accumulation of twenty-six inches of snow in a span of two days. A travel ban was ordered although a standstill. Luckily we had no power outages. Cape Cod was not so fortunate.

February 1st The NE Patriots defeated the National Football Conference Champions Seattle Seahawks 28-24 for their fourth title at the University of Phoenix Stadium in Glendale, Arizona. Exciting Time!

February 2nd Another foot of snow fell with very cold and slippery conditions. No school for days. In seventeen days more than sixty inches of snow fell, breaking the previous record of 58.8 inches in thirty days in 1978. Snowstorms continued faithfully until March. Record snowfall for Boston: 110 inches in 2015.

February 7th Connor took honors at Boston University: first place for Sectional in freestyle swimming among school teams.

February 7th We attended the funeral of my cousin Dorothy's husband

Frank, in Woburn MA. We met many relatives.

A surprise discovery at St. Brendan Church: I met Marguerite Boucher from Shediac Bridge, New Brunswick, Canada. We had attended the same high school in our hometown. We were unaware of each other's whereabouts.

March 24th A most welcomed visit from my old hospital coworker and friend Maryellen from Jamestown RI.

April 12th A surprise seventy-fifth birthday party at Eaton Place. There was a great turnout. Even old friends from nursing school were present. Thanks to my two wonderful daughters for planning the event.

April 28th At Carson Beach, the Boston 5K walk/run for MMRF with Nancy, Dave and I walking; Lori-Ann, her family and friends, Josh and Kate, running. Lori-Ann's time was 26:51. A good time for all.

June 5th Ficco's Bowladrome, a candlepin bowling alley in Franklin, shut its lanes after seventy-nine years in business. The founder Albert Ficco opened in 1936. His son Paul took over the business in the 1960s. The business grew from ten lanes to twenty lanes and moved to a different location through the years. "I was always around people who were having a good time", exclaimed Mr. Ficco. There are numerous stories to be told… One lady has been in the same league for forty-seven years. "I will miss seeing the jubilant faces of people when they bowled, especially the children" he said, and added: "The alley has been the venue for uncountable first dates, many of which blossomed into happy marriages". For me personally, as well as for my family, happy times were enjoyed at that famous Franklin establishment. The founder, Albert, was a golfer, not a bowler. Interesting!

June 14th Brianna's spring dance recital was AMAZING! She was awarded a $3,000.00 scholarship for her dedication, her good attitude and hard work. We were so proud!

June 21st Father's Day After a long wait, Tyler entertained us at the conclusion of the musical classes he attended. It was well worth the wait.

June 24th A trip to New Hampshire and Maine with the Medway Senior Center members was most enjoyable. A 45-minute harbor cruise from Portsmouth NH, with a good narrator, was very informative. A welcoming delicious lunch at Warrens in Kittery ME was followed by our visit to Hampton Beach NH, where we viewed the famous sand sculptures. Amazing work! Cheers to our excellent bus driver, Jeff, who took us safely home.

July 21st We took a trip to Lenox MA and received a cordial welcome from Bill Cotter, Dave's brother-in-law. We spent some time at Tanglewood and listened to classical orchestras during their morning practices. I recited eight rosaries with many intentions. We visited the Shrine of the Divine Mercy in Stockbridge MA. There were many pious visitors present. The chapel is beautiful and very impressive. St. Mary's Church in Lee is very lovely with a small chapel in the back where eucharistic adoration is available from 6:00 am to midnight daily. Wonderful!

August 12th to 18th We took a trip to New Brunswick and visited many friends and relatives.

August 16th At a family reunion at the Collette's residence in New Brunswick, we celebrated our eighteenth wedding anniversary. Our vacation was much too short.

September 12th We celebrated my sister-in-law Cécile's seventy-fifth with a surprise birthday party at her son Michael's home.

September 27th Nancy's first marathon in Keene NH. Her time was 4:03:28. Great!

October 10th A condominium explosion in Franklin killed a 66-year-old couple. The cause of the explosion is unknown.

October 27th My former daughter-in-law Juliette died unexpectedly, leaving our family devastated. Julie was the loving mother of two daughters and had two grandchildren. She was a very talented young lady.

October 31st to November 25th I suffered an embolism near the site of my pacemaker and my planned corneal transplant surgery had to be postponed. Following visits to vascular and cardiac surgeons, and the use of a compression arm sleeve, in addition to anticoagulant treatment, the embolism was dissolved and the pacemaker was not compromised.

December 4th to 15th Margot was hospitalized at Cape Cod Hospital in Hyannis MA.

December 24th Marcel attended the midnight mass at St. Brendan Church with me and made me very happy. We enjoyed the beautiful angelic voices of the choir of which Dave is a member. We enjoyed unusual temperatures of 70 degrees overnight and upper 60s on Christmas Day. Pansies, five of them, were still alive in our front yard.

December 29th Our first snowfall of the season, a scant amount. December records were smashed for above normal temperatures.

CHAPTER 73

2016

We were having a mild winter as far as snowfall amounts are concerned but we had frequent frigid temperatures in January and early February.

February 19th A right eye corneal transplant was performed by Dr. Joseph Williams at St. Vincent Hospital in Worcester. It was successful and restored my vision to 20/20 after the laser treatment. Thanks be to God.

February 28th Brie's hip hop performance at Milford High School with Dancin' Spirit earned her an "Elite Gold".

Early March Night driving was tolerated well, even on a rainy night. Interesting. My birthday was celebrated at Medway Cafe Restaurant with my family; while my friend and neighbor Edna was having her fractured hip repaired after a fall earlier in the day.

March 18th I purchased a 2012 Chevy Cruze at Imperial Dealer in Mendon MA.

March 24th Holy Thursday service was attended by a large number of our faithful and pious parishioners at St. Brendan Church.

March 27th Easter Sunday. Mother Angelica, founder of the Eternal Word Television Network (EWTN), returned to her Maker.

March 30th I bade adieu to my 2003 Buick Century for a poor trade-in on the Cruze due to the condition of my "old Silver". Cosmetic repair to the Cruze was needed; we did not reunite until well into April. I was anxious.

April 2nd Uncle Bill's one hundredth birthday celebration, Dave's maternal uncle. Great party!

April 21st We spent a wonderful day in Newport, Rhode Island, with the Bellingham Seniors.

April 23rd A surprise twenty-fifth wedding anniversary party for John and Laura Darling in New Hampshire was SUPER!

May 1st The Multiple Myeloma Research Foundation (MMRF) walk/run 5K at Carson Beach took place in Boston. Dave and I participated with other family members.

May 25th A freak accident happened in Franklin, in which I suffered a fractured right foot, a badly bruised right leg and an embolism in my right thigh, and a totally demolished vehicle. All right side injuries were caused by the airbag deflation. Wearing a walking orthopedic boot was no fun but still preferable to crutches.

June 3rd Brianna's high school graduation with a party to follow on June 11th and her final dance recital on June 18th.

June 23rd to 25th Memorable period for our beloved pastor Father Mullen who suffered a myocardial infarction and open heart surgery. He experienced a remarkably speedy recovery.

July 15th Margot moved to Massachusetts from Bethlehem, New Hampshire.

July 17th Matt and Lori-Ann's twentieth wedding anniversary party at Eaton Place and Margot's seventy-first birthday.

July 30th I purchased a Chevy Spark 2014 with low mileage, great to park and good on fuel, a light blue mini vehicle.

August 9th To North Conway NH for a mini-vacation that we well enjoyed.

August 19th Lori-Ann's fortieth birthday celebration at Homestead in Medway was a blast.

October 8th John sought help at Exeter, Rhode Island, with success.

October After another interesting season, David Ortiz, a leader All-Star and champion is retiring. His fourteen years with the Red Sox team brought much joy to the Boston fans. At last this legend walked off the field for the last time. THANKS BIG PAPI !

October 28th Jack Ashburne, Janice's fiancé, was diagnosed with two types of stage 4 cancer affecting four different organs. He was given a life expectancy of two to four months. So sad! A fundraiser was held. It was very successful and helpful to the family.

November 8th, 2016 changed our country as came the end of the most controversial election ever seen. The campaign was actually ridiculous! Donald J. Trump was elected as our forty-fifth president. What have we done? There are no "do-overs" in politics. I am not ashamed to say that I did not vote for either one of those two candidates. My conscience would not permit me to do so.

This message was sent to me prior to our infamous ELECTION:

Regardless of who wins the presidential election in November, we will witness history being made.

If Hillary Clinton wins the US presidential election, it will be the first time in history that two US presidents have slept with each other.

If Donald Trump wins the US presidential election, it will be the first time in history that a billionaire moves into public housing vacated by a black family.

Is this a great country or what?

President Barack Obama's farewell speech, ten days before President Trump's inauguration, was forceful and tearful. After nearly a decade in the limelight, he will become a private citizen. His plans: to take some time off, write a book and immerse himself in a democratic redistricting campaign.

CHAPTER 74

2017

January 1ˢᵗ Our Christmastime celebration at our usual Eaton Place in Franklin were somber this year, with our good friend Jack being so sick. In spite of his suffering, he was with us for a few hours and sat for a last family gathering photo. The whole Bourgeois family was present, except Mark and his family in Texas and David Jr. and Tina. The holidays had been painful for the two families, Jack's and ours.

On January 11ᵗʰ, Lori-Ann, David and I spent some time with Janice. Jack was still coherent and he could still walk with one assist. His mom, Janet, was a great asset in Jack's care. Janice was amazing, performing tasks that I never would have imagined her doing, like administering Jack's medication with a syringe.

January 20ᵗʰ This was a very sad day indeed. I was present along with the hospice chaplain Tobias, and close family members. Jack was uncomfortable and in need of his comforting medication more frequently. Jack being non responsive in early afternoon, the family was called in. This was the initial sign of Jack's last hours and immediate family members were expressing their farewell in a variety of ways. Tobias and the Ashburne family pastor were most supportive by their presence and their prayers.

January 21ˢᵗ At 12:45 am, Jack expired, six days after his fifty-third birthday. God rest his soul!

January 29ᵗʰ Jack was a most generous individual with a multitude of friends; calling hours proved so. There was a great turnout at the Darlington / Theroux Funeral Mortuary in Pawtucket RI.

January 30th The funeral service was followed by the eight-mile ride to Highland Memorial Park, in Johnston RI. The urn containing Jack's ashes was carried by Janice, his step-son Corey, and his best friend Jimmy, in his own remodeled truck, his pride and joy. Also present in the special vehicle were Jack's step-daughter Mandy, and Brianna. Jack is sadly missed by all and his memory will always be alive in our family.

January 31st As planned, Phil, Dave, myself and Lori-Ann went to the Hanover Theater in Worcester MA to attend an Elvis Presley impersonator concert, courtesy of the Zajac family. In spite of a snowy drive, we had a great time. The show was superb!

February 5th Brianna's nineteenth birthday was celebrated with family and friends at the Empire Restaurant in Woonsocket RI.

February 5th On this day history was made when the New England Patriots won the Super Bowl L1 by defeating the Atlanta Falcons 34-28. It was a miracle victory, after trailing by 25 points in the third quarter. They made the biggest comeback in Super Bowl history to claim their fifth championship in overtime. Their winning years were: 2001, 2003, 2004, 2014, and 2016. Quarterback Tom Brady and coach Bill Belichick became the first in their respective positions to win five Super Bowls. The city of Boston was in a high festive mode and it was a great success in spite of the weather, a wintry mix typical New England weather.

February 13th Our uncle Bill Symmes, a hundred and a half years old, was hospitalized with pneumonia. He had suffered a fall in his apartment earlier and recuperated at Blair House Rehabilitation Facility in Milford. After a few weeks, he moved to an assisted living facility and was doing well.

February 21st I purchased a 2015 Chevrolet Sonic in exchange for my 2014 Chevy Spark. My tiny Sparky being unsafe, as judged by my family. I am happy with my choice, and so is my family, and I feel safe.

February 23rd On that day, temperatures reached 73 degrees in Boston. Records were broken for the day and for the month since the 1800s.

February 27th A 50th birthday party for my special niece Nancy.

March certainly came in like a lion and continued during the entire month to act like a ferocious one.

March 4th was the coldest day at 3 degrees above 0. On my birthday.

March 14th was a cold day with blizzard conditions.

March 23rd Dave's carpal tunnel right hand surgery was successful.

March 2017 exited the same way it entered: in a cold and blustery manner. April brought us warmer days with the arrival of our beautiful feathered friends the robins, as well as Easter Sunday, the Boston Marathon, the Zajac family's trip to Valencia, Spain, to visit my grandson Matthew who is studying at the Berklee School of Music. Chloe celebrated her eighth birthday while visiting her big brother.

Bursting with activities, the month included the talent show at Chloe's school, the Davis Thayer, with Lori-Ann as chairlady. Saydee, aged six, had a play at the Stadium in Woonsocket. The New England Patriots' visit to the White House, a get-together for a few former nursing school students to honor one of our own, Helen Brule's eighty-sixth birthday.

A trip to Boston to accompany a friend to a medical appointment proved to be on the rainiest day of the year. The cliché "raining cats and dogs" was most appropriate on that day.

In April 2017, my grandson Matthew wrote from Valencia, Spain:

Hi Mammy! Thank you for your letter. It's really good to hear you are making progress on your book. I admire your patience and willpower. I look forward to reading every chapter and learning more details from your life. You have inspired me to pursue my writing skills, and I always think of you when I run. I hope you are all doing well in Massachusetts.

Say hi to Papa Dave,

Love you, see you in May,

Matthew

April 3rd The birthday celebration in honor of our friend and classmate Helen Brule at her home with Vicki, Natalie, Mary and myself. We had a good time.

April 16th Easter was celebrated quietly at home with a few family members.

April 17th The Boston Marathon was viewed at home. As I watched the Boston Marathon on television, I was reminiscing on my Boston Marathon runs in the past. It is truly a unique event unlike any other one I ran, but I believe Heartbreak Hill is not as scary as it is said to be. But it is somewhat challenging because of its placement in the race: 17-21 miles.

April 28th A second corneal transplant, the left eye, was successfully done at St. Vincent Hospital, Worcester, by Dr. Joseph Williams.

May 1st Bad News! The second post op visit found a detached cornea.

May 5th The corneal revision was done, successfully. The healing process continued with frequent visits to the surgeon.

Nephew Danny Darling's fiftieth birthday was observed with the Finkelstein family.

David's second of both hand surgeries took place on May 25th, with good results.

May 26th Dave's uncle Bill's one hundred and one birthday was observed with pride. He is a great role model to follow for his intelligence, his patience and his good disposition.

June 13th The start of a much enjoyed mini-vacation in Mystic, Connecticut, and surrounding towns, accompanied by our good friend Beverly-An from Long Island NY. During our short stay at the Quality Inn, where we felt so welcomed by the staff (it was truly remarkable), we visited beautiful grounds and parks. We had wonderful dining experiences, saw the great movie Churchill and we observed the ducklings' adventures at the duck pond. A most relaxing time for three good friends.

CHAPTER 75

Running

Next to my family, running was my passion. It all started in the summer of 1978 while vacationing in Shediac, New Brunswick, Canada, when my six-year-old Jamie kept me running around the trailer park, in order to keep him safe. I caught the running bug and upon our return home, I started jogging up the street to Art's Grocery Store, seven tenths of a mile away, a few mornings a week. My son John joined me to improve his speed for soccer. That soon ended, however, but I persevered, even though I felt light headed after my run. I increased my mileage and, one year later, I entered my first race: a 5.6-mile in Franklin with a time of 48:02.

I was invited to join the Franklin Bolts Running Club by Joanne Lippert, whose husband Dale was the founder of the club and also John's soccer coach, and by their son Gary, John's friend. At my first road race, as I was running through Franklin Center, a young boy on his bicycle spotted me and said to his friend: "Here comes the old ladies". I was thirty-nine years old! I felt insulted but that did not deter me from continuing to run as much as my busy schedule permitted.

On May 17th, 1980, after returning from my trip to Florida, I entered a 10-km race in Milford. About a hundred yards from the finish line, I was overwhelmed by the heat. I was assisted and transported to the hospital by ambulance. I remained there for the weekend, suffering from heat exhaustion and dehydration. I was on the fourth floor, on the opposite end of the department where I worked, by request.

As a Master Runner (age 40-49) there is less competition, it is therefore easier to place in your category. In September 1980, I ran my fourth race; 6.7 miles in 54.06 minutes (8.42 pace), which is slow, but I got the First Master award. Then I became an avid runner and I got involved with the Franklin Bolts Running Club's activities. Jamie, Mark and Lori-Ann became active members as well, and made friends with other club members' children and participated in several races. On Wednesday evenings was our weekly 8-mile run from Franklin to Norfolk MA.

In 1981, during the month of June, I ran 200 miles in America's Love Run for Muscular Dystrophy and I was invited to the The Jerry Lewis Labor Day Telethon at the Channel 5 Studio, in Boston, to receive a gold medal for my efforts, along with four other runners who had raised $1,000.00 or more for the charity. We were honored to be presented these awards by Natalie Jacobson. My children and I also enjoyed a free limousine ride to the studio from Yaz Limousine Service, which was arranged by my friends Dr. John Hoell and Bill Flynn.

In November 1981, I ran my first marathon in Foxborough MA where there were more cows than people as spectators. Missing the qualifying time for the Boston Marathon by ten minutes was disappointing but I kept running and after running the same course in November 1982, I was accepted to compete in the Master's Division of the BAA Marathon in the spring of 1983. I ran that marathon and finished in a time of 3:31:33 minus 4 minutes and 10 seconds allowance to cross the starting line, therefore an official time of 3:27:23. I qualified for the following year's BAA race.

It was a glorious year for the American runners as Greg Meyer won the men's division with an impressive time of 2:09.00. Joan Benoit ran a super race, breaking the women's world record by nearly three minutes with a time of 2:22:42.

On February 17th, 1983, my friend Sue Aronovitz ran the Silver Lake Dodge Marathon in Wellesley MA in 3:22:47. What a feat! It was her first marathon ever and her longest previous run had been fifteen miles. How proud we were!

I ran several races in 1984, including the Bonne Bell in Boston, 6.2mi I ran the Sturdy Memorial Hospital 5-miler in Attleboro where I received a

$100.00 gift certificate to London's Department Store for the First Master prize and got myself a jacket. On October 20th, 1984, I participated in the Cape Cod Relay as a member of the Franklin Bolts. My leg was 14.8 miles, including the Sagamore Bridge. That was a memorable run. Our mixed team finished 143 out of 238 teams with a time of nine hours and forty six minutes. This relay race was from Plymouth to Provincetown. I participated in that race for several more years and I enjoyed it.

On November 4th, I ran the Ocean State Marathon in Newport, Rhode Island, with a time of 3:40:42. It was a very scenic race and enjoyable in spite of an annoying left knee discomfort for the last three miles of the course. Road racing can vary in hardship due to road conditions, hills, potholes, but more so with the weather as foot races are not usually cancelled due to weather conditions. I have run in all kinds of weather, in extreme heat, rain, snow, and high winds.

While training for any race, I did some speed work on the Franklin High School track and some hill work at the Middle School. I always tried to improve my running skill and speed. I worked hard at it. It became an addiction. Some days I would get up at 5:30 am and run a few miles before work. One morning, a car seemed to be following me. I became scared and pretended to go to a neighbor's house. I fell off their back porch and sprained my ankle. Not good. I also realized that my follower was the newspaper delivery vehicle...

Jamie, Mark and Lori-Ann participated in several races, mostly the ones sponsored by our running club. Mark finished in second place in a mile race once, with a time of 6:00 minutes flat. Great! Lori-Ann trailed with a time of 6:18 and was the first female finisher in her age division. They made me a proud mamma! They showed interest in watching the Boston Marathon from Wellesley with my friend Vicki and her two boys, Marcus and Matthew. After I had run by their post, Vicki took them to the Boston Museum of Science, which they loved to visit, especially Mark. He still enjoys it today.

The Boston Marathon always takes place on Patriots' Monday, during the third week of April and during school break in Massachusetts. The Boston Red Sox usually play at Fenway Park on that very festive day in Boston. Note that Massachusetts and Maine are the only two States that observe that holiday.

On April 20th, 1981, Johnny Kelley, aged seventy-three, of East Dennis MA, ran his fiftieth Boston Marathon and his hundred and seventh marathon, at the loud cheers of thousands of fans. He finished with a time of 4:01:25 and with a pulse of only 64 per minute. FANTASTIC! Although disappointed in his time, but not in his physical condition, he exclaimed "I feel wonderful!" He added: "Marathons after the age of seventy are for the birds: but I believe I'm an exception to the rule." His favorite song, which he often sang, Young At Heart, described him to a T. He ranked seventh overall in the Boston Marathon several times.

Four-time winners of the Boston Marathon were: Bill Rodgers, Gerard Cote and Clarence DeMa. Kathrine Switzer, then a twenty-year-old university student from Syracuse, New York, was the first woman to run the Boston Marathon (incognito) and ran it again fifty years later on April 17th, 2017.

My first Boston Marathon was very memorable, not only for the prestige, but for my adventure after the long run. I had left a change of clothes with two different friends in case we separated and that was exactly what happened. I wrapped in my silver foil cover up and roamed around until I met Mark Bush, a member of my runners' club, who graciously offered me a warm-up suit. I gratefully accepted, no matter the size of the suit. Mark's six-foot plus frame and my five-foot stature were not compatible; but his suit kept me warm. I got a ride home with a physician from Holliston, whom I knew and who was working at the medical tent.

In April 1984, I ran the Boston Milk Run, a 10K, with Bill Flynn and Louise Nelson on a very cold and rainy Sunday. The Boston Milk Run serves as a "tune up" for many runners for the Boston Marathon. It is sponsored by The Dairy Farmers of New England and the Massachusetts Dietetic Association.

The year 1985 was a very active year in my running career. On March 30th, I ran a 15km (9.3 miles). The weather was warm and the course somewhat hilly, in Upton MA, with a time of 68.23 minutes and I earned Second Master. In May I ran the Maine Coast Marathon from Kennebunk to the University of New England in Biddeford ME. Running through Kennebunkport and along the coast was a feast for the eyes. A few of my fellow club members also ran and made the event more fun. My 3:35:03 official time qualified me for Boston '86.

Two short-distance races, with a low turnout of participants, one in Hopkinton and one in Upton were lucky for me as I was the first woman finisher. It never happened again. I ran a few half marathons, including one in Hopkinton MA in 1981, followed by the popular New Bedford half marathon in the 1990s, finishing fourth in the Masters division twice.

Post 1985 Marathon, I received a survey from the Harvard University School of Public Health, department of Epidemiology. I completed the questionnaire. The reason for the survey was to help provide information for a study of marathon runners' health and the likeliness of injury or illness. In 1985, over eight hundred runners required some form of medical treatment following the Boston Marathon. I also obliged to an interview with a Boston University female student regarding women marathoners.

The Franklin Bolts Running Club made its membership proud to be part of such a dedicated group of individuals. I enjoyed the camaraderie and some lasting friendship that ensued. We also fared fairly well in competition. The Franklin Bolts welcomed runners and would-be runners of all ages; and made a concerted effort to attract youngsters. The July Fourth Fun Run around the Franklin Commons was open to children ages 6-12. During the summer the Club held a track clinic at the High School for youngsters ages 6-14, supervised by members of our Club. My three younger children participated and I assisted as needed. Several road races were organized by the Bolts and sponsored by the Ben Franklin Savings Bank, where prize money was awarded.

The 1986 Boston Marathon was a rainy last few miles. My finishing time was 3:37:06. A thirty-eight-year-old man from Salt Lake City, Utah, suffered pain in his right leg off and on from mile seven on during the Boston Marathon. He was unaware of a right thigh bone fracture. At the finish line he collapsed and was hospitalized and underwent a five-hour surgery the following day. The doctors were amazed at his finishing the race, nineteen miles with a broken leg. According to the medical staff, Guy Gertsch's strong thigh muscles acted as a splint and held the bone together. After crossing the finish line, the muscles relaxed and the bone fell apart. What courage that young man had! Sometimes, runners with increased endorphins and with the adrenaline pumping surprise themselves with what they can accomplish. In 1984, Joan Benoit Samuelson had won the Olympic Trials Marathon seventeen days after knee arthroscopic surgery. On a smaller scale, I had run a race eleven days after a bunionectomy in 1982 and a half marathon while recovering from pneumonia. This shows the mentality of an addicted runner, whether a high profile athlete or a beginner.

Running for a cause usually energizes a runner and increases the perseverance in finishing the race. One of our best Franklin Bolts runners, George Crerar (a great guy!) not only beat his personal best with a time of 2:53:56 but also raised thousands of dollars for Multiple Sclerosis, which he had done repeatedly since 1978. He was supported by his fellow employees at Sun Life Of Canada in Wellesley. I also ran the Boston Marathon for Multiple Sclerosis, my biggest support was from the physicians of the Milford Hospital. They were very generous.

I ran ten marathons including five Boston Marathons:

November 1981 Foxtrotter Foxborough MA

November 1982 Foxtrotter Marathon Foxboro MA

April 1983 Boston Marathon

November 1984 Ocean State Marathon Newport RI

May 1985 Maine Coast Marathon Kennebunk ME

April 1986 Boston Marathon

October 1989 Cape Cod Marathon Woods Hole MA

April 1990 Boston Marathon

April 1991 Boston Marathon

April 1992 Boston Marathon

After a back injury in 1987, I did not run much until 1989. I earned eight numbers for the Boston Marathon but ran with five of them due to the injury or to the PIE syndrome, missing 1984, 1987 and 1993.

The most difficult Boston Marathon for me was in 1990, running with sciatica. My friend Dolores, a Henry O. Peabody School of Nursing alumni, and I although we had never run together prior to this day, ran in a synchronized manner for fifteen miles. Then started the sciatic pain. At the hills (miles 17-21) there was more walking than running. She was an inspiration to me by her encouragement and her patience and she saw me through my trials and stayed with me all the way. We finished in 4:03:39, my slowest time. Dolores is a super lady, a true friend and a good Christian.

On March 24th, 1991, on a beautiful Sunday afternoon, my good friend Phil Morin and I went for a training run on the Boston Marathon course. The trek from Natick Center to Boston College, a ten-miler and return, turned out differently than planned as we got separated somehow and an extra one and a half mile was run in search for Phil. We reunited and returned to Phil's vehicle but we were unable to enter it as the only key in his possession was the ignition key. The friendly policeman took us in his cruiser to the line of the next town of Framingham, then another cruiser brought us to the Ashland border, where another cruiser took us to the Hopkinton line, where my vehicle was waiting. After picking up the appropriate car key at Phil's house, we drove back to his vehicle in Natick. It made for a very long afternoon. My 20-miler turned out to be twenty-three. What an adventure! The next day I called out from work... I was a little tired.

In 1991, Dolores and I ran with some of her friends and we got separated early in the race and finished at the approximate same time 3:47:34. How cool! There was a welcome improvement in our time in 1992 at 3:41:19.

According to the USA Track & Field Directory, my credentials were:

10km 42:42 6:49 pace

10-miler 73:34 7:20 pace

Half marathon 1:39:19 7:34 pace

25km (15 + miles) 2:03 7:53 pace

Marathon 3:27: 21 7: 55 pace

When my children could not be race spectators to cheer me on, they would convey their wishes on short notes which are still in my "special memories envelope". Here are excerpts:

Janice wrote:

> Mom, I thought I'd write you a little note to let you know
>
> I'll be thinking of you tomorrow.
>
> I hope you break your record. Well, good luck and have fun.
>
> See you soon.
>
> I love you.
>
> Janice

Jamie wrote:

Hey Mom! Good luck tomorrow. I hope you do well.

Sorry that I cannot go watch, but that is not my choice.

I will be watching on TV. I hope 2CU on TV.

Good Luck again!

Your #1 Fan,

Your #1 son (Ha!)

You're cool!

Have a good run!

Love ya,

Jamie

P.S. I will be praying 4 you.

Mark wrote:

Mom, Good Luck! I hope you get a PR and have a great run.

Hopefully I'll be watching; if not, I'll see you on TV.

Best wishes! Good Luck.

Love,

Mark

Lori-Ann wrote:

Mom, Good Luck! I'm sorry I will not be going,

but I'll be watching you on TV.

I love you and I know you will do well;

you better if you know what's good for you.

Good luck again.

Love always,

Lori-Ann

P.S. I hope you don't have to take the train home. (which I did once)

One of the highlights of all my years of running, over 30 years, was running the Falmouth Road Race in August 2003 with Lori-Ann and I finishing together, holding hands, on a very hot and humid day. Then we were left behind, but were rescued later on by my husband and David Jr.

The Bolts Club brought back to life the Cape Cod Relay in the early millennium, in 2006, 2007 and 2008. I participated as well as did my niece Nancy. David and I enjoyed joining in the running fun as well as meeting new people. It was always interesting to reminisce on the old running days, when we were in our prime.

Along with nineteen trophies, I accumulated a few other prizes such as gift certificates to sport and running stores, an alarm clock, Nike running shoes, and cash prize of $50.00, twice, a plaque and a cup. And, yes! you guessed it: I still possess these, except the cash.

What do you do with old trophies?

CHAPTER 76

Salvatore Pilla

Our 97 year young Sal is everyone's friend and acts as the mascot at the grocery store where he is still employed. A WWII veteran, battling the Battle of the Bulge, he certainly has earned love and respect from our community. A faithful parishioner at St. Brendan Church in Bellingham, he loves to proclaim the Alleluia as loud as he can. One of my early morning prayers was given to me by this man who, even though he knows everyone by name, calls me Mrs. Darling. Still performing his duties as an usher at the church after so many years, he teaches us perseverance and loyalty. May God bless our pillar of the community. And may we learn to be as generous as he has been for so many years.

This is the prayer I was given by this fine gentleman, which I recite every morning:

Good Morning, God.

You are ushering in another day, untouched and freshly new.

So here I come to ask you, God, if you'll renew me too.

Forgive the many errors I made yesterday

And let me try again, dear Lord, to walk closer in your way.

But, Father, I am well aware I can't make it on my own.

So take my hand and hold it tight for I can't walk alone.

CHAPTER 77

The New Pledge of Allegiance

BY A 15-YEAR-OLD SCHOOL KID WHO GOT AN A+ FOR THIS ENTRY.

TOTALLY AWESOME!

Since the Pledge of Allegiance and the Lord's Prayer are not allowed in most public schools anymore because the word "God" is mentioned, a kid in Arizona wrote the new school prayer.

NEW PLEDGE OF ALLEGIANCE

Now I sit me down in school, where praying is against the rule.

For this great nation under God finds mention of Him very odd.

If Scripture now the class recites, it violates the Bill of Rights.

And anytime my head I bow, becomes a Federal matter now.

We should learn from this fifteen-year-old as this is really happening in our world today. Let's not be ashamed of our beliefs and values.

CHAPTER 78

A Gift of Love and Comfort

A GIFT OF LOVE AND COMFORT

Youngsters donate stuffed animal collection to Franklin Fire Department

By Heather McCarron

My seven-year-old granddaughter Chloe and her eight-year-old friend Harriet had a very special delivery packed inside a plastic laundry basket for the Fire Department, with armloads of plush animals of all sizes and shapes, with arms, legs, tails and snouts poking out here and there - a mound of pink, purple, gray, brown, white and yellow cheerfulness.

The girls said they had all the love and comfort out of the animals they needed, and were ready to share them with others, so other children can enjoy the stuffed animals in situations that call for such objects of consolation. As they looked at their extensive stuffed collections, they realized how fortunate they were and decided to donate.

Chloe had already made a similar donation a couple of years ago after a fire in which a family had lost everything. "They lost all their favorite things and that stuck with me", explained Chloe. It feels good to see that she is thinking of others and cares and understands how it might feel. The memory of her previous toy donation inspired the idea to donate again for those unexpected emergencies encountered by the firefighters and paramedics all of the time.

Accepting the donations were Fire Chief Gary McGarraher and Jon Chalk, firefighter/paramedic and Harriet's dad.

CHAPTER 79

The House at Rest

How does one hush one's house,
each proud possessive wall, each sighing rafter,
the rooms made restless with
remembered laughter
or wounding echoes, the permissive doors,
the stairs that vacillate from up to down,
windows that bring in color and event
from countryside or town,
oppressive ceilings and complaining floors?

The house must first of all accept the night.
Let it erase the walls and their display,
impoverish the rooms till they are filled
with humble silences; let clocks be stilled
and all the selfish urgencies of day.
Midnight is not the time to greet a guest.
Caution the doors against both foes and friends,
and try to make the windows understand
their unimportance when the daylight ends.
Persuade the stairs to patience, and deny the passages
their aimless to and fro.
Virtue it is that puts a house at rest.
How well repaid that tenant is, how blest
who, when the call is heard,
is free to take his kindled heart and go.
Author unknown

CHAPTER 80

My Niece Nancy

Nancy started her running while in her teens and she still runs regularly and has run numerous races including half marathons. I had the pleasure of running a few races with Nancy, which included the CVS 5K in Providence RI, the Falmouth Road Race, a 7-miler, and the Cape Cod Relay. She did well in the Hyannis Marathon Relay on a cold February 2006. Her first marathon was in September 2016 in Keene NH, with a time of 4:03:28. She made us proud.

In 2010, when responding to a questionnaire regarding her running career, Nancy wrote:

Running has been a wonderful part of my life. I began running in high school to get in shape for the sports I played. It improved my stamina tremendously. I was motivated by my aunt Doris and ran my first 10k-race at the age of 18. Running was a great way to get back into shape after having my children. I ran up to my 6th month of pregnancy. It's a great workout in a short amount of time,

ideal for a working mother. I ran a lot of 5km- and 5-mile races in my 20s. My desire to take my running to a new level was realized when I ran my first 10-mile race, followed by a 15k, 4 half marathons, several relay races, six Falmouth races and a sprint triathlon. Running is enjoyable to me especially in the warmer months, when I can go outside and connect with the natural surroundings. I love how running makes me feel physically and mentally. I love the challenge and how rewarding it is to reach the goals I've set for myself. It's a terrific stress reliever and has helped me to manage my weight over the years.

====== CHAPTER 81 ======

My Daughters~in~law

I have three wonderful daughters-in-law: Marian, Tracy and Kristine.

Another daughter-in-law, Juliette Gralla, who was married to my son John, is now deceased. Julie was extremely gifted with multiple talents and left this world too soon. Her legacy: her two daughters and her two beautiful grandchildren, Saydee and Bradley. Her memory will remain with us forever.

Marian, Marcel's wife, is always there when needed. She is supportive of her husband's passion for golf and is a doting grandmother to her two grandsons, Dylan and Nicholas. She is passionate about horses, which she rides as often as she can. Here is the content of a beautiful plaque I received from Marian on their wedding day:

OUR MOTHER

You are the mother I received

the day I wed your son

and I just want to thank you, Mom,

for the things you have done.

You have given me a gracious man

with whom to share my life.

You are his lovely mother

and I his lucky wife.

You raised in love a little boy

and gave to me a man.

Tracy helped Jamie become a more disciplined man and also encouraged him to pursue his plumbing career. Her stability and her sense of responsibility have created a comfortable home for their family. As a mother, her children's behavior reflects their good upbringing. Tracy and I used to have a great time opening USPE boxes to find the surprises hidden inside. Tracy knows my taste and style in clothes and home decor and I am always pleased at Christmastime. Her swimming expertise has been inherited by her two children. Her cosmology profession as well as her culinary talents impress me. Tracy knows where to find a greeting card when needed. Good choice, JP.

'Outgoing, smart, witty, dramatic, loves a good time' describes Kristine, Mark's wife. She is very family-oriented and a caring mother. Her husband and children are her priority and she is a conscientious worker. And she may devote her time to a good cause if she believes in it. She spends much energy helping her daughter's girl scouts troop. Kristine is very loyal and has a marvelous sense of humor. She is knowledgeable and assertive. She is always ready to taste new foods of any ethnicity and she has taught her children to do the same. She is fun to be around and has many friends. Her young daughter has her demeanor, with her sense of fun, her imagination, her gift of gab and charming personality.

CHAPTER 82

Special Cousins

There are two cousins in Shediac, New Brunswick, Canada, who are special to me: Alice and Bernice.

They are both very dedicated to their family, and are hard working women who have seen harsh times.

Alice has proven her warm-hearted disposition by caring for her significant other for over thirty years.

Bernice, as a young widow, was the heart of her loving family by her devotion to all.

I admire them both for their strength and their courage through all the kinds of adversities which they have experienced in their lifetime.

May God bless them both!

There is another Canadian cousin, Rachel, who deserves credit for playing an important role in this project. She used her literary knowledge and her editing expertise to make me aware of what to look for in my manuscript that would bring out the best from the heart of a simple story. I am so grateful for the immense amount of time and effort she devoted to this meticulous task, by her vigilant watch in observing the whole project and her constant interest and patience in providing me with valuable recommendations and productive criticisms at all times. She has been the push I needed to complete this manuscript. My sincere appreciation to you, dear cousin.

CHAPTER 83

2017 Trip to New Brunswick, Canada

July 9th to 18th, 2017 The eleven-hour trek to New Brunswick, Canada, went as planned and, upon our arrival at Shediac Bridge, we were graciously welcomed with a delicious supper quickly prepared by my sister-in-law Louise. The Bay Vista Lodge, our cozy, clean and private cabin #3, felt very inviting to our tired bodies.

The highlights of our visit, besides being with family, were the visits to two museums. The first museum was a schoolhouse formerly called la p'tite école, The Little Schoolhouse, where I started my education in 1947 in my parish of Grande-Digue. That one-room schoolhouse brought back many memories. It is now part of the village museum, "Le Musée des Pionniers".

The other memorable sight was the convent where I passed my last high school year under the direction of the religious order of the Sisters of Our Lady of the Sacred Heart: the Immaculate Conception Convent in Bouctouche, now called Le Musée de Kent. I was honored to meet Pierre Cormier, the facility's curator. I was given a plaque with a replica of my Alma Mater, which made me feel special. I will cherish it.

We also visited the theme park in Bouctouche called Le Pays de La Sagouine, created as a tribute to the renowned local author Antonine Maillet, and where the pages of her novel and dramatic play La Sagouine come alive. Our personal tour guide, Ti-Loup, made it so interesting as he explained how it depicts the way of life of the Acadians in the province of New Brunswick in the 1940s and 1950s.

The Bourgeois and Arsenault families showed their true colors as we were treated as special guests everywhere we went, which included barbeques, home-cooked meals, and restaurant treats. We enjoyed visiting, and saw most of my late sister's children, some old friends and some former classmates. All a pleasure to see.

Toby's welcome was much appreciated after a blinding rain on Interstate 495 where the extremely heavy traffic made difficult the last part of our journey home. But that aside, we had a great trip to my old home country, New Brunswick, Canada.

Addendum: September 11th, 2017 In memory of our Country's worst disaster, we pause, remember, and pray for all who are still suffering from their loss on that dreadful day.

On that September day during my daily morning walk, I witnessed an event which was a first for me. A gentleman, in a parking lot, was freeing pigeons, approximately fifteen at a time, sending them home to his house in Hanson MA, a distance of about thirty-one miles (as the crow flies) from Bellingham MA. I also learned from Mr. MC that Queen Elizabeth II belongs to the same hobby club as he and his son do. That made my day.

My daughter Lori-Ann has been in remission from Multiple Myeloma for five years at present time and has trained and run the London marathon in April 2018, we are very proud of her accomplishment.

Printed in the United States
By Bookmasters